Charles Coppens

A Brief Text-Book of Logic and Mental Philosophy

Charles Coppens

A Brief Text-Book of Logic and Mental Philosophy

ISBN/EAN: 9783337068394

Printed in Europe, USA, Canada, Australia, Japan

Cover: Foto ©Thomas Meinert / pixelio.de

More available books at **www.hansebooks.com**

A. M. D. G.

A BRIEF TEXT-BOOK

OF

LOGIC

AND

MENTAL PHILOSOPHY.

BY

REV. CHARLES COPPENS, S.J.,

Author of "A Practical Introduction to English Rhetoric" and "The Art of Oratorical Composition."

———

"Christ is the Restorer of the Sciences." LEO. XIII

NEW YORK
SCHWARTZ, KIRWIN & FAUSS
42 BARCLAY STREET

Copyright, 1891,
by
THE CATHOLIC PUBLICATION SOCIETY CO.

Transferred to CATHOLIC SCHOOL BOOK CO.

ALL RIGHTS RESERVED.

PREFACE.

THESE pages are a modest contribution towards the accomplishment of an important purpose. They are written in compliance with an earnest desire repeatedly expressed in the solemn utterances of our venerated Supreme Pontiff Leo XIII. "The more active," he says, "the enemies of religion are to teach the unlearned, the young especially, what clouds their intellect and corrupts their morals, the more should you exert yourselves to establish not only a well-adapted and solid method of instruction, but a method in perfect conformity with the Catholic faith, especially as regards Mental Philosophy, on which the right teaching of all the other sciences in a great measure depends—a Philosophy which shall prepare the way for Divine Revelation instead of aiming at its overthrow."

Thus spoke the Holy Father in his Encyclical "Inscrutabili" at the opening of his Pontificate. What this Philosophy should be, he soon after explained in a special Encyclical "On the Higher Studies." It should be the Philosophy of the Schoolmen, the system founded upon the teachings of Aristotle, which was carried to its perfection by St. Thomas in the thirteenth century, and which has held its place in most of the Catholic Colleges and Universities to the present day. "Among the doctors of the Schools," he says, "St. Thomas stands forth by far the first and master of all. . . . . To this we must add," the Encyclical continues, "that this Angelic Doctor extended the sphere of his philosophic conclusions and speculations to the very reasons and principles of things, opening out the widest field for study, and containing within themselves the germs of an infinity of truths, an exhaustless mine for future teachers to draw from at the proper time and with rich results. As he used the same intellectual process in refuting error, he succeeded in combating single-handed all the erroneous systems of past ages, and supplied victorious weapons to the champions of truth against the errors which are to crop up in succession to the end of time."

Of this Philosophy there exist many excellent text-books in the Latin, but very few in the English tongue; the present little volume does not attempt to rival their perfection. Its aim is simply: to present to pupils unfamiliar with Latin a brief outline of a sound Philosophy conformable to the teachings of the Schoolmen. It was composed before the excellent Stonyhurst Series of English Manuals of Catholic Philosophy was published; but it is chiefly meant for a different purpose, viz.: for class use in Academies and similar institutions, for which that collection of Manuals is too voluminous, though invaluable as works of reference for professors and pupils. The author sincerely hopes that his modest efforts will contribute to the propagation of sound Philosophic learning.

THE AUTHOR.

DETROIT COLLEGE, August 20, 1891.

TABLE OF CONTENTS.

                                                        PAGE

INTRODUCTION, ... 7

LOGIC.

BOOK I.—DIALECTICS.

CHAPTER I.	Simple Apprehensions and Judgments:	11
Article	I. The Nature of Simple Apprehensions;	11
"	II. Distinctions regarding Ideas;	12
"	III. Judgments and Propositions.	18
CHAPTER II.	Reasoning:	22
Article	I. The Categorical Syllogism;	22
	§ 1. Constructing Syllogisms;	23
	§ 2. Criticising Syllogisms;	26
Article	II. The Hypothetical Syllogism;	30
"	III. Other Species of Demonstrative Arguments;	32
"	IV. Probable Reasoning;	36
"	V. Indirect Reasoning;	38
"	VI. Fallacious Reasoning;	40
"	VII. Method in Reasoning;	42
"	VIII. Exercise in Reasoning.	45

BOOK II. CRITICAL LOGIC.

	PAGE
CHAPTER I. The Nature of Certainty:	48
Article I. Truth and Falsity;	49
" II. States of the Mind with Regard to Truth;	51
" III. Elements that Make up Certainty.	54
CHAPTER II. The Existence of Certainty.	56
CHAPTER III. Means of Attaining Certainty:	62
Article I. A Sketch of our Cognoscive Powers;	62
" II. The Intellect in Particular;	65
§ 1. Consciousness;	66
§ 2. Primary Ideas;	68
§ 3. Immediate Analytical Judgments;	70
§ 4. Memory;	72
§ 5. Reasoning;	73
Article III. Sensation;	74
§ 1. The Inner Sense;	75
§ 2. The Outer Senses;	77
Article IV. Authority;	87
" V. Common Sense;	90
CHAPTER IV. The Ultimate Criterion of Certainty.	94

INTRODUCTION.

1. **Philosophy** is the science which investigates the highest causes of all things in as far as they are knowable by reason. That portion of Philosophy which terminates in theory or speculative knowledge is called *Theoretical* or *Mental Philosophy*, or *Metaphysics*. That portion which applies first principles to practice, directing the moral conduct of men, is styled *Practical* or *Moral Philosophy*, or *Ethics*.

2. Since reason is to be our guide in all these investigations, we must begin by examining, (*a*) What process our reason must follow that it may guide us with safety, and (*b*) How far our natural powers of mind can give us unerring certainty. This double task is the scope of **Logic**, which science must first be studied, because it is the foundation of the mental and moral structure. It is as truly a part of Philosophy as the foundation is a part of the building.

3. **Human reason and Divine Revelation** are two means by which truth is manifested to man; they cannot contradict one another: as a matter of fact, that which is evident to reason is never found in conflict with Revelation. Hence arises a precious advantage for the Christian philosopher, of which he were foolish not to avail himself. For, knowing that the path of reason, often difficult to trace correctly, must run parallel to the high road of supernatural Revelation, he will be guarded by the clear and infallible teachings of the

Faith against the vain pursuit of false theories. Thus, Faith, far from enslaving, liberates his intellect from the shackles of ignorance and error. Philosophy looks not for novelties, nor does it aim at originality of thought, but it studies the eternal and unvarying principles of truth.

4. Among the purely human sciences, Philosophy is the **noblest and most important;** for its final purpose is the most exalted, its process the most intellectual, and its teachings secure the foundation of the other sciences. These receive from it their principles, the laws of their investigations, and the ends or purposes to which they should be directed.

PART I.

LOGIC.

5. **Logic** is the science which directs the mind in the attainment of truth. By a **science** we mean the knowledge of things in connection with their causes. Logic is properly called a science, because it considers not only the rules which direct the mind in the attainment of truth, but also the causes or reasons why they do so.

6. It comprises **two parts**. That portion which considers the modes or forms of mental action, and, in particular, the rules to be observed in reasoning or discussing, is called *Formal Logic* or *Dialectics* (διαλέγομαι, I discuss); that portion which studies the matter or truth attained, criticising the reliability of mental action, is *Material Logic*, also styled *Critical* or *Applied Logic*.

BOOK I.

DIALECTICS.

7. In treating of Dialectics, the **main purpose** of a text book is to teach pupils how to reason correctly themselves, and readily to detect flaws in the false reasonings of others. To this practical purpose we shall almost exclusively confine ourselves. Setting aside, therefore, all other details usually insisted on in works on Formal Logic, we shall here treat of reasoning only, and of a few such preliminary matters as must be understood before the reasoning process itself can be properly explained. We shall therefore treat, in Chapter I., of *simple apprehensions and judgments*, and, in Chapter II., of *reasoning* itself.

CHAPTER I.

SIMPLE APPREHENSIONS AND JUDGMENTS.

8. We shall consider: 1. *The nature of simple apprehensions.* 2. *The most important distinctions regarding ideas,* and 3. *Judgments,* together with the expression of them in *propositions.*

ARTICLE I. THE NATURE OF SIMPLE APPREHENSIONS.

9. **Simple apprehension** is the act of perceiving an object intellectually, without affirming or denying anything concerning it. To *apprehend* is to take hold of a thing as if with the hand; an *apprehension,* as an act of the mind, is an intellectual grasping of an object. The mind cannot take an object physically into itself; but it knows an object by taking it in intellectually, in a manner suited to its own nature, forming to itself an intellectual image, called a *species* of the object. The act of forming this mental image is called a *conception,* and the fruit of it, the image itself, is the *concept, idea,* or *notion* of the object. The word *simple* added to apprehension emphasizes the fact that the apprehension neither affirms nor denies the existence of the object; it affirms nothing and denies nothing, it simply conceives the idea of the object.

10. This intellectual image should not be confounded with the sensible image, or **phantasm**, which is a material representation of material objects, and which is formed by the imagination, by means of the material organ of the brain.

The difference between these two images is great, and distinction between them is of vital importance in Philosophy. For instance, I intellectually *conceive* a triangle by apprehending a figure enclosed by three lines and thus having three angles. My notion or idea contains this and nothing more; it is very precise, and every one who conceives a triangle conceives it exactly the same way. But when I *imagine* a triangle, I cannot help imagining it with sensible material accidents, as being of such or such a size and shape, a foot long at one time, a mile long at another. The picture may be vague, various pictures of triangles may be blended together; but it can never be universal, representing all possible triangles, as my idea does. This imagination is a *phantasm*. True, phantasms are often called 'ideas' by English writers; in fact, the whole school of Berkeley, Hume, and their followers fail to trace any difference between them; it is the fundamental error of their pernicious philosophy. Thus, for instance, Huxley maintains that God, the soul of man, etc., are unknowable and unthinkable,* because we can form no phantasm of them. This makes them simply unimaginable, not unknowable nor unthinkable; we know what we mean when we speak of them. (On the difference between ideas and phantasms see, further, *Logic*, by Richard Clarke, S.J., c. vi.)

Our ideas are expressed by words, or *oral terms;* the ideas themselves are often called *mental terms.*

ARTICLE II. DISTINCTIONS REGARDING IDEAS.

11. Logicians go into much detail on a variety of distinctions with respect to ideas; it will be sufficient for our present purpose briefly to notice a few of them.

* *Essay on Science and Morals.*

A first distinction lies between *abstract* and *concrete* ideas. A **concrete** idea expresses a subject, *e. g.*, 'this gold,' 'some men,' 'all flowers'; or a quality as belonging to a subject, *e. g.*, 'heavy,' 'virtuous,' 'fragrant.' An **abstract** idea expresses a quality by itself, drawn forth, as it were (*abstraho*, I draw away), from the subject to be separately considered, *e. g.*, 'heaviness,' 'virtue,' 'fragrancy.'

12. A second distinction exists between *singular*, *particular*, and *universal* ideas. An idea is **singular** if it expresses a definite single object, *e. g.*, 'this book,' 'that army,' 'that gold,' 'James,' 'the Angel Gabriel,' 'the United States,' meaning this one country.

An idea is **particular** if it represents one or more objects without determining which, *e. g.*, 'a man,' 'an army,' 'a Nero,' 'a spirit,' 'three books,' 'some states.'

An idea is **universal** when it expresses a note or notes common to many objects, found in each of them, no matter how much those objects may differ in other respects; *e. g.*, 'animal' and 'rational' are notes common to all men; they are conceived in the universal idea 'man,' and each of ther corresponds to a universal idea. The term *note* designates anything knowable in an object.

13. All universal ideas can be ranked under five heads, called **the five heads of predicables**, because it is always in one of these five ways that a universal idea is predicated of an object.

> 1. What is apprehended as common to many objects, found in each of them, and therefore predicable of them all in exactly the same sense, may be the whole nature, the essence of those objects, *i. e.*, all that without which those objects cannot exist nor be conceived. For instance, it is the nature or essence of all men to be 'rational animals'; unless I conceive an

object as being both 'rational' and 'animal,' I do not conceive a man at all. <u>This common essence</u> of a <u>class is called a *species*</u>. The **species**, therefore, is defined as all that constitutes the common nature or essence of a class of objects; *e.g.*, 'man,' 'rational animal.'

2. The universal idea may express a part only of the nature common to many objects. Thus, when I conceive 'animal,' I conceive only a part of man's nature, a part found in other species of objects as well, viz., in brutes. 'Rational' is the other part of man's nature, and it is not found in brutes, but it distinguishes man from the brute. Now, that universal concept which seizes upon what <u>is common</u> to different <u>species</u> is the idea of the **genus**; *e.g.*, 'animal' is the genus, to which belong the two species 'man' and 'brute.'

3. On the other hand, <u>the universal concept</u> which expresses <u>the peculiar note by which one species differs from another species of the same genus</u> is styled the **specific difference**; *e.g.*, 'rational' is the specific difference of the species man as distinguished from the species brute.

4. When the concept <u>expresses something that flows or results so necessarily from the very</u> essence that the essence cannot exist without it, and that note never exists but in such an essence, such note is called a **property or attribute** of that essence. Thus, 'the power of laughing,' 'the power to express one's thoughts by articulate speech,' cannot be found but in a being that is both animal and rational, and they result as natural consequences from its compound nature. The use of them may be accidentally im-

peded, as is that of reason itself in the infant and the idiot; but they belong to human nature as such, as distinct from other natures, and are therefore properties of man, proper or peculiar to man. Properties need not be conceived in order to apprehend the nature from which they flow; thus, to conceive man, I need not think of his risible power.

5. Lastly, the universal may express what is found in one or many individuals of a class, or even perhaps in all of them, yet in such a way that it could be absent without the individuals' ceasing to be of the same nature. In that case it expresses an **accident** of the species. For instance, a man may be white or black, tall or small, gentle or fierce, young or old, a European or an American; all these are accidental notes of man. All men are larger than ducks; and yet, if a dwarf should be born, who, when full-grown, should not be so large, being nevertheless a rational animal, he would be truly a man, his particular size being only an accident, not a property of his essence.

14. When we conceive a note common to two or more genera, *e.g.*, 'living,' which note belongs to animals and to plants alike, we have then a **higher genus**, of which the former genera may be considered as the species. 'Body' expresses a still higher genus; for it is predicated not only of living but also of non-living substances, such as stones and metals. 'Substance' itself is the **highest genus,** to which not only bodies but also spirits belong.

Reversing the process, we may start with the highest genus, say 'substance,' and call 'material' and 'immaterial' substances, or 'body' and 'spirit,' its species. The species 'body' becomes next a **subordinate** genus, of which 'living,' or 'organic,' and 'inorganic' will be the two species. Of 'organisms,' as a new subordinate genus, the species will be 'sentient' and 'non-sentient,' 'animals' and 'plants.' Of 'animals' we have two species, 'rational' and 'irrational,' 'man' and 'brute.' We have various species of 'brutes,' but not of 'man'; for, while brutes have very different natures or essences, and, flowing from these, very different properties, all men have the same essence and the same properties; these differ not in kind but in accidental degrees of perfection. Therefore 'man' is not a genus, but the **lowest species**; 'animal' is his proximate or **lowest genus**. The genera and species between the highest and the lowest are called *subaltern, subordinate,* or *intermediate.*

15. This ramification of a highest genus into subaltern genera and species is presented to the eye in the **Porphyrian** tree. The trunk of the tree contains the genera and the species, the branches the specific differences, the top exhibits individuals. (See page 17.)

16. In connection with universal ideas we must explain, as matters of the very highest importance in Logic, the *comprehension* and the *extension* of an idea. **Comprehension** means the total signification, all the notes comprehended or contained in an idea; thus, the concept 'man' comprehends the notes 'animal' and 'rational'; 'animal' itself means 'sentient, living, material substance.'

Extension means the total number of individuals to which the idea extends or applies; the extension of the concept 'man' is all men, that of 'animal' is wider still, extending to all men and all brutes. It is thus apparent that *the greater the comprehension of an idea is, the less is its extension,* and *vice versa;* because the more numerous the qualities apprehended, the fewer the individuals that will possess them all; thus, the genus 'animal' has more extension but less comprehension than the species 'man.' 'Animal' has more

I. e., substance is corporeal or incorporeal; corporeal substance, called matter or body, is organic or inorganic; an organic body or organism is sentient or insentient, etc.

THE PORPHYRIAN TREE.

extension than 'man,' because there are more animals than men; it has less comprehension, because the term 'animal' signifies fewer notes than 'rational animal' or 'man.'

When a term is taken in its full or widest extension, it is said to be **distributed**; it denotes then every one of the objects to which it can apply. Thus, when we say 'all men are creatures,' we mean 'every man is a creature.' Terms expressing particular ideas (No. 12) are **undistributed**; *e. g.,* 'gold is found in California'—*i. e.,* 'some gold.'

A distributed term is applied to all its objects in exactly the same meaning or acceptation. Now, many words are capable of two or three different acceptations: 1. When the meaning of a word is exactly the same, the term is called **univocal**; as when we give the name of 'box' to a case or receptacle of any size or shape. 2. When the meanings are entirely different, without any connection between them, the term is styled **equivocal**; as when the word 'box' is applied, now to a case, then to a blow on the head. 3. When the meanings are different but connected with one another, the term is **analogous**; thus the same word 'box' may stand for a case and for the wood out of which cases used often to be made, the box-tree.

ARTICLE III. JUDGMENTS AND PROPOSITIONS.

17. A **judgment** may be defined as *an act of the mind affirming or denying the agreement of two objective ideas*. The mind in judging compares two ideas, and consequently the objects represented by those ideas, and affirms or denies that they agree with one another; *e. g.*, 'modesty is praiseworthy,' 'ebriety is not worthy of man.' If, as in these examples, the agreement or disagreement is seen to exist by the mere consideration or analysis of the ideas compared, the judgment is **analytic**; it is also styled *a priori, i. e.,*

formed antecedently to experience; or *pure, i. e.*, formed by pure reason, not learned by sense-perception; or again, it may be called *necessary, absolute*, or *metaphysical*, according to the obvious meanings of those terms. But if the agreement or disagreement is discovered consequently on experience, *e. g.*, 'gold is malleable,' the judgment receives the opposite appellations of **synthetic**, *a posteriori, experimental, contingent, conditional*, and *physical*.

18. If a judgment of either kind is arrived at by reasoning, it is **mediately evident**; if the agreement or disagreement is seen without the aid of reasoning, the judgment is **immediately evident**. That 'ice is cold,' is an immediate *a posteriori* judgment; that 'there is nothing without a reason for it,' is immediately known *a priori;* that 'the sum of the angles of a triangle is equal to two right angles,' is known mediately *a priori;* the physical laws are known mediately *a posteriori*.

19. A judgment expressed in words is called a **proposition**. The subject and predicate together are its **matter**, and the affirmation or negation its **form**; the **copula** is always the verb 'to be' in the present indicative, expressed or implied: 'I see' is equivalent to 'I am seeing,' 'He said' to 'He is one who said,' etc.

That a proposition be **negative**, it is necessary that a negative word affect the copula. Now, it often requires some reflection to see what word is intended to be affected by the negation: 'No criminal is a happy man' means 'A criminal *is not* a happy man'; 'A tyrant has no peace' means 'A tyrant *is not* one having peace.'

20. In propositions it is of the highest importance for correct reasoning that we carefully attend to the *extension* and the *comprehension* of the terms used and of the ideas for which they stand.

I. If we consider **the extension of the subject**, a proposition is styled *singular, particular, or universal*, according as its subject expresses a singular, particular, or universal idea (No. 12). The form of the term expressing that idea may be misleading, the meaning must be carefully considered. Thus, 'a man is a creature,' 'man is a creature,' 'all men are creatures,' 'every man is a creature,' 'no man is necessary,' are all universal propositions; while 'a man was slain' is particular (for here 'a man' means, not every man, but 'some one man'), and 'that man is generous' is a singular proposition.

II. If we consider **the extension and the comprehension of the predicate**, we have the following rules:

1. *In an affirmative proposition the predicate is taken in its full comprehension, but not (except in definitions) in its full extension.* For instance, 'gold is a metal' means that gold has all the notes constituting a metal, but not that it is every metal. We say 'except in definitions,' for in these the defining words, which are the predicate, must have the same extension as the thing defined, expressed in the subject; *e. g.*, 'man is a rational animal,' *i. e.*, 'any rational animal.'

2. *In a negative proposition the reverse holds true, i. e., the predicate is taken in its full extension, but not in its full comprehension.* For instance, 'a diamond is not a metal' denies that the diamond is contained in the whole class of metals; but it does not deny that it has qualities in common with metals, since it is a substance, material, lustrous, etc., as well as metals. The extension of the subject determines the **quantity** of a proposition; its **quality** depends on its form, *i. e.*, on its being affirmative or negative.

21. In reasoning we must distinguish between *hypothetical* and *categorical* propositions.

The **hypothetical** proposition does not affirm or deny the agreement of subject and predicate absolutely, but dependently on some supposition or condition, or with a possible alternative. It is distinguished from the **categorical**, which directly affirms or denies the agreement between a subject and a predicate without any condition or alternative.

The hypothetical may be of *three kinds :*

(*a*) The **conditional**, consisting of two parts, one of which is declared to be the condition of the other. The part expressing the condition is called the *condition* or *antecedent*, the other the *conditioned* or *consequent*. If the connection is true, the proposition is true. Thus, 'If you knew God well, you would love Him,' is certainly true; 'If you get old, you will be wise,' may be false.

(*b*) The **disjunctive**, which connects incompatible clauses by the disjunctive particle 'or'; as, 'A being is either created or uncreated.' The proposition is true, if it leaves no alternative unmentioned.

(*c*) The **conjunctive**, which denies that two things can exist, or hold true, at the same time; as, 'A being cannot be created and independent.'

CHAPTER II.

REASONING.

22. **Reasoning** is the mental act or process of deriving judgments, called conclusions, from other judgments, called premises.

The principle underlying all valid reasoning is that the conclusion is implicitly contained in the premises; therefore whoever grants the truth of the premises thereby really grants the truth of the conclusion. For instance, in this reasoning, "Every good son is pleased to see his mother honored; but Christ is a good Son; therefore He is pleased to see His Mother honored," whoever grants the first two propositions must grant the third, since it is contained in them.

Reasoning is styled *pure*, if the judgments are analytic judgments; *empiric*, if they are synthetic, and *mixed*, if one premise is analytic and the other synthetic. Reasoning expressed in words is called **argumentation**.

ARTICLE I. THE CATEGORICAL SYLLOGISM.

23. All argumentation may be reduced to the *categorical syllogism*. A **syllogism** is an argument consisting of three propositions so connected that from the first two the third follows. If all the propositions are categorical, the syllogism is categorical. It will be remembered that a proposition is called **categorical** if it affirms or denies absolutely the agreement of a subject with a predicate. (No. 21.) "All virtues are desirable; but sobriety is a virtue; therefore sobriety is

desirable," is a categorical syllogism. This conclusion, "Sobriety is desirable," is implicitly contained in the first or major premise, "All virtue is desirable"; and the second or minor premise, "Sobriety is a virtue," points out the fact that it is therein contained. Such reasoning is, therefore, perfectly valid.

§ 1. *Constructing Syllogisms.*

24. To prove a thesis by a syllogism we begin by finding a proposition which really involves the truth of the thesis, and in a second proposition we state that it does so. Thus, if I am to prove that every one must honor his father and mother, I may start with the premise, "Every one must do what God commands"; I add the minor premise, "But God commands to honor father and mother." Hence I legitimately draw the conclusion, "Therefore every one must honor his father and mother."

25. We must next examine in what ways premises may contain conclusions. If the major is a universal proposition, it may contain the conclusion in four different ways:

1. The proposition being universal, the subject is distributed or taken in its widest extension; thus, "Every stone is matter," means that the predicate 'matter' applies to everything that is a 'stone.' If, therefore, the minor states that something, say 'marble,' is a stone, the conclusion will follow that marble is matter. Thus *the major affirms that a predicate belongs to a whole class; the minor affirms that a certain thing is of that class; the conclusion affirms that the same predicate belongs to that certain thing.*

2. Similarly, if the major is negative, as, "A stone is not a spirit," and the minor declares that "Marble is a stone of some kind," the conclusion will be that "Marble is not a spirit." That is: *the major*

denies a predicate of a whole class; *the minor affirms that a certain being is of that class; the conclusion denies that same predicate of that same being.*

3. A third form reasons thus: *The major denies a predicate of a whole class; the minor affirms that a certain being has that predicate; the conclusion denies that said being is of said class;* for if it were of that class, it would not have that predicate. Thus, "A stone is not a spirit; but an Angel is a spirit; therefore an Angel is not a stone."

4. In the three cases just explained the minor is affirmative. A fourth form of syllogism arises if *the major affirms some predicate of a whole class, and the minor denies that a certain being has that predicate; the conclusion will then be that said being does not belong to said class;* since all the individuals of that class have been affirmed to possess that predicate. "Every stone is matter; an Angel is not matter; therefore an Angel is not a stone."

In these four forms the major is a universal proposition, and the reasoning is founded upon the wide extension of the subject. The major need not be universal in the **fifth form**, which derives its validity from the full **comprehension of the predicate**.

5. The fifth form reasons thus: *The major affirms that a being has a certain predicate*, *i. e.*, that it has all the notes comprehended in that predicate; *the minor affirms that a certain note is comprehended in that predicate; the conclusion affirms that said being has said note.* Thus, "This stone is matter; but all matter is extended; therefore this stone is extended." By changing the order of the premises, this fifth form is reducible to the first.

26. The **first and second of these five forms** are the most obvious modes of argumentation and the most constantly used. The reasoning so familiar in Mathematics, $A=B$, $B=C$, $\therefore A=C$, is an application of the first form. The argument, if expressed in full, would read thus: "Any two things equal to a third thing are equal to each other; but A and C are equal to a third, B; therefore they are equal to each other." Similarly, from the second form we have the following reasoning: "Two things, one of which is equal to a third thing and the other unequal, are not equal to each other; but A is equal to B, and C is not equal to B; therefore A is not equal to C.

27. In these two special modes of reasoning the major propositions are usually suppressed, because they are so obvious; and the arguments assume an **abridged form**, so constantly in use and so practically useful, that we must explain it with special care. In fact, many logicians reduce all syllogisms to these two abridged forms, which they call the *affirmative* and the *negative syllogism*.

28. The **affirmative syllogism**, *i. e.*, that in which both the premises are affirmative, is based on the principle that *two things equal to a third are equal to each other*: $A=B$, $B=C$; therefore $A=C$

The **negative syllogism**, *i. e.*, that in which one premise is negative, is based on the principle that *two things, one of which is equal and the other unequal to a third, are unequal to each other*: $A=B$; B is not equal to C; therefore A is not equal to C.

29. The purpose of comparing A with B, and B with C, in the premises is to bring A and C together in the conclusion, as equal or unequal to each other. A and C are to be brought together; they are therefore called the **extreme terms**, and B, which brings them together, is **the middle**

term. The subject of the conclusion is styled the *minor extreme;* its predicate, the *major extreme.* The premise containing the major extreme is the *major premise,* and that containing the minor extreme is the *minor premise;* still, practically the first expressed is usually called the major, and the second the minor premise. All the propositions together are the **matter** of the syllogism; the proper connection between them is its **form** or **sequence**, a term not to be confounded with consequent or conclusion.

30. A syllogism is valid when both the matter and the form are without a flaw. The following is materially true, formally false: "All virtue is good; intemperance is not a virtue; therefore intemperance is not good." The following is materially false, formally true: "Gloomy things are hateful; but virtue is a gloomy thing; therefore virtue is hateful."*

§ 2. *Criticising Syllogisms.*

31. In the mathematical formula, $A=B$, $B=C$, $\therefore A=C$, there is no danger of error; but when we substitute ideas for the letters, there is need of great care to avoid mistakes. Thus, suppose that for A I substitute "silver," for B "a certain metal," for C "yellow," and instead of the formulas, $A=B$, $B=C$, $\therefore A=C$ I write: "Silver is a certain metal; but a certain metal is yellow; therefore silver is yellow," the conclusion is not legitimate; for 'a certain metal' is taken in two different significations, and consequently 'silver' and 'yellow' are not compared to one thing, but to different things. To

---

* **Exercises** like the following will be found to be of great advantage: Construct syllogisms proving the following theses: The Saints deserve to be honored, No man is to be hated by his fellow-man, Theft should be punished, Good books are valuable treasures, Bad books are injurious, Riches are not lasting possessions, The study of music should be encouraged, Jealousy cannot please God, No time is useless.

avoid and to discover errors in syllogistic reasoning, the following eight rules must be applied:

1. The terms are only three, to this attend;
2. Nor let the consequent a term extend.
3. Conclusions ne'er the middle term admit;
4. At least one premise must distribute it.
5. Two negatives no consequent can show,
6. From affirmations no negations flow.
7. A universal premise you'll provide,
8. And let conclusions take the weaker side.

32. *Rule* 1. *The terms are only three, to this attend.* There must be three terms, representing three ideas, and only three terms and ideas; this is the most important rule of all: it virtually contains most of the other rules. We evidently need three terms, that two things may be compared with a third; and, as each term must occur twice, there is no room for a fourth term. This rule is often violated by using one of the terms in two different meanings, especially the middle term; as:

Chewing is a bad habit;
But *chewing* is necessary to man;
Therefore a bad habit is necessary to man.

Rule 2. *Nor let the consequent a term extend.* Let no term have a wider meaning in the conclusion than in the premises; else there would really be more in the conclusion than is contained in the premises; as:

You are not what I am;
I am a *man*;
Therefore you are not a *man*.

'A man' is distributed in the consequent; for it stands for 'any man at all,' 'you are not any man at all'; but 'man' is particular in the minor; it means 'a certain man,' 'some man.'

Rule 3. <u>*Conclusions ne'er the middle term admit.*</u> This rule is evident, as the conclusion has nothing to do but to compare the extremes. We could not argue:

>Lincoln was President;
>Lincoln was of Illinois;
>Therefore *Lincoln* was President of Illinois.

Rule 4. *At least one premise must distribute it.* The middle term must be used in its widest meaning in at least one of the premises. If the middle term were taken twice in a particular meaning, it might denote different objects; as:

>*Some monks* were very learned;
>Luther was a *monk;*
>Therefore Luther was very learned.

Notice that a *singular term* is taken in its widest meaning, as 'Cicero,' 'Columbus,' 'the Eternal City,' etc.; *e. g.*, "Columbus discovered America; but Columbus was disgraced; therefore the discoverer of America was disgraced."

Rule 5. <u>*Two negatives no consequent can show.*</u> From the fact that two things are not equal to a third, it does not follow that they are equal to each other, nor that they are unequal.

Rule 6. <u>*From affirmations no negations flow.*</u> If the two premises are affirmative, they declare that two things are equal to a third; whence it follows that they are equal, not unequal, to each other.

Rule 7. <u>*A universal premise you'll provide.*</u> If both premises are particular, no conclusion will follow. For their subjects are particular (No. 20), and if both are affirmative, their predicates are particular (No. 20); thus all their terms are particular, and the middle term is not distributed as it should be by Rule 4. If one is negative, its predicate is distributed (No. 20), but that is not enough; we need then two universal terms, one for the middle term and one for the predicate of the conclusion. For that conclusion will be negative (Rule 8), and therefore must have a universal predicate (No. 20). We cannot reason thus:

> Some Inquisitors were cruel;
> Some good men were Inquisitors;
> Therefore some good men were cruel.

Rule 8. And let conclusions take the weaker side. The meaning is that, if one of the premises is negative, the conclusion is negative; if one is particular, the conclusion is particular. The first assertion is evident: it regards the negative syllogism explained above (No. 28). As to the second, if one premise is particular, two cases may occur: 1. If both are affirmative, they can contain only one distributed term, since one subject and both predicates are particular. The distributed term must, of course, be their middle term, for the middle term must be at least once distributed; and therefore the subject of the conclusion must be particular. 2. If one premise is negative, there may be two distributed terms in the premises, viz., the subject of the universal proposition, and the predicate of the negative—one of these is needed for the middle term, and one for the predicate of the negative conclusion; thus the subject of the conclusion will again be particular.*

33. These same rules apply to all syllogisms having

---

* **Exercise.** Criticise the following syllogisms:
  1. "The beings conjured up by spiritists are spirits;
     But the souls of the dead are spirits;
     Therefore the beings conjured up by spiritists are the souls of the dead."
  2. "Blessed are the poor in spirit;
     The Apostles are blessed;
     Therefore the Apostles are poor in spirit."
  3. "Scientists deal with physical laws;
     But Huxley and Darwin are scientists;
     Therefore they deal with nothing but physical laws."

categorical premises, even though the premises be **compound** propositions. The rules may seem at first sight to be violated, but they will be found, on careful inspection, to be observed in all correct reasoning of this kind. Attend especially to that part of the compound premises in which the stress of the argument lies. Thus, when we say, " God alone is *eternal*, but Angels are not God; therefore they are not *eternal*," the term 'eternal' is distributed in the conclusion, while it seems to be the predicate of an affirmative proposition in the major premise. But the major is compound, and contains a negative part, " Whatever is not God is not eternal." Hence the rule is not violated.

ARTICLE II. THE HYPOTHETICAL SYLLOGISM.

34. **A hypothetical syllogism** is one whose major is a hypothetical proposition (No. 21); and such it always is when the syllogism is not categorical. We have seen that there are three kinds of hypothetical propositions: the *conditional*, the *disjunctive*, and the *conjunctive*. Hence there are three species of hypothetical syllogisms.

35. I. **Conditional** syllogisms derive their force from an affirmed connection between a condition and a consequent; so that, if a certain condition is verified, a certain consequent must be admitted. Therefore, if the consequent does not exist, the condition is thereby known not to be verified. Hence this argument may validly conclude in two ways:

 4. " Monopolists are rich:
    Some rich men are proud:
    Therefore monopolists are proud."
 5. " Many men are rich:
    Many men oppress the poor:
    Therefore the rich oppress the poor."
 6. " The free-traders wish to reduce the tariff:
    Mr. C. wishes to reduce the tariff:
    Therefore Mr. C. is a free-trader."

1. *Affirmatively: The condition being affirmed, the consequent must be affirmed;* but not *vice versa.* Thus we say rightly:

> "If the sun shines, it is day;
> But the sun shines;
> Therefore it is day."

But if the minor were "It is day," it would not follow that the sun shines. Or, 2. *Negatively: The consequent being denied, the condition must be denied;* but not *vice versa.*

> "If the sun shines, it is day;
> But it is not day;
> Therefore the sun does not shine."

If the minor were "The sun does not shine," it would not follow that it is not day.

These and all other conditional syllogisms can be reduced to the categorical form. For instance, we can reason thus:

> "All times of sunshine are day;
> But this is a time of sunshine;
> Therefore it is day."

36. II. The **disjunctive** syllogism has a disjunctive major premise; *e. g.*, "Either the father, or the mother, or the child is the natural head of the family." It is supposed that the disjunction is complete, *i. e.*, that no fourth alternative is possible. From this major we may reason in three ways:

1. *The minor may deny one member of the disjunction, and the conclusion affirm the other members disjunctively.*

> "But the child is not the natural head of the family;
> Therefore either the father or the mother is such."

2. *The minor may affirm one of the members, the conclusion deny the other members copulatively:*

> "But the father is the natural head;
> Therefore neither the mother nor the child is such."

3. *The minor may deny all the members but one, the conclusion affirm that one:*
"But the mother and the child are not;
Therefore the father is."

37. III. The **conjunctive** syllogism has a conjunctive major premise; as: "No one can love God and hate his neighbor." From this premise we can reason validly by affirming one of the incompatible predicates in the minor, and denying the other in the conclusion: "But the Martyrs loved God; therefore they did not hate their neighbor," or "But Nero hated his neighbor, therefore he did not love God."

ARTICLE III. OTHER SPECIES OF DEMONSTRATIVE ARGUMENTS.

38. 1. The **Enthymeme**, as now usually understood,* is an elliptical syllogism, one of the premises being understood (ἐν θυμῷ, in the mind); *e. g.*, "The world displays a wonderful adaptation of means to an end; therefore it is the work of an intelligent Maker." The major is understood, viz., "Whatever displays a wonderful adaptation of means to an end is the work of an intelligent maker." To criticise the validity of an enthymeme we have only to supply the omitted premise, and then apply the ordinary rules of the syllogism.

39. 2. The **sorites** (σωρός, a heap) is an abridged series of syllogisms; it is an argument consisting of more than three propositions so connected that the predicate of the first becomes the subject of the second, the predicate of the second the subject of the third, etc., till the conclusion joins the subject of the first with the predicate of the last premise. "Man is accountable; whoever is accountable is free; whoever is free is intelligent; whoever is intelligent cannot be mere matter; therefore man cannot be mere matter."

---

* The word was differently derived and explained by Aristotle.

40. *To test such reasoning*, it should be resolved into connected syllogisms, thus:

"Whoever is accountable is free; but man is accountable; therefore man is free."

"Whoever is free is intelligent; but man is free; therefore man is intelligent."

"Whoever is intelligent cannot be mere matter; but man is intelligent; therefore man cannot be mere matter."

41. 3. The **dilemma** ($\delta \iota \varsigma$-$\lambda \tilde{\eta} \mu \mu \alpha$, a twofold assumption) is an argument which offers an adversary the choice between two or more alternatives, from each of which a conclusion is drawn against his position. The alternatives are called the *horns* of the dilemma. Such was the reasoning of one whom a Protestant parent was preventing from becoming a Catholic. He answered: "Either Protestantism or Catholicity is right. If Protestantism is right, every one must be guided by his own judgment in religious matters, and you should not prevent me from judging for myself. If Catholicity is right, you ought not only not to prevent me, but even to follow my example."

42. To be **conclusive**, the dilemma must leave no escape from the alternatives presented; thus, the dilemma just quoted would not be conclusive against a Pagan; for he would deny the major. Besides, the partial inferences must follow strictly from their respective premises; else the argument may often be retorted. A young man, striving to dissuade his sister from devoting herself to the exclusive pursuit of holiness, argued thus: "Either you have still a long or but a short life before you: if a long life, you will forego countless pleasures; if a short life, you cannot get far on the path of holiness." She retorted: "If a short life, I shall forego few pleasures; if a long one, I can get far on the path of holiness."

43. 4. When proofs of the premises or of one of them are inserted in a syllogism, the argument is called an **epichirema** (ἐπὶ χείρ, at hand, ready for use), which is rather an oratorical form of the syllogism than a distinct species of reasoning; *e. g.*, "Education should promote morality; but it fails to do so when severed from religious teachings, since morality derives all its force from religious convictions; therefore education should be religious."

44. 5. **Induction** requires careful consideration, on account of its constant application to the Physical Sciences. It follows a process the reverse of the syllogistic; for it argues not from universals to particulars, but from particulars to universals. It may be defined as an argument in which we conclude that what is found by experience to hold true of single objects of a class holds true of the whole class. Induction may be *complete* or *incomplete*.

45. **Complete induction** examines every single object of a class, and then enunciates universally that all the class has certain properties; for instance, after exploring every zone of the earth, we may conclude, "All the zones of the earth's surface are capable of supporting human life." Complete induction rests for its validity on this **syllogism**: "Whatever is true of every individual of a class is true of the whole class; but a certain proposition is true of every individual of a class; therefore it may be predicated of the whole class."

46. **Incomplete induction**, the ordinary process of Physical studies, does not examine every single object of a class, but a sufficient number of such objects, and under sufficiently varied circumstances, to make it certain that the property or action observed cannot be owing to any accidental cause, but must be due to the very nature of the objects, and therefore must always accompany them, even in such cases as have not been examined. As long as any doubt remains whether, perhaps,

the peculiarity constantly observed may not be owing to some accidental circumstances, induction cannot give truly scientific certainty; but when all such doubt is excluded, the argument is conclusive. It rests then upon this clear **syllogistic reasoning**: "Whatever property or action flows from the very nature of objects must always accompany those objects; but a certain property or action is known by a sufficient variety of experiments to flow from the very nature of certain objects; therefore it must always accompany them." For instance, heavy bodies when left unsupported have been found in most varied circumstances to fall to the earth, and therefore we judge without fear of error that this tendency must be due to their very nature, and we formulate the natural law: "Heavy bodies when unsupported fall to the earth."

47. The only **danger** is that scientists, in their eagerness to formulate general laws, will not always examine a sufficient variety of cases to exclude all doubt as to the real cause of the phenomena observed. Thus, Laplace laid it down as a natural law that all the parts of the solar system revolve from west to east; while it is now known that some of the solar planets and their satellites perform motions in the opposite direction.

48. It is evident that no conclusion is **valid**, except in as far as it is contained in the premises from which it is derived. Therefore the fact that an assertion is found to hold in ninety-nine cases is no certain proof that it will hold true in the hundredth case, since this hundredth case is not contained in the cases observed. Incomplete induction, therefore, cannot by itself, without resting on a syllogism, furnish a scientific proof. But we have scientific proofs of many things. Hence it is evident that Materialists and Positivists (*i. e.*, those pretended philosophers who admit nothing but matter and sensible phenomena) are entirely mistaken when they teach that the

mind has no knowledge of any universal propositions whatever, except as far as it has observed and generalized individual facts; that all reasoning, therefore, is only the generalizing of facts, or that all the elements of our knowledge are only inductive, without any universal proposition on which their certainty rests. Some of these philosophers maintain that we do not even know that a circle must be round, but only that it is always known to be so on this earth, while elsewhere it may, for all we know, be square. But the proposition, "A circle is round," is self-evident, independently of observation and induction. A system is known to be false if it leads logically to absurd consequences, as their system does.

Article IV. Probable Reasoning.

49. In all the forms of argumentation so far explained, the process is every way reliable and the conclusion certain; such reasoning is called **demonstrative**; to distinguish it from **probable** reasoning, which fails to remove all prudent fear of error.

A syllogism one or both of whose premises are only probable will, of course, yield only a probable conclusion; it is called **dialectic**, *i. e.*, open to discussion (διαλέγομαι, I discuss). We shall here consider two important species of probable arguments, *Analogy* and *Hypothesis*, both of frequent application, chiefly in the Physical Sciences.

50. I. **Analogy** (ἀνάλογος, parallel reasoning) is an argument by which we conclude that a certain line of reasoning will hold in one case because it is known to hold in a similar case. Thus, because we see that the actions of brutes are to a great extent similar to those of men, and in men they are prompted by certain feelings, we conclude, with very strong probability, that in brutes also they are prompted by similar feelings.

51. **The principles underlying analogical reasonings** are such as these: "Similar causes are apt to produce similar effects," "Similar properties suggest similar essences," "Things similarly constructed appear to be governed by similar laws," etc. Sometimes the probability thus obtained is very strong; at other times the argument is deceptive, because, though alike in many other ways, the two cases may differ on the very point in question. Such are many of the analogies urged in support of the Evolution of Species. "The vile grub is evolved into a beautiful butterfly; why may not a hawk be developed into an eagle?" asks the popular scientist. But from the egg of the butterfly comes the vile grub again, and the species remains ever the same. Varieties of type within the same species of animals are numberless, but no single case of an evolution from one species into another has ever been scientifically established.

52. The argument of analogy is more useful to the orator than to the philosopher. It supplies the former with the topics of Similitude and Example. It suggests much effective reasoning *a majori, a minori,* and *a pari.*

In scientific investigations analogy is often suggestive of solutions, which may afterwards be proved demonstratively to be correct; till they are so proved, they are called *hypotheses.*

53. II. An **hypothesis** (ὑπόθεσις, a supposition) is a proposition provisionally assumed as if true, because it accounts plausibly for many facts. For instance, it was formerly supposed that light consisted of particles emitted by luminous bodies; the present hypothesis explains the phenomena of light more plausibly by the vibrations or undulations of ether. When an hypothesis is so far confirmed by experience that it leaves no reasonable doubt as to its correctness, it ceases to be an hypothesis and becomes a *thesis.*

That an hypothesis may be probable and truly **scientific,** it is necessary: 1. That it explain a considerable portion of the facts in question. 2. That it do not certainly contradict any well-established truth; for, as two contradictories cannot both be true, whatever hypothesis contravenes a well-established truth is thereby known to be false. Numerous important discoveries have been made, especially in the Physical Sciences, by means of ingenious hypotheses. On the other hand, science has often been much retarded by false hypotheses, which led investigations into wrong directions. To point out such false assumptions is to render most important services to the cause of progress. For one Copernican theory retarded a while till supported by stronger proofs, numerous wild vagaries have been discountenanced by the Roman tribunals, and the energies of the learned diverted from wasting themselves in the pursuit of idle fancies.

Article V. Indirect Reasoning.

54. Reasoning, whether demonstrative or probable, is styled **indirect** when, instead of proving the thesis, it simply aims at clearing away objections against it, or at establishing some other proposition from which the truth of the thesis may be inferred. Indirect reasoning may assume various forms:

1. The **self-contradiction**, or *reductio ad absurdum*, is a form of argument showing that the denial of the theses leads to absurd consequences; thus we argue the necessity of admitting certainty from the fact that the denial of all certainty leads a man to stultify himself.

2. The **negative argument** points out the absence of all proof from an opponent's assertions. "Mere assertions go for nothing," " *Quod gratis asseritur gratis negatur,*" are received axioms of discussion.

3. The **instance** or **example** adduces a test case in

which the assertion or the reasoning of an opponent is shown to be at fault. Thus, if one asserted that all history is unreliable, we might instance our Declaration of Independence as an undeniable fact of history.

4. An **argumentum ad hominem** draws from an opponent's principles, true or false, a conclusion against him; *e. g.*, when a Fatalist philosopher was about to flog his slave for the crime of theft, the latter argued that he could not be justly punished for a crime which he was *fated* to commit.

5. A **retort** turns an adversary's argument or some portion of it against himself; as when the same philosopher answered that he likewise was *fated* to flog the slave.

6. We **evade** an argument when, without discussing his proofs, we call on an adversary to explain what he is unwilling or unable to explain; thus many a specious theorizer is silenced by summoning him to explain the consequences of his theories.

7. The argument **ad ignorantiam** shows that an opponent is unable to prove his point or answer our objections.

8. The argument **ad invidiam** makes an adversary's thesis or his proofs odious or ridiculous.

55. In **answering objections** we should attend with special care to distinguish what is true from what is false in the arguments of our opponents.

Most objections contain some element of truth; for falsity, as such, is not plausible: it is the truth blended with falsity that gives plausibility to an objection. To separate the one from the other, by drawing clear lines of demarcation, is the keenest test of logical skill, and the direct road to complete victory. To facilitate for the student this task of neatly dis tinguishing the true from the false, we shall now point out the chief forms which fallacious arguments are apt to assume.

ARTICLE VI. SOPHISMS OR FALLACIES.

56. A **sophism** or **fallacy** is an argument which, under the specious appearance of truth, leads to a false conclusion. The deception is caused either by some *ambiguity in the expression*, or by some *confusion in the thoughts expressed*.

57. 1. The fallacies arising from **ambiguity in the expression** are chiefly two:

1. The **equivocation, or ambiguous middle,** uses a middle term in two different meanings; *e. g.*, "The soul is immortal; but a brute animal has a soul; therefore a brute animal has something immortal." We answer by distinguishing the two meanings of the word 'soul.' In the major it denotes the human soul, in the minor the principle of life in any animal: there are four terms.

2. The fallacy of **composition and division** confounds what holds of things separate with what holds of them united; *e. g.*, "It is absolutely impossible that the dead should live" is true in the sense that they cannot live and be dead at the same time, *i. e.*, in the sense of *composition;* but it is not true in the sense of *division:* those now dead can, by the power of God, be made to live again.

58. II. Fallacies result from **confusion of thought** in six ways, chiefly:

1. The fallacy of the **accident** confounds an essential with an accidental property; *e. g.*, "We buy raw meat, and we eat what we buy; therefore we eat raw meat."

What we eat has the same essence as what we buy, but not the same accident of rawness.

2. What is true in the proper sense of the word, '*simpliciter*,' is often confounded with what is true in a qualified sense or **under a certain respect** (*secundum quid*); *e. g.*, "A sea-captain who willingly throws his cargo overboard ought to indemnify the owner; but A did so; hence A ought to indemnify the owner." The major would be true, if the captain were absolutely willing to destroy the cargo entrusted to him; but not if he is willing in a way only, *i. e.*, as a necessary means to save vessel and crew.

3. An **irrelevant conclusion**, *ignoratio elenchi*, or *missing the point*, proves what is not in question, refutes what is not objected; as when Evolutionists prove elaborately that the body of man resembles in various ways the bodies of brutes—a fact which no sensible man denies.

4. The *petitio principii*, or **begging the question**, consists in taking for granted the point which is to be proved; when this very point is used as a premise in the reasoning, the fallacy is called a **vicious circle**.

5. The **fallacy of the false consequence**, often called a *non-sequitur*, or want of sequence, is used when a conclusion is drawn which is not contained in the premises; *e. g.*, "There exists a wonderful gradation in the perfection of plants and animals; therefore the more perfect are evolved from the less perfect."

6. The **undue assumption**, or false cause, *non causa pro causa*, assumes as a cause what is not a cause; as when the Reformation is assumed to be the cause of scientific progress. This fallacy often arises from

the fact that mere priority in time is mistaken for causality; *post hoc; ergo propter hoc.**

Article VII. Method in Reasoning.

59. **Order** is a proper arrangement of parts for any purpose whatever, theoretical or practical; **method** is a suitable arrangement of parts with a view to a practical end. In reasoning, the end is the acquisition or the communication of knowledge.

60. All reasoning must **begin with undoubted premises**, which themselves need not to be supported by reasoning: no science is expected to prove its first principles. Thus, Geometry starts out with a number of axioms, from which the whole science is derived by logical reasoning. Such axioms are not blindly or arbitrarily taken for granted; but they are self-evident, they need no proof. Thus, too, in Philosophy the first principles are self-evident and need no proof.

61. As the mind must, of course, apprehend the premises before it draws conclusions from them, we say that in the **logical order**, *i.e.*, in the order of thought, the premises are always prior to the conclusions. But in the **ontological order**, *i.e.*, in the order of being, a truth stated in the premises may be really posterior to the truth expressed in the conclusion. Such is the case whenever we reason from an effect to its

---

* **Exercise.** Point out the fallacies contained in the following arguments:

1. "Liberty is desirable; but the laws restrict liberty; therefore the laws restrict what is desirable."

2. "The liberty of the press is a blessing; but blessings should not be restricted; therefore the liberty of the press should not be restricted."

3 "The Inquisition was the cause of much cruelty; but the Popes approved the Inquisition; therefore the Popes approved the cause of much cruelty."

4. "The Spanish Inquisitors were often cruel; but St. Peter Arbues was a Spanish Inquisitor; therefore the Saints are often cruel."

5. "Galileo was condemned by a Roman tribunal; therefore the Pope is not infallible."

6. "The Supreme Court of the United States is a fallible tribunal; therefore its decisions are not to be regarded."

cause, say from a beautiful picture to the skill of the painter; for the effect is posterior to the cause, is dependent on the cause.

62. Reasoning thus from effect to cause is reasoning **a posteriori**, and, *vice versa*, reasoning from cause to effect is called **a priori**, since causes are ontologically prior to their effects.

63. It will be noticed that the terms *a priori* and *a posteriori* have not exactly the same meaning when applied to reasoning and when applied to judgments. A **judgment a priori**, as explained above (No. 17), is one formed independently of experience, while a **reasoning a priori** is one proceeding from a cause to its effect.

64. While in *a priori* and *a posteriori* reasonings we consider relations between two things, one of which is ontologically prior to the other, in **analytical** and **synthetical** reasonings we consider only one thing, studying the relations between the whole being and its parts, between a substance and its qualities. If we are first acquainted with the whole being and from the study of it strive to discover its parts, we are said to analyze the subject (ἀναλυω, I take apart): we then proceed analytically. But if we know the parts first, and put them together to find the whole, we proceed synthetically (σύνθεσις, a putting together). The chemist analyzes a mineral to discover its simple ingredients; the apothecary combines simples into compounds. The synthetic geometrician puts together lines and angles to find the properties of surfaces and solids; while the analytical geometrician finds the particular mathematical relations implied in a general formula.

65. The metaphysician considers **an idea as a whole**, and the **notes of it as its parts**. For instance, knowing that an oak is a tree, he examines the notes involved in the concept

'tree,' and finds analytically that an oak is a substance, material, vegetable, etc. On the other hand, seeing that the human body is a substance, extended, living, sensitive, he concludes synthetically that it is of an animal nature. Now, it is obvious that the idea analyzed is less extended than the notes; *e. g.*, 'tree' is less extensive than 'substance,' for every tree is a substance, but not every substance is a tree. Therefore, when we reason analytically, we proceed *from the particular to the universal*, and *vice versa* we reason synthetically *from the universal to the particular*.

66. A science may use either **analysis or synthesis,** or now the one and then the other. Thus, in this treatise on Dialectics, while first explaining ideas, next the union of ideas into judgments, then the combination of judgments into arguments, we have used synthesis; and, in analyzing the nature of reasoning to discover the rules that must guide it, we have used analysis. This latter process is, in most studies, better suited for the investigation of truth, synthesis for the imparting of truth to others.

67. While treating of scientific methods, it is proper to speak of the **distinctions existing between various sciences.** These are distinguished according to their objects; thus, Astronomy is evidently distinct from Botany, because it treats of a different class of objects. When sciences treat of the same object, as do Geology, Geometry, and Geography, all of which study the earth, they view that object differently; and the view they take of their objects is called their *formal object*, the object itself being called the *material object*. Sciences are therefore more correctly said to be **specified by their formal objects.** It naturally follows that a science is esteemed as more or less noble in proportion as its formal object is more or less worthy of man. Theology is therefore the noblest of all, since it views all its objects as they are known

by the highest light, viz., by the supernatural light of Divine Revelation. Philosophy is the noblest of the merely human sciences, since its formal object is what is most intellectual in all things, viz., their very essences and their relations to the highest good.

68. The true teachings of any science can never come into **conflict** with the true teachings of any other science; for truth objectively considered is something absolute, not merely relative; it is *that which is*. In the case of an apparent conflict between two sciences, it will always be found that one of the conflicting teachings is not demonstrated nor capable of demonstration.

ARTICLE VIII. EXERCISE IN REASONING.

69. The most useful exercise in philosophic studies is the manner of discussion called **The Circle.** We shall here explain it at some length:

One pupil is appointed to defend on a given day, during about half an hour, any thesis that has been explained in the class; two others are appointed to object; and the whole discussion is to be conducted in strict syllogistic form. The discussion is opened by the first objector, who challenges the defender to prove the thesis. The latter begins by explaining the exact meaning of the thesis; he next gives the proof in a formal syllogism, adding, if necessary, the proof of the major or the minor, or both. The objector then attacks the thesis or its demonstration: he offers a syllogism the conclusion of which is contradictory to the thesis or to the validity of the proof. The defender repeats the objection in the very words of the opponent; next, he replies separately to each of its propositions.

Let us suppose that the third thesis of *Critical Logic*—**the theory of universal scepticism is self-contradictory** (No.

94)—is the subject of discussion. The defender, at the summons of the first objector, explains and proves the thesis. Then the first *objector:* "That is not self-contradictory which does not affirm and deny the same thing; but the theory of universal scepticism does not affirm and deny the same thing; therefore it is not self-contradictory." The *defender* repeats the objection word for word, and then adds: "The major, 'That is not self-contradictory which does not affirm and deny the same thing,' I grant. The minor, 'The theory of universal scepticism does not affirm and deny the same thing,' I deny." *Objector:* "I prove the minor: that does not affirm and deny the same thing which affirms nothing whatever; but the theory of universal scepticism affirms nothing whatever; therefore it does not affirm and deny the same thing." The *defender* repeats the syllogism, and adds: "The major, 'That does not affirm and deny the same thing which affirms nothing whatever,' I grant. The minor, 'The theory of universal scepticism affirms nothing whatever,' I deny." *Objector:* "I prove my new minor: the theory which doubts of everything affirms nothing whatever; but the theory of universal scepticism doubts of everything; therefore it affirms nothing whatever." *Defender,* after repeating the syllogism, adds: "The major, 'The theory which doubts of everything affirms nothing whatever,' let that pass. The minor, 'The theory of universal scepticism doubts of everything,' I deny." *Objector:* "I prove the last minor: universal scepticism is defined as the theory which doubts of everything; therefore universal scepticism doubts of everything." *Defender* repeats the enthymeme, and adds: "The antecedent, 'Universal scepticism is defined as the theory which doubts of everything,' I distinguish: as the theory which pretends to doubt of everything, I grant; as the theory which really doubts of everything, I deny; and therefore I deny the consequent."

Objector: "But the sceptic really doubts of everything; therefore the distinction is of no avail." *Defender* repeats, and adds: "The antecedent, 'The sceptic really doubts of everything,' I deny." *Objector:* "May I ask your reason for denying it?" *Defender:* "I deny it because no man can really doubt of everything; even his own existence; the fact that he is reasoning, speaking, etc." *Objector:* "But the sceptic sincerely affirms that he doubts of everything." *Defender:* "Then he affirms something, and thereby contradicts himself."

The Second Objector: "That should not be maintained as a thesis which cannot be validly proved; but it cannot be validly proved that universal scepticism is an absurd theory; therefore it should not be maintained as a thesis." The *defender* repeats, then adds: "The major, 'That should not be maintained as a thesis which cannot be validly proved,' I will let that pass for the present. The minor, 'It cannot be validly proved that universal scepticism is an absurd theory,' I deny, and therefore I deny the conclusion." *Objector:* "I prove the minor: that proof is not valid which takes for granted what cannot be proved; but the proof of this thesis does so; therefore it is not valid." *Defender* repeats, and adds: "'That proof is not valid which takes for granted what cannot be proved,' I distinguish that major: if that which is taken for granted needs proof, I grant; if it needs no proof, I deny. As to the minor: 'But the proof of this thesis takes for granted what cannot be proved,' I distinguish this the same way: it takes for granted what is evident, and therefore needs no proof, I grant; it takes for granted that which needs proof, I deny. And therefore I deny the conclusion, etc., etc."

BOOK II.

CRITICAL LOGIC.

70. We have studied, in *Dialectics*, the laws which govern the *form* of reasoning; in **Critical Logic** we are to examine the certainty of the propositions, *i. e.*, of the *matter* of reasoning, and the validity of the reasoning process itself. For this purpose we are to consider: 1. *The nature of certainty;* 2. *The existence of certainty;* 3. *The means of attaining certainty, and* 4. *The ultimate test or criterion of certainty.*

CHAPTER I.

THE NATURE OF CERTAINTY.

71. **Certainty** is defined as that state of mind in which we firmly adhere to a truth, on account of motives that exclude all fear of error. To study its nature, we must examine: (*a*) *The nature of truth and of its opposite, falsity;* (*b*) *The various states of our minds with regard to truth, and* (*c*) *The elements that make up certainty.*

Article I. Truth and Falsity.

72. Truth *denotes conformity between a mind and an object.* This conformity may be differently viewed:

1. When we consider the knowledge of the mind as conformable to the object known, we have **logical truth;** thus we speak of 'true judgments,' 'a true understanding of a fact or of a theory,' etc.
2. When we consider an object as cognoscible, *i.e.*, as conformable to real or possible knowledge, we have **metaphysical truth.** In this sense the truth of an object is really identical with the very being of the object, for an object is cognoscible inasmuch as it has being; therefore all things have metaphysical truth.
3. When we consider language as conformable to the knowledge of him who uses it, we have **moral truth;** thus we say: 'a true account,' 'a true statement,' etc.

Logic treats of logical truth.

73. Falsity is the opposite of *truth*. The mere absence of truth is sometimes called *negative falsity;* but this is not falsity in the proper sense of the word. We never speak of metaphysical falsity, for all things have metaphysical truth: even a false coin is truly what it is, and cognoscible as such; when we call it 'false,' we use a figure of speech by which we mean 'calculated to deceive.' **Logical** falsity exists when there is something in the intellect which is not conformable to the object; **moral** falsity, or falsehood, exists when there is something in the expression not conformable to what is in the mind.

74. Logical falsity may occur in a judgment in three ways;

1. The intellect may affirm something which is not in the object; as when it affirms that matter can think, or it counts six stars where there are but five.

2. It may affirm as real what is only apparent; *e. g.*, that the sun moves around the earth.

3. It may deny what really is, *e. g.*, the motion of the earth.

75. The terms 'true' and 'false' are chiefly applied to **judgments** and propositions. Still, a mere **apprehension** or idea may also be called true; for it contains conformity between the mind and an object. But a mere apprehension is never called 'a truth'; this expression is confined to a judgment or a proposition.

76. **Thesis I.** *A mere apprehension, as such, cannot be false.* *Proof.* A mere apprehension, as such, is merely a mental image of something real or possible (for we cannot have an image of something absolutely impossible, *e. g.*, of a square circle, nor of a mere nothing); but every image, as such, *i. e.*, in as far as it is an image, is necessarily conformable to that of which it is the image; else it would not be the image of it. Therefore, inasmuch as it is an image at all, it is true, not false. A portrait may not resemble the person who sat for it, but it represents what it represents, and so far it is a true image.

77. If it be **objected** that we may have a wrong idea or notion of a thing, *e. g.*, of a spirit, conceiving it as a being composed of thin air, we *answer* that our concept of a being composed of thin air is a true idea; for such a being is possible; but, if we go on to judge that such a being is what is called a spirit, we do more than conceive an idea—we join two ideas, we pronounce a judgment. It is not then the mere apprehension but the judgment which is false.

But can we not have an idea to which no possible being corresponds, *e. g.*, of a 'square circle'? We have ideas of 'square' and of 'circle'; but we cannot either imagine or conceive a square circle. If we proceed to form a judgment that these ideas are compatible with each other, the error is in our judgment, not in our apprehensions. We do not deny that many men have wrong ideas, *e. g.*, of religion, of the Catholic Church, of indulgences, of literary excellence, of honor, etc.; but the falsity in those ideas is due to the false judgments which those ideas implicitly contain, not to the ideas as ideas. For instance, a man conceives of an indulgence as 'leave to commit sin,' and he judges that this is the meaning of the word in Catholic doctrine.

ARTICLE II. STATES OF THE MIND WITH REGARD TO TRUTH.

78. 1. **Ignorance** is the state of a mind to which the truth is not presented at all; thus, we are all ignorant whether the number of the stars is odd or even. Ignorance is *vincible* if it is in our power to remove it; else it is *invincible*.
2. **Doubt** is the state of a mind hesitating whether to assent to a truth or not. A *positive* doubt sees reasons for and against assent; a *negative* doubt sees no reasons for either side; it comes to the same as ignorance. A mere doubt inclines the mind to neither side; but doubt may be accompanied by suspicion or opinion.
3. **Suspicion** is the state of a mind which has more leaning to one judgment than to its contradictory, but still pronounces no judgment.
4. **Opinion** is the state of a mind pronouncing a judgment, but not without fear of error. The motives for assenting are called the *probability* of a judgment. **Probability** is said to be *intrinsic* when the motives for assent are drawn from the consideration of the matter; *extrinsic*, when they are drawn from the statements of other persons.

5. **Certainty** is the state of a mind assenting to a truth without fear of error. If this fear of error is excluded by motives which leave no room for reasonable doubt, we have certainty in the *proper* sense of the word; if the fear of error is excluded without such motives, we have certainty *improperly* so called. In the latter case, the fear of error is excluded by the free action of the will, which turns away the intellect from considering all reasons of doubt.

79. It is useful to distinguish **speculative** from **practical** judgments: the former regard the certainty of knowledge, *e. g.*, "The bread before me is not poisoned"; the latter, the prudence of action, *e. g.*, "I may eat that bread without further examination." We act prudently when we look for the best guidance of reason that circumstances allow; strict certainty cannot be had concerning every step of daily conduct.

80. Since prudence is not inconsistent with a possibility of error, there may be **invincible error** connected with prudent practical judgments; but all error is inconsistent with strict certainty, and there can be no invincible error connected with judgments which are strictly certain.

81. Error in judgments of any kind, speculative or practical, is always **traceable to free will.** It cannot, of course, be caused by the objective truth; nor can the intellect be necessitated to judge falsely, since its very essence consists in the power of knowing, *i. e.*, grasping, truth. There remains only one possible cause of error, viz., man's freedom to embrace a proposition. The free will of man can often bend the intellect so to fix its attention on the probabilities of a proposition as to overlook all reasons to doubt, and thus form a false judgment, firmly adhering to it without fear of error: this is not certainty, however, in the proper sense of the word (No. 78. 5)

The Nature of Certainty.

82. Error or falsity cannot strictly be predicated of *ignorance*, *doubt*, or *suspicion ;* for these states of the mind neither affirm nor deny anything whatever. Ignorance may be culpable, doubt may be unreasonable, suspicion unfounded and rash; but none of these is properly called false. Error can be predicated of nothing but *opinion* and *certainty* improperly so styled, *i. e.*, of that state of mind which excludes the fear of error by the force of the will.

83. While the will is the ultimate source of all error, there are various **proximate sources**; the chief are:

1. *Prejudices*, *i. e.*, judgments formerly assented to without proper examination.
2. Imperfect *teaching* or false information regarding facts and principles.
3. *Confusion of ideas*, whether resulting from dulness, *i. e.*, slowness to distinguish between things similar, or from present inattention, owing to fatigue, negligence, multiplicity of cares, etc.
4. *Passion*, *i. e.*, violent desire or aversion, which prompts our will to accept as true what is pleasing to us.
5. *Impatience* to arrive at a conclusion, either because we are eager to act, or too conceited to doubt our judgment, or too vain to acknowledge our ignorance. From all this it is evident that virtue is favorable to the acquisition of sound knowledge.
6. Another frequent source of erroneous judgments in many persons is a diseased condition of the nervous system or a portion of it. This abnormal state of the body may give rise to a variety of phantasms so vividly presented to the mind as to prevent calm consideration of the reasons for or against the formation of a judgment.

Article III. The Elements that Make up Certainty.

84. We have defined *certainty proper* as the state of mind in which we firmly adhere to truth, on account of motives which exclude all fear of error. Several **elements** are here combined: 1. **Subjectively**, *i. e.*, considering the acts of the mind, we have a firm adhesion (a positive element), and the exclusion of all fear of error (a negative element). 2. **Objectively**, *i. e.*, considering the object known, we have such a manifestation of a truth as is sufficient to exclude all fear of error. The subjective adhesion is caused by the objective manifestation of truth. It is called *subjective certainty*, the manifestation of the truth being designated as *objective certainty*.

85. When the mind reflects on the fact that it has this firm adhesion, its certainty is called **reflex**; when it does not reflect on this fact, its certainty is **direct**. **Philosophical certainty** does not differ from ordinary reflex certainty except in this, that it notices distinctly and scientifically the motives of adhesion to a truth.

86. If we examine objective certainty still further, we find that the truth manifested may be of *three species*, which give respectively three different names to certainty; viz.:

1. Certainty is called **metaphysical** when the mind sees that a proposition is essentially true because its contradictory would be absurd; in such a case an exception is absolutely impossible; *e. g.*, "Virtue is praiseworthy," "A triangle has three sides."
2. Certainty is **physical** when a fact is seen to be so necessary, according to the laws of material nature, that no one but the Author of those laws can make an exception; *e. g.*, "The dead do not return to life."
3. Certainty is **moral** when the mind sees that something

is constantly and universally true in the conduct of men, although dependent on their free choice; *e. g.*, "Serious men do not tell a falsehood on important points without weighty motives."

87. The term 'moral certainty' is often used in a **looser sense** to denote a strong probability; *e. g.*, I have a moral certainty that this house is not on fire just now, though I have no real certainty on the subject.

88. Subjectively considered, all kinds of certainty are alike in the **negative element**, *i. e.*, all exclude fear of error; but the **positive element**, *i. e.*, the intensity of the mind's adhesion to the truth, may be more or less firm: in some cases, as in axioms, and generally in all that is immediately evident, the mind cannot doubt the agreement of subject and predicate. Thus, we cannot help seeing that a whole is greater than its parts, that some bodies exist, that virtue and vice differ from each other, etc. Even in many things that are only mediately evident we cannot entertain a doubt; *e. g.*, no well-informed man can doubt that ancient Rome existed. In many matters, however, we can refuse to admit the objective truth; and in others we even find it difficult to steady our attention sufficiently on the object to exclude all doubt. Metaphysical certainty admitting no possible exception is, as such, nobler than the other kinds; still, it is not always stronger in a given case; thus, I am more intensely convinced of Cæsar's death, which is a matter of moral certainty, than of many theses in Mathematics or Philosophy, which rest on metaphysical principles.

CHAPTER II.

THE EXISTENCE OF CERTAINTY.

89. Scholastic Philosophy begins, as the Physical Sciences pretend to do, by ascertaining and examining **undeniable facts;** in this particular it differs strikingly from many false systems in Philosophy which commence with theories directly contradictory to all experience. When entering on the subject of the existence of certainty, we are at once brought face to face with a patent fact which may be stated thus: *All men having the full use of reason exhibit a direct and natural adhesion to many truths as objectively certain.*

90. We are not yet maintaining that those truths *are* objectively certain; we are only stating the undeniable fact that all men adhere to them as objectively certain. We call this adhesion *direct*, *i. e.*, antecedent to reflection and to philosophic analysis. For instance, all men consider their own existence, the existence of bodies, the connection between cause and effect, the difference between right and wrong as objectively certain. (See Balmes's *Fundamental Philosophy*, cc. 1, 2, 3; Kleutgen's *Philosophie*, 3d Treatise.) No fact on which any physical science relies is more undeniable. We have called this adhesion *natural*, because in science we call any effect natural if it is found constantly and universally to attend a given cause. Now, this adhesion is constantly and universally found in man; therefore it must be natural to man.

91. **Thesis II.** *This direct and natural adhesion of all men*

to many truths as objectively certain is (*a*) *certainty properly so called ;* (*b*) *not indeed philosophical certainty, but* (*c*) *capable of becoming such.*

Proof: (*a*) Certainty properly so called is a firm adhesion to a truth, on account of motives which exclude all fear of error. But the adhesion here spoken of is such; therefore it is certainty properly so called. *We prove the minor:*

1. *It is firm ;* in fact, man cannot rid himself of it.*
2. *It excludes fear of error ; i. e.,* we do not mistrust these judgments.
3. This fear of error is excluded by the evidence of the *objective truth.* As St. Thomas expresses it: " It is the property of first principles that they not only are necessarily true, but also manifest themselves evidently as objectively true." If this fear of error were not excluded by the evidence of the objective truth, it would be excluded either by the free will of man or by a blind necessity compelling man to judge wrongly. But it is not excluded by our will, for we adhere to the truth even against our will. Nor by a blind necessity to judge falsely; for then our intellect would be no intellect at all, since an intellect is a power to see the truth, not a power to act blindly.

(*b*) *This direct adhesion is not itself philosophic certainty;* for it is antecedent to reflection and analysis, while philosophic certainty is subsequent to both.

(*c*) *It is capable of becoming philosophic certainty ;* for, when reflected on and analyzed, it is distinctly seen to contain motives sufficient to exclude all fear of error, and thus the

---

* The sceptic Pyrrho, when laughed at for fleeing from a falling stone with as much earnestness as if he had no doubt of its reality, replied ingenuously: ' It is hard entirely to throw off human nature." If any votary of philosophy should begin to have any real doubts of the existence of certainty, he would need rest of mind and healthy exercise of body, not abstract reasoning, to convince him of objective certainty.

element is supplied which constitutes the accidental difference between ordinary certainty and philosophic certainty, viz., the distinct perception of the motives for adhesion to truth (No. 85).

92. **Objections:** 1. This reasoning supposes several things that have not yet been demonstrated; *e. g.*, that we have understanding. *Answer.* It does not suppose anything that needs demonstration or that could reasonably be doubted.

2. Some judgments in which all men concurred were false; *e. g.*, that the sun moved round the earth. *Answer.* All men *judged* that the sun moved around the earth, we distinguish; they judged about the scientific question whether it was the earth's or the sun's motion that caused the phenomena perceived, we deny; few men gave this question any thought, and those who did would naturally judge that the motion *appeared* to be in the sun. If any judged that it *was* in the sun, they erred freely. All judged that the sun was seen in different directions successively, we grant. They called that change 'motion,' and so do even the learned to-day, when they speak of the sun as rising and setting, and they distinguish apparent from real motion, relative from absolute motion.

93. The only escape from the thesis just proved is that attempted by the **Sceptics,** *i. e.*, by those few philosophers who pretend that man can really be certain of nothing. Sceptics are of two kinds: *universal* or *subjective* Sceptics, who refuse to admit any certainty at all, even that of their own existence; and *partial* or *objective* Sceptics, who admit their own existence and nothing or very little more.

94. **Thesis III.** *The theory of Universal Scepticism is self-contradictory.* *Proof.* That theory is self-contradictory,

which affirms and denies the same thing; but such is the theory of universal Scepticism. Therefore it is self-contradictory. *We prove the minor:* Scepticism denies that there is any certainty at all; at the same time it implicitly affirms several things as certain; *e. g.*, that certainty is something different from doubt, that the words used have certain meanings, that those using them exist, etc. If the Sceptic should plead that he does not hold even those points as certain, he must then grant that, for all he knows, he may be saying and even meaning just the contrary of what he teaches, which would be an absurd theory; but even this would implicitly affirm that the Sceptic exists, speaks, etc.

95. In connection with Scepticism, we must consider the **Methodic Doubt** recommended by Descartes, who, under the Latinized name of Cartesius, wrote in the middle of the seventeenth century. He was not a Sceptic; but he traced out a false system of studying the existence of certainty: destroying the solid basis of Philosophy, he substituted for it a weak fabric of his own invention, and left little in the minds of his followers but ruin and confusion. He maintained, (*a*) That every philosopher should begin his speculations by doubting of everything. (*b*) Next, the philosopher will find that he cannot help granting the fact of his own thought, and he will conclude from it his own existence: *Cogito, ergo sum*— "I think, therefore I am." (*c*) Hence the would-be philosopher will infer the general rule that whatever is clearly perceived is true. (*d*) Then finding that he clearly perceives the idea of God, he thence concludes to the existence of God. (*e*) From the veracity of God he infers the reliability of his own faculties. (*f*) Thence, at last, he reasons to the certainty of his knowledge.

96. **Thesis IV.** *Descartes' Methodic Doubt is absurd. Proof.* That is absurd which affirms and denies the same thing; but

the doubt in question does so. For in it the philosopher begins by denying the reliability of reason, and at once implicitly affirms its reliability by using it to prove his own existence: "I think, therefore I am." He pretends to doubt all his faculties, and still he treats the guidance of those same faculties as reliable. Besides, Descartes moves in a vicious circle: he proves the reliability of our faculties by the veracity of God, and the veracity of God by the reliability of our faculties, etc.

97. The error of Sceptics arises from their **false supposition** that nothing is certain which is not demonstrated by discursive reasoning. Now, the science of Mathematics begins by the admission of axioms which are self-evident; *e. g.*, that "the whole is greater than a part," that "two things equal to a third are equal to each other," etc. The science of Philosophy must follow a similar process: it must draw its first conclusions from premises which are evident without proof. Besides, like Mathematics and all other sciences, it must admit without proof the reliability of the reasoning process. If the first premises and the reliability of reason required proof, man could never make the first start in scientific studies; in fact, he would be incapable of reasoning at all: he would not be a rational being.

98. Every philosopher, therefore, must, on entering the field of science, affirm with certainty: 1. His own existence; called *the first fact*. 2. The principle of contradiction, viz., that a thing cannot ' be and not be ' at the same time; called *the first principle*. 3. The power of the intellect to know truth; called *the first condition*. These truths are not blindly admitted: they are seen to be objectively evident. There is no alternative between admitting them and admitting the self-contradiction of universal Scepticism.

99. To refute **partial Scepticism**, we must prove the reli-

ability of the various means by which certainty may be attained, as we shall do in the following chapter. Still, the arguments which we shall adduce will, in many cases, be rather *scientific explanations than strict proofs : scientific explanations*, because they will show distinctly what causes or reasons we have for firm adhesion to the truths; *not strict proofs*, because the reliability of the means in question is in several cases proved while taking their reliability for granted, as having no need of demonstration.

CHAPTER III.

MEANS OF ATTAINING CERTAINTY.

100. The **means at our disposal to attain certainty are**, *directly*, our own cognoscive powers or faculties, viz., intellect and sensation, and, *indirectly*, the authority of other men. To explain these clearly we must treat: 1. Of *our cognoscive powers in general;* 2. Of *Intellect* in particular; 3. Of *sensation;* 4. Of *authority*. To all this we shall add a chapter on *common sense*, which, though proceeding from the intellect, requires for the discussion of its certainty the previous understanding of the reliability of intellect, sensation, and authority.

ARTICLE I. A SKETCH OF OUR COGNOSCIVE POWERS.

101. I. **The outer senses.** Our first step in the acquisition of knowledge is the perception of material objects by means of material instruments which are parts of ourselves, and are called the organs of sense.

102. An organ is a part of a living body peculiarly constructed by the Creator for the purpose of exercising a function of life. Living bodies are made up of such organs. In man, and in the higher animals generally, five of these organs are intended for the perception of exterior bodily objects; these are called the organs of the five outer or exterior senses, viz., of the *sight*, *hearing*, *smell*, *taste*, and *touch*.*

* Physiologists now split up the touch into two senses, the tactual or skin sense and the muscular sense: the former perceives heat and cold, roughness and smoothness, etc.; the latter perceives resistance, exteriority, and extension. President McCosh.

103. II. **The inner sense.** There is, besides, an internal or inner sense, whose organ is some portion at least of the nervous system; it perceives interior modifications of the animal body, such as cause the feelings of hunger, thirst, fatigue, pain, comfort, etc. It also perceives the actions and affections of the various external senses; for an animal not only sees, hears, tastes, etc., but it also *feels* that it sees, hears, tastes, etc. This inner sense, in as far as it takes cognizance of what is done by the outer senses, is often called *the common sense*, and its organ is styled the common sensory; but the term *common sense*, without the definite article 'the,' stands for a very different idea, viz., for the common judgment of men on matters of universal importance to mankind.

104. The inner sense does not perceive the causes of the affections which it perceives, but only the fact that those affections exist. As both the objects of sensation and its organs are material, the action of all sensation is material, organic, and is common to man and brute. But the organ is, of course, not dead but living matter; it is one substance with the soul, *i. e.*, with the principle of life; hence the actions of any sense are actions of the living compound soul and body.

105. III. **The imagination.** When an animal perceives

describes it thus, quoting Wundt's *Beiträge zur Theorie der Sinneswahrnehmung:* "When we move our members we come upon external resistances. We observe that these resistances sometimes give way before our pressure; but we find at the same time that this takes place with very different degrees of facility, and that, in order to put different bodies in motion, we must apply very different degrees of muscular force; but to every single degree of the contraction-force there corresponds a determined degree in intensity of the muscular sensations. With these muscular sensations, the sensations of the skin which cover our members of touch so continually mingle, that the intensity of these touch-sensations goes parallel to the intensity of the accompanying muscular sensations. We succeed in this way in connecting the degree of intensity of the muscular sensations in a necessary manner with the nature of the resistances which set themselves against our movement" (*Defence of Fundamental Truth*, p. 173).

material objects, it forms and retains of them material images or representations, called *phantasms*. The organ used for these purposes is the brain. The imagination is the power of forming and retaining those images, of recalling them on occasions, and of combining them in wonderful varieties, thus forming new phantasms which in turn may be recorded and retained, etc. We should not suppose those images to be pictures, for we can have no picture of taste, smell, etc.; they are modifications of some kind.

106. IV. **The sensile memory.** This name denotes that portion of the imaginative power which retains and recalls the phantasms, but it adds a further function, viz., that of recognizing, not intellectually however, present sense-perceptions and present phantasms as identical with former phantasms and former sense-perceptions. By this faculty "The ox knoweth his owner, and the ass his master's crib," as Holy Writ expresses it. The inner sense, the common sense, the imagination, and the sensile memory need not be considered as distinct faculties, but rather as various functions of the same faculty, which may be generally designated as *the inner sense*.

107. V. The intellect, understanding, or mind, in the proper meaning of this term, is an entirely different faculty; it does not confine its perceptions to the material qualities of objects, as all sense-action does, but it penetrates into the very essences of things material and immaterial (*intus legit*, it reads within), and it forms concepts or ideas representing essences, *e. g.*, of 'plant,' 'tree,' 'spirit,' etc. Even when it considers mere accidents, *e. g.*, 'color,' 'shape,' 'size,' it need not simply consider this individual color, shape, or size, as material faculties must do, but it can consider the essence of color, shape, and size; so that, by a power peculiar to itself, it forms ideas representing qualities as abstract—*i. e.*, drawn

forth, as it were, from the subjects in which they are found and thus stripped of their individuality.

108. VI. **The judgment.** Besides conceiving ideas, the intellect judges; *i. e.*, it compares two ideas together and pronounces on their agreement or disagreement. This act of the intellect is called *judgment;* it was explained in *Dialectics* (No. 17).

109. VII. **Reason** is not a faculty distinct from the intellect and the judgment; it is the intellectual act or process of deriving judgments from other judgments; it, too, was sufficiently explained above (No. 22).

110. VIII. **The intellectual memory** is another function of the intellect; it enables us to perceive and reproduce ideas, judgments, and reasonings formerly elicited, and to recognize identity or difference between present and former objects of knowledge. The intellectual memory is greatly assisted in its action by the sensile memory, which associates phantasms with mental concepts.

111. IX. **Consciousness** is the intellectual power of perceiving our own internal acts, whether of intellect and will or of our interior sense; it will be more fully explained in the following article.

ARTICLE II. THE INTELLECT IN PARTICULAR.

112. **The intellect** or understanding may be called the *universal means* by which certainty is to be acquired; for certainty is a state of the mind or intellect, and therefore it cannot be reached except by the intellect. That the intellect may begin to act, it must be excited by sensation; and therefore those whose senses are very imperfect remain idiotic. But sense, no matter how perfect, can never elicit a judgment. Still, sense is a means by which the human intellect is brought into communication with many objects of knowledge, and

the reliability of sense-perception will be examined in the next article.

113. We are just now concerned with **the certainty of intellectual knowledge as such.** We must begin this study by recalling to mind that *the first condition* for the attaining of all certainty is the capacity of the intellect to reach truth. We need not, then, prove the reliability of our intellect. But we must here examine *what is involved or included in this capacity of the intellect to know truth.*

It involves the certainty, 1. Of *consciousness;* 2. Of our *primary ideas;* 3. Of *immediate analytical judgments;* 4. Of the *intellectual memory;* 5. Of the *reasoning process.* We shall examine the reliability of these functions of the intellect in detail; in doing so, we shall *scientifically explain* rather than *prove* our theses; for the first condition of certainty needs no proof.

§ 1. *Consciousness.*

114. **Consciousness is the reflex perception of our own acts**, *i. e.*, of ourselves as acting. We not only think and feel, but, when we reflect, our mind perceives that we think and feel. This reflection consists, as the word indicates (*reflectere*, to bend back), in the bending back of the mind upon itself, upon its own acts. Reflection is, of course, not the beginning of our knowledge; for we must first think and feel before we can perceive that we think and feel. But when we scrutinize our own knowledge, this reflection on self is the first act to be examined in the process of our study.

115. This reflection should not be confounded with reflection in the sense of *remembrance.* **Nor should consciousness be mistaken for the inner sense**, explained above (No. 103). It differs from it: (*a*) In the *subject* that elicits the act: consciousness is elicited by the simple intellect, sensation by the human compound; (*b*) In the *object* perceived: con-

sciousness perceives both <u>simple and organic actions</u>, the inner sense <u>organic actions</u> only; (c) In the *manner* of perception: the perception of <u>sense</u> terminates in <u>phantasms</u>, that of consciousness in <u>ideas and judgments</u>, affirming that the facts exist, *i. e.*, that we really think or feel as we are conscious we do. But consciousness is not the function which perceives what are the causes of our feelings, *e. g.*, the causes of pain or comfort experienced; such causes are made known to us by reasoning and repeated observation united, *i. e.*, by induction.

116. **Thesis V.** *The reliability of consciousness is included in our capacity to know truth.*

Explanation. We are not proving our capacity to know truth; this capacity needs no proof (Nos. 97, 98); but we maintain here that this same capacity of our intellect to know truth could not exist unless our consciousness were reliable.

Proof. That is included in our capacity to know truth, without which we could never know whether we know or not, but without the reliability of consciousness we could never know whether we know or not. Therefore—

We prove the minor. It is only through consciousness that we know our own intellectual acts; therefore, if consciousness were not reliable, we could not really know whether we are eliciting acts of knowledge.

117. It will be noticed that the field of **consciousness covers** the following objects of knowledge: <u>1. Our own existen</u>ce; for we perceive ourselves as being the subjects of our intellectual acts and of our sensations. <u>2. The existence of our intellectual acts.</u> 3. <u>The existence of our internal sense</u> and of <u>its acts.</u>

118. **It may be objected:** 1. We are not conscious of all our internal acts. *We answer:* We claim certainty for those only of which we are conscious.

2. Many persons are conscious of affections which do not exist; *e. g.*, that they are ill when they are not ill. We *answer:* They are conscious of certain feelings, from which they infer by faulty reasoning that they are ill. Consciousness reveals only the existence of the feelings, not their causes.

3. Lunatics are conscious of being kings, princes, etc. *Answer.* They are conscious of judging themselves to be kings, etc., and they do judge so owing to their diseased imagination. For lunacy supposes an inability to distinguish between imaginations and real perceptions; but the consciousness of even a lunatic is reliable.

4. No one can know that his certainty is not owing to a diseased imagination. *Answer.* If so, universal Scepticism would follow, and the intellect would be incapable of knowing truth.

5. The proof takes for granted the reliability of our consciousness, the point to be proved. *Answer.* We are not giving a strict proof, but only a scientific explanation; for the first truths cannot be strictly proved and need no demonstration.

§ 2. *Primary Ideas.*

119. By **primary ideas** we do not mean inborn ideas; for no ideas are inborn in us: we have no ideas antecedently to sense-perception. But whereas by sense we form phantasms or material images of bodies observed, we form by our intellect ideas or immaterial images of what is cognoscible in those bodies; *e. g.*, of 'being,' 'substance,' 'size,' 'color,' etc. The objects of sense are necessarily individual, extrinsic, and concrete qualities; the proper objects of the intellectual idea are universal and abstract notes.

120. **We call primary ideas** those of 'being,' 'truth,' 'substance,' 'cause,' 'effect,' etc.; all those, namely, that are involved in our commonest perceptions. Of these we assert that they have *objective truth*, and that their objective truth is implied in the very capacity of our intellect to understand truth. Kant makes them *subjective forms* only, to which nothing objective corresponds.

121. **Thesis VI.** *Our primary ideas are objectively true, i.e., conformable to objects really existing.*

Proof. If these ideas were not objectively true, not conformable to objects really existing, our commonest knowledge would be but an illusion; if, for instance, 'being,' 'truth,' 'substance,' etc., were mere figments of the imagination or of the intellect, we could never know anything. Therefore they are objectively true.

122. It must be carefully noticed, however, that the *object of a universal idea* does not really exist as a universal object: everything that really exists is an individual thing. Likewise, the object of an abstract idea does not really exist as an abstract object: every existing being is concrete. For instance, there exists no real abstract or universal cause, nor any real abstract and universal effect, substance, being, etc., just as there exists no real abstract or universal animal, which would be neither rational nor irrational, but simply have the qualities that make up the genus animal. How, then, is the idea 'animal' objectively true? Because the qualities expressed by the term 'animal' really exist in every individual animal. Nothing, then, in nature *exists* in the abstract; but anything may be viewed in the abstract by the intellect, and abstract notes are the distinctive objects of intellectual cognition.

123. Now, the abstract idea is the same as the universal idea: the word **abstract** denotes the manner in which such an idea is formed, while the word **universal** denotes its

applicability to many objects. Thus, I form the abstract idea 'animal' by attending to the notes, which I perceive in any individual animal, viz., 'a material substance endowed with life and feeling'; these notes I draw forth, or abstract (*abstraho*), for separate consideration, or, if you wish, I withdraw my attention from the other qualities of that same individual animal which I am considering. Since these same notes conceived are common to all animals, my concept of 'animal' is a universal concept, *i. e.*, it is predicable of a whole class. In as far as my idea 'animal' denotes only the qualities or notes that make up its *comprehension*, it is called a **direct universal**; but when I reflect besides that the idea is applicable to many beings, *i. e.*, when I consider also its *extension*, the idea is then called a **reflex universal**.

124. Philosophers have warmly disputed upon the nature of these reflex universals: the **Nominalists** call them *mere names*, which are given to a confused collection of individuals, but to which no concepts correspond; the **Conceptualists** call them *concepts*, but they suppose those concepts to be mere figments of the intellect to which no real objects correspond; the **Exaggerated Realists** supposed that *universal beings* really exist corresponding to the universal concepts; the **Moderate Realists** maintain that *some reality* in objects corresponds to the abstract idea, yet that such reality does not exist objectively as an abstract or universal being without individualizing notes, but it exists concretely in each individual object. The explanation we have given in the two preceding numbers is that of the moderate realists; but the scientific proofs of our doctrine and the refutation of other systems belong to Psychology.

§ 3. *Immediate Analytical Judgments.*

125. **Analytical judgments**, as explained above (No. 17), are those judgments in which the agreement or disagreement

of the subject and predicate is perceived by the mere analysis of their meaning, without the aid of experience. If this agreement or disagreement is perceived at once, without reasoning, the judgments are said to be **immediate**.

126. **Thesis VII.** *Immediate analytical judgments can never be false.*

Proof 1. That such judgments cannot be false is made evident by considering their very nature; for they consist in affirming or denying explicitly what the very idea of the subject contained or excluded implicitly; *e. g.*, when I conceive ' a part,' I conceive something as distinct from ' the whole,' and distinct from it by being less. Thus all immediate analytical judgments, *e. g.*, 'The part is less than the whole,' do no more than affirm or deny explicitly what the subject of them contained or excluded implicitly before the judgment was formed.

Proof 2. Our intellect has the power to know truth (No. 98). Therefore that can give us real certainty which is implied in the capacity of our intellect to know truth, or which must be objectively true if the intellect can know truth at all. But such are these judgments. For if our intellect could not be relied on in these judgments, *e. g.*, that 'a circle is round,' that 'a part is less than the whole,' etc., then the intellect could never be relied on in any judgments; for none are more evident. Therefore it can be relied on in these: they give us real certainty.

127. **Objections:** 1. This thesis cannot be demonstrated. *Answer.* It need not be; for it is evident.

    2. Some of the judgments are false, *e. g.*, " The whole is greater than the part "; for the whole Blessed Trinity is not greater than any of the Persons. *Answer.* The Divine Persons are not parts of God; each of them is the infinite God whole and entire.

3. Another of these judgments is false, viz., "Out of nothing nothing can be made"; for the world was made out of nothing. *Answer.* This analytical judgment means that nothingness cannot be a material out of which a thing can be made, while, in creating, God made the world without using any material; He did not make nothingness the material of His creation.

4. All our judgments are empirical; for they presuppose sensation. *Answer.* They presuppose sensation before we can conceive the ideas, we grant; they compare the ideas by attending to experience and sensation, we deny. Now, the latter is required for empiric judgments. (No. 17.)

5. No judgments are certain; for to err is natural to man. *Answer.* To err sometimes in his opinions, yes; to err in his certain judgments, no.

6. Analytical judgments are useless; for their predicates are contained in their subjects, even though no judgments be elicited. *Answer.* They formally and explicitly discover and express what predicates are implicitly contained in tneir subjects.

§ 4. *Memory.*

128. **Memory** is the power of retaining and re-awaking former knowledge, and of recognizing it as former knowledge. It is twofold:

1. **The sensile memory** retains and re-awakes phantasms—*e. g.*, of a whip formerly seen or heard and of a pain felt—and it perceives a connection or association between those phantasms. In this way brutes remember as well as men. (No. 106.)

2. **The intellectual memory** retains and re-awakes ideas —*e. g.*, of what we formerly saw, felt, read, thought, or

willed—and it judges that the objects of those ideas were formerly perceived. In man the sensile and the intellectual memory work together and assist each other.

129. The memory acts **voluntarily** when it recalls the past at will; **spontaneously,** when the will has no share in the act. To act spontaneously, the memory must be aroused by a perception in some way associated with a former perception; *e. g.*, the fragrance of a fruit may recall its taste; the idea of eternity may recall the shortness of this present life.

130. **Thesis VIII.** *The reliability of our memory is contained in our power to know truth.*

Explanation. We do not maintain that we can recall all our former perceptions; but simply that, when our memory does recall a former perception, and judges with certainty that the object now recalled is identical with an object perceived before, it is reliable in such a judgment, and that this reliability of the memory is contained in the power of our intellect to know truth.

Proof. That is included in the intellect's power to know truth, without which all connected thought and all expression of thought would be impossible. But the reliability of our memory is such. For, unless our memory were reliable, we could not think connectedly, since one judgment would be forgotten before another could be compared with it; and no thought could be expressed, because no words could be remembered to express them.

131. If it be **objected** that our memory often deceives us, we *answer :* Not when it gives us, on careful consideration, positive testimony, excluding all fear of error. But men are often too careless, impatient, or presumptuous to examine their recollections properly.

§ 5. *Reasoning.*

132. When we attempt to reason in order to prove the

reliability of reasoning, we evidently do not pretend to give a strict proof; we simply give a **scientific explanation**, showing why it is that a conclusion logically derived from true premises must be as certain as the premises themselves.

133. **Thesis IX.** *Whoever grants the premises of logical reasoning cannot deny the conclusion.*

Proof. All logical reasoning, as explained above (Nos. 22, etc.), is based on this principle, that the conclusion is implicitly contained in the premises. Hence, he who would grant the premises and deny the conclusion would thereby affirm and deny the same thing; but one cannot deny what he affirms. Therefore whoever grants the premises of logical reasoning cannot deny the conclusion.

134. **Objections:** 1. If the conclusion were contained in the premises, nothing new would be learned by reasoning. *Answer.* The knowledge of the conclusion is new to us; for, although the conclusion was implicitly contained in the premises, we did not know this conclusion in particular till we arrived at it by reasoning. Thus, all the theorems of Geometry are derived from the preceding theorems and ultimately from the axioms.

2. Reasoning leads men into many errors. *Answer.* Not when it is materially and formally correct.

3. The proof given holds only for the syllogism. *Answer.* All reasoning is reducible to the syllogistic. (See Nos. 35, etc.; in particular, for induction, No. 46.)

ARTICLE III.   SENSATION.

135. The faculty of **sensation** distinguishes all animals from all vegetable substances; for 'sentient' is the *difference* which, added to the *genus* 'living material substance,' con-

stitutes the *species* 'animal.' By saying man is an 'animal' we mean exactly this, that he is a living material substance endowed with sense.

136. Now, sense is a cognitive power, *i. e.*, a power of knowing; its action, or knowledge, is elicited by a living material substance, and its organs consist of the living material nerves. It is a clear and certain principle that no action can be superior to the agent, else the effect would exceed the cause; therefore, as sense is a material power, **it can know nothing higher than material objects.**

137. Besides, any matter is a concrete individual portion of matter; both the organs and the objects of sense are such, and therefore every sense-action will be a concrete individual modification of a concrete individual portion of matter. But it is evident that a concrete individual modification of a concrete individual portion of matter can picture or represent by its own nature nothing but a concrete and individual modification of matter; now, perception of sense consists in such representation, hence **sense can perceive nothing but concrete and individual modifications of matter.**

138. When sense perceives the material modifications that take place within its own animal body, it is called **inner sense**; when it perceives the material modifications that take place outside of its animal body, it is called **outer sense**. Inner sense was more fully explained above (Nos. 103, 104).

§ 1. *The Inner Sense.*

139. The **inner sense** does not testify to the causes of our feelings or affections; for by our inner sense we merely feel a certain affection called pain or comfort; by our animal instinct we are prompted to seek relief of the pain or increase of the comfort; but it is only by a process of inductive reasoning that we have learned intellectually to refer this

certain feeling to a special cause. Thus we have learned by long experience that a peculiar feeling of discomfort arises from want of food, another from want of drink, etc.

140. **Thesis X.** *Inner sense is reliable in its perceptions; i. e., the material modifications perceived by it really exist.*

Proof. To say that the inner sense is not reliable in its perceptions, is the same as to say that those identical affections, or inner modifications of the animal body, which are perceived, do not really exist. But this cannot be said without absurdity; for 'to be perceived' means 'to be that which is perceived' or 'to exist as the object of perception.' If, then, those affections did not really exist, they would 'exist and not exist'; which is absurd.

141. **Objections:** 1. The inner sense sometimes testifies to the feeling of a pain in an amputated limb. *Answer.* It testifies to the feeling of a pain, we grant, and there really is a pain; but it does not testify to the exact cause of that pain. The feeling experienced now may be similar to that experienced before the limb was amputated. Then the feeling of pain arose from some lesion in that limb; and now, the imagination reproducing this former relation, affords us an occasion for judging that the present sensation is again owing to the limb which is no longer there. We feel a lesion, which we may be inclined, by the force of habit, to locate in the amputated limb, whereas the nerves are affected elsewhere, namely at their extremity, which is exposed and very sensitive.

2. The inner sense fails to report all affections. *Answer.* We simply maintain that those affections exist which it does report.

3. The proof supposes that the inner affections are really felt and therefore must really exist; but perhaps we

only imagine that we feel them. *Answer.* We know by consciousness that we can imagine a certain pain, for instance the pain of burning, and that we can feel that pain, but that there is a vast difference between these two acts.*

§ 2. *The Outer Senses.*

142. We stated before (No. 102) that we perceive objects outside of us by the five outer senses of sight, hearing, smell, taste, and touch. **Two very different questions** present themselves on this subject: 1. How far is the testimony of our external senses reliable? 2. How do the senses work so as to give us reliable testimony? The full treatment of the latter question belongs to Psychology, that of the former to our present study of Critical Logic. We are absolutely certain of many facts, though we cannot satisfactorily explain how they are brought about: a man exhausted with hunger and fatigue is absolutely certain of the pleasure and the restoration of strength which he derives from a wholesome meal, although he cannot explain the exact process by which the senses and the digestive power contribute to these results; similarly, all men are certain that the outer senses often give reliable information, though few are able to describe the manner in which this is accomplished.

143. **The obvious facts in the case** are these: (*a*) We have various sensations of outer objects in and by our external senses; (*b*) *We judge the cause of these to exist in bodies, i. e.*,

---

* The objective reality of both sense-perception and intellectual perception is well expressed in the following words of Very Rev. I. T. Hecker (*Cath. World*, Oct., 1887, p. 6): "To see, if one is not a fool or a lunatic, is to see something. To act on any other view of human life, is to tend to imbecility. This law of objective reality applies to the entire realm of human activity. Life is real. 'Wherefore,' says St. Augustine on the Trinity (book ix), 'it must be clearly held that everything whatsoever that we know begets in us the knowledge of itself, for knowledge is brought forth from both, from the knower and the thing known.'"

in substances distinct from our mind, having extension and peculiar powers of action; (*c*) We adhere to this judgment firmly without fear of error. **We maintain** that our firm adhesion to this judgment is due to the objective existence of bodies, and that therefore our external senses are reliable in their sensations of outward objects.

144. But some philosophers argue that we do not know bodies except by means of phantasms and ideas, which are subjective in us, and which, for all we know, may have no objective reality corresponding to them. These philosophers are called **Idealists**. They are divided into two schools: 1. Fichte, the leader of the **subjective school**, maintains that there exists nothing but his own mind which is ever imagining unrealities: "The *Ego* posits itself." 2. Berkeley, the leader of the **objective school**, makes God the direct cause of our phantasms and ideas.

145. Such speculations, instead of resting on solid facts, as all sciences should do, are in direct conflict with all known facts and with the firmest judgments of all mankind. Every sound mind knows for certain **the difference between real perceptions and mere imaginations;** and unsoundness of mind consists precisely in the inability of some men to distinguish between objective realities and mere phantasms. But there is no likelihood that any philosopher of note ever doubted the existence of bodies. Such as pretended to doubt did violence to their own good sense in order to support some pet theory, by which they earned the name of original thinkers.*

---

* Hume writes in his *Treatise on Human Nature:* "I dine, I play a game of backgammon, I converse and am happy with my friends; and when, after three or four hours of amusement, I would return to these speculations, they appear so cold, so strained, and so ridiculous that I cannot find it in my heart to enter into them any farther" (vol. i. p. 467). Why did Hume and Fichte write books if they really believed that no readers existed?

146. Thesis XI. *By our external senses we really perceive bodies*, i. e., *substances distinct from our mind, extended and resisting.*

Proof. Nothing exists without a reason for it; but there exist in us, as we know by consciousness, (*a*) Sensations; (*b*) Irresistible judgments that those sensations are caused by bodies, *i. e.*, by substances distinct from our mind, extended and resisting; therefore a reason must exist for those sensations and for those irresistible judgments. But that reason can be none other than bodies really existing; therefore they really exist.

We prove the last minor: If that reason were not in the bodies, it would be either, 1. In our minds, as Fichte maintains; or, 2. In God, as Berkeley supposes. No other reason is assigned by our opponents. Now, it is, 1. Not *in our minds*. If it were, we should produce those sensations and judgments necessarily or freely; but we do neither: (*a*) Not freely, for we see, hear, feel, etc., many things which we are totally unwilling to see, hear, feel, etc.; (*b*) Not necessarily; for if we were so constituted that we necessarily elicited false judgments, our intellect would be essentially unreliable; it would be a power, not of knowing truth but of deception and falsification. 2. Not *in God*. Those who admit the existence of God at all, as Berkeley and his followers do, admit that He is the infinitely perfect Being; but a perfect being is essentially truthful and cannot be the source of a universal deception, as He would be if He produced those phantasms and gave us at the same time an irresistible impulse to judge falsely of their cause.

147. Objections: 1. An evil genius could produce the deception. *Answer.* We deny this; for the deception, if such it were, would be, not accidental, but natural and essential to man, and therefore it would be essential to man to judge falsely; and thus universal Scepticism would become reasonable.

2. God would not be omnipotent if he could not directly produce on us all the effects that bodies can. *Answer.* He cannot give us an irresistible propensity to judge falsely; this would be against His own perfect nature, and it would leave us incapable of having certainty, of knowing truth.

3. God does so in visions, *e. g.*, when He made Tobias see an Angel. *Answer.* The Angel had assumed a material body.

4. Sometimes a vision is merely subjective. *Answer.* Then the intellect sees reason to suspect the truth.

5. In dreams we judge irresistibly that we perceive real objects. *Answer.* In dreams we do not examine the certainty of our judgments; we have not that reflex certainty which we are here considering. Besides, in dreams we are not in the normal state of rational beings.

6. Those suffering of *mania a potu* cannot rid themselves, even on reflection, of the perception, as they suppose it to be, of snakes, demons, etc. *Answer.* From the fact that a disordered mind cannot know the truth, it does not follow that a sound mind cannot; besides, they no doubt perceive their own abnormal condition and see reasons, when they reflect at all, to doubt their visions.

7. From any act which is only subjective we cannot infer the existence of the objective reality; but sensation is only subjective. *Answer.* Our sensation is not merely subjective; for it is a perception, and a perception is the subjective act of taking in an object: a perception without an object perceived is a self-contra-

diction: there can be no taking in of nothing. Besides, we invincibly judge that our perceptions are due to objects (Nos. 143, etc.)

148. To understand **how far the reliability of our senses extends**, we have only to examine on what points sensation prompts us irresistibly to elicit judgments. As this is a question of great importance, we shall consider it with some detail.*

1. We may see a painting in the distance and judge it to be a statue; we may judge a sound to come from a greater distance than it does. Do our senses deceive us on those occasions? Not at all: in fact, the sight, as such, does not inform us whether all the parts of the object seen are equally near, as in a painting, or unequally, as in a statue. Neither sight nor hearing, as such, tell about distances: sight deals with color and, consequently, with the outlines of colored objects; hearing deals with sound, of which we perceive countless varieties. Each sense has thus its own **proper object of sense-perception** (*sensibile proprium*). The proper object of sight is *color;* of hearing, *sound;* of smell, *odor;* of taste, *flavor;* of touch, *temperature* and *resistance*. The perception of resistance enables us to distinguish between varieties of surfaces, some of which are noticed to be yielding or soft, others unyielding or hard; some are even or smooth; some uneven or rough; some are bounded by straight, others by curved lines; some extend over a large, others over a small space, etc.

2. As extension, outline or figure, number, etc., are perceptible by touch and sight, they, and in general all

---

* See *The Old Philosophy and Relativity of Knowledge*, by Henry Brown. (*The Month*, September, 1888.)

those qualities of bodies which are perceptible by more than one sense, are called the **common objects of sense-perception** (*sensibile commune*).

3. Sense does not perceive color, sound, resistance, etc., in the **abstract**; but it perceives something colored, sounding, resisting, etc., in the **concrete**.

4. While by our senses we perceive some concrete body as colored, resisting, etc., **our intellect**, by its power of abstraction, abstracts, or considers apart, various notes or marks of that body, such as 'color,' 'resistance,' 'existence,' 'quality,' 'substance,' etc., and thus forms **abstract ideas**; next, by its power of judging, it compares these ideas and the objects perceived together, and pronounces **judgments**, such as 'this substance is colored,' 'something resisting exists,' etc.

5. **The senses usually assist each other**: the eye beholds what the hand touches; the ear perceives the sound, the eye the figure of the rattle or the string which the fingers move. Thus from earliest infancy we have learned by practice to associate our sense-perceptions with one another and with our intellectual acts; we have perfected our associations of phantasms by inductive reasoning, till we have acquired great readiness to judge of the qualities revealed to one sense by the proper object of another sense. For instance, on hearing a familiar human voice we know the presence and the very expression of countenance of a well known person; from the fragrance of a fruit we can tell its taste; from the aroma we judge the form of a flower.

6. We see many reasons to judge, and on many points no reason to doubt, that **the senses of brute animals** work in the same way as our own. Brutes perceive

the proper and the common objects of sense; and, as their organs and their instincts are often more perfect than ours, brutes may associate phantasms, derived from various senses, more readily and perfectly than we do, as is well exemplified in the scent of the dog and the cunning ways of the fox.

7. Sense does not perceive substance as such; *i. e.*, as distinct from quality; but still, by perceiving the concrete qualities, it puts us into relation with substance. What is thus intellectually perceived on account of sense, is said to be **indirectly sensible** (*sensibile per accidens*). Brutes do not judge at all, in the proper sense of the word; they merely associate, *e. g.*, the stone thrown with the man who throws it, and they do not always do even that: the dog will often bite the stone itself. The Creator, in His wisdom, has given brutes as perfect a power of associating phantasms as is beneficial to themselves and to man, for whose advantage they are evidently intended.

8. Man both associates and judges; for he has instinct and reason. It is, however, only on occasions of some importance that we stop to consider whether our judgments are well enough founded to exclude all doubt. We find them to be such when, on careful examination, we perceive that they give us evidence of the objective truth. That they may do so with regard to our sense perceptions, the following **conditions** must be fulfilled: (*a*) We must be conscious that we are in a normal or healthy condition; else we can see reason to suspect the testimony of our senses. (*b*) We must be aware that our surroundings appear normal; *e. g.*, it all around us looked yellow, we should see reason to suspect that our eyes were jaundiced. (*c*)

We must find that our senses are concordant with one another and constant in their testimony; *e. g.*, if a passing glance makes me perceive an unusual appearance, I look again with care, I shift my position to dispel all possible illusion of the sight; or I even apply my hands to touch what excites my surprise.

149. **Thesis XII.** *The external senses, acting under proper conditions, are reliable with regard to their proper and their common objects of sensation.*

The proper conditions here spoken of have just been explained. This thesis defines the extent to which the outer senses are perfectly reliable.

Proof. The senses are reliable in their testimony if they perceive nothing but the objective truth; but such is the case. For, being physical powers, they work necessarily, and therefore they can only perceive the objects presented to them; else they would perceive what does not exist; *i. e.*, that which does not exist would be an object of perception; which is absurd.

150. We do not, then, **claim certainty** for every judgment that is formed on occasion of sense-perception, but only for what the senses really report, *i. e.*, the existence of those sensible qualities which are the proper and the common objects of sensation. The substance itself in which those sensible qualities exist is not apprehended, by the senses, as distinct from those qualities. From the knowledge of the qualities perceived by sense, the intellect judges the nature of the substance in which those qualities inhere. In forming its estimate of that substance, the intellect may often be mistaken; *e. g.*, it may judge that to be an orange which is a lump of wax; it may mistake a picture for a body. But even in such cases the intellect is not led necessarily into error, but it can suspend its judgment till all fear of error has been removed.

151. **Objections:** 1. The senses tell us that sugar is sweet, fire hot, etc., while Descartes and others prove that these qualities are not in the bodies perceived, but in the senses. *Answer.* When we say that sugar is sweet, fire hot, etc., we mean that those bodies have real qualities which produce in us corresponding sensations of sweetness, heat, etc.; both the qualities that are in those bodies and the sensations that are in us are denominated by the same terms analogically. Certainly sugar and fire have real qualities which are causes of our sensations.

2. We know by science that the sun is not exactly there where we see it; here the sight deceives us. *Answer.* We know by the sight nothing but the color of the sun; its place, size, etc., are inferred by inductive reasoning.

3. But even the color of the sun is not such as we see it when modified by the atmosphere. *Answer.* We do not claim certainty except for what we perceive; now, we perceive by the sight the color such as it is when it reaches our eyes; with anything else the sense of sight has nothing to do.

4. But the sight distorts its objects; thus, a square tower appears round in the distance. *Answer.* The sight reports only the colors of the different parts of the tower; all inference as to its shape, size, etc., are conclusions of inductive reasoning, which is often too imperfect to give certainty.

5. By admitting that the senses must be concordant and constant in their testimony, we imply that each sense singly can be mistaken in certain cases, at least for a while. *Answer.* All we imply is that the senses give no sufficient ground for certainty till we have

examined whether all the conditions are complied with.

6. When I see a stick plunged into water, I see it broken where it touches the surface; here my sight deceives me. *Answer.* My sight reports the truth, viz.: that the stick appears as if broken.

7. Then our senses can report appearances only; *e. g.*, that I see the appearance of a man, not that I see a man. *Answer.* Sense apprehends appearances only; but our intellect understands that appearances are accidents which naturally exist in substances. When I see the appearance of a man, I understand there must be a cause for that appearance; and, by attending to all the circumstances of the particular case, my mind soon forms a judgment, often absolutely certain, that on the present occasion the appearance of the man is due to the reality of his presence.

8. That our senses may be relied on, we must first know that the order of nature is constant; but we cannot learn this except from the testimony of the senses; therefore we cannot reason on this subject except in a vicious circle. *Answer.* We deny the major and the supposition that we need to reason at all in order to see the evidence of the common and the proper objects of sense, when the required conditions are attended to. We see color, we feel heat and resistance immediately.

9. A color, odor, taste, etc., may please one man and displease another; therefore different men must apprehend objects differently; therefore all do not apprehend them correctly. *Answer.* The apprehensions are the same, but they do not suit all alike. As the organs of men are substantially alike in structure, with

only accidental differences, we reasonably judge that the apprehensions of all men by sense are substantially the same, with only accidental differences. But the pleasure arising from colors and sounds is mostly due to associations of phantasms and sentiments; thus, orange and green please persons of different parties. Odors and tastes, being intended by the Creator to guide us in the selection of suitable food according to our varying bodily conditions, though identical in kind, will often please one and displease another, according to our several needs, thus displaying the wonderful wisdom with which Providence adapts means to an end.

10. In the Holy Eucharist the senses are deceived. *Answer.* They apprehend the appearances which really exist, and thus there is no deception of the senses.

11. Persons who are color-blind misjudge colors. *Answer.* Rather, they are unable to distinguish colors sufficiently to judge with certainty.

Article IV. Authority.

152. Consciousness and intellect put us into direct communication with objective truth, of which they see the evidence. Their perceptions are called intuitions, *i. e.*, visions of truth. It is the same with our sense-perceptions of the proper and the common objects of sense: they, too, give us intuitions or immediate evidence. Reasoning brings evidence to us in a more circuitous way; it gives **mediate evidence**. Such, too, is the evidence of sense-perceptions with regard to all testimony that implies the process of induction; *e. g.*, I have only mediate evidence by my sight of the distances of objects; for any judgment I pronounce on that subject is derived from observation and induction united.

153. **Authority** gives us certainty in a still more circuitous way; for it brings us into communication with truth by means of the statements of other persons. The truth thus reached is said to be *believed*, and authority is called an *extrinsic* motive of certainty. **Belief**, or faith, is Divine or human, according as the authority on which it rests is Divine or human. In Philosophy we are concerned with human faith; and the question to be now considered is, whether the authority of human witnesses can be relied upon to give perfect certainty.

154. **Thesis XIII.** *The testimony of men, under proper conditions, can give perfect certainty.*

The **conditions** required are: 1. That the facts testified to are sufficiently open or accessible to observation; 2. That they are of great moment; else they might not be noticed carefully; 3. That the witnesses are sensible men; 4. That they are either undoubtedly sincere, or, if not, that they are many, of sufficiently different characters, opinions, parties, interests, etc., to exclude all reasonable suspicion of collusion in the support of false statements. *Proof.* That testimony gives perfect certainty which convinces us beyond all reasonable doubt that the witnesses could not have been deceived themselves and did not wish to deceive us. But such is the testimony which fulfils the conditions just stated.

For: 1. *The witnesses could not have been deceived*, since: (*a*) The facts are supposed to be open, accessible to observation; (*b*) They are of great moment, so as to invite careful examination, (*c*) The witnesses are sensible men, who do not act rashly and are not easily imposed upon; and, besides, they are of different opinions, characters, etc., so as not to make a mistake in common.

2. *They do not wish to deceive us;* since either they are known for certain to be sincere, and, of course, such men do

not wish to deceive; or, if not certainly sincere, they are supposed to be many, of different characters, opinions, parties, interests, etc. Now, sensible men do not lie wantonly, especially on matters of importance; and, least of all, would they combine to propagate an important falsehood, unless some common grave interest led them into so disgraceful a crime. But they are supposed to have no such interest in common. There is, consequently, no reason to doubt their testimony.

155. **Objections:** 1. Each witness gives only probability, and no number of probabilities can make up certainty. *Answer.* Even one witness who is certainly intelligent, prudent, and sincere may give perfect certainty; but if the testimony of one or several still leaves special reasons to doubt, the testimony of others may show that the doubt is unfounded in the present case; certainty is thus attained, not by an accumulation of probabilities, but by the elimination of all motives for reasonable doubt.

2. Every witness is free to deceive. *Answer.* We can know from the conditions laid down that, in a given case, there was no actual attempt at deceit. Every man is free to commit suicide, and still it is certain that they will not all do so.

3. History contains many falsehoods. *Answer.* We do not defend all history.

4. At least, we cannot be certain of events long since past, because traditions are gradually changed. *Answer.* We can often be certain of such events, viz., when we know that, in a given instance, the tradition was not changed; *e. g.*, we know for certain that Christ died on a cross; that He rose again; that His disciples preached His Resurrection; that they had no motive to do so if He had not risen; that they laid

down their lives in testimony of their sincerity, etc. (See this argument more fully treated in Schouppe's *Course of Religious Instruction*, p. 6.)

5. At least, no amount of testimony can make miracles certain; for it is physically certain that they never occurred, while it is at most only morally certain that they did. *Answer.* It is not physically certain that they never occurred; all that is physically certain is that nature has no power to produce them, but the Lord of nature has; and it is morally certain that they have occurred.

6. Still, plain men could not assure us that any particular miracle was performed; for they are not fit judges of what is miraculous. *Answer.* Sensible men, even though unlearned, can give reliable testimony about obvious facts, of which learned men will judge whether they were natural or beyond all natural power.

Article V. Common Sense.

156. There are many unwavering judgments or convictions common to all men of sound minds; all these may in a wider meaning be called dictates of **common sense,** *i. e.*, of that sense or intellect which belongs in common to all men. Some of these judgments proceed from the testimony of consciousness, others from the immediate intuitions of identity between two ideas, others from intellect and sense-perceptions combined, others are the obvious deductions of reason from intuitive principles and from the perceptions of the senses. But the term common sense, when considered as a special motive of certainty, is taken in a **more restricted meaning**; it comprises those judgments only, common to all sensible men, which are not immediately or intuitively evident, and which are concerned with the direction of moral conduct.

157. The following are **examples** of common-sense judgments: "There is a sovereign Lord and Master of all things," "His Providence directs human affairs," "We must reverence Him," "We must obey His laws," "He is the rewarder of good and evil," "Our soul will survive our body," "There are rewards and punishments after death," "Children must honor and obey their parents," "Friends must help each other," "Brutes may be killed for the use of man," "Men cannot be killed without just cause," etc.

158. To find how far the judgments of common sense are reliable, we must carefully consider whence they proceed and what evidence they give us of the objective truth. We should not suppose that they proceed from the universal consent of men; men agree because each of them individually forms the same judgments, but each one separately does not form them because all agree: **universality is a character, not a cause** of them.

159. True, we may accept a judgment on the authority of men if their united testimony is known to us; but we are then influenced by another motive of certainty, viz., **common consent**. Thus, we may believe that man is fallen from an originally happier condition, because most nations have traditions to that effect; but the judgments of common sense are very different, being formed by each one independently of the consent of others.

160. Nor should we suppose that the judgments of common sense proceed, as Reid and his followers of the Scottish School maintain, from a mere **instinct to believe** certain truths. These writers wished to refute the Scepticism of Hume by the weapon of common sense; but they failed to establish the reliability of common sense by making it a mere blind instinct.

161. Whence, then, do the judgments of common sense

derive their validity? From the evidence of the objective truth, which is presented with sufficient clearness to every sound mind. The objective truth in such cases is not intuitively beheld; we do not see immediately God's existence, nor the action of His providence, nor the soul as surviving the body, nor one being called virtue and another vice; but, starting with premises supplied by sense-perceptions and intellectual action, we go through an **obvious process of reasoning**, of which the evident conclusions are the dictates of common sense. For instance, my senses seize upon the fact of the world's existence, my intellect sees there must be a reason for its existence; and, not finding that reason in the world itself, my mind concludes by an obvious process of reasoning that there is a first cause of the world, distinct from it; besides, since we also understand that a thing made belongs to its maker, we conceive the Cause of this world as the Sovereign Lord and Master of all things, etc. The judgments of common sense, therefore, are reliable, because they are evident conclusions derived from evident premises.

162. This motive of certainty is, then, not entirely distinct from the motives already considered; but it has a special **advantage,** viz., that it furnishes us with a summary proof of many most important propositions, the detailed study of which would require lengthy explanations.

163. **Thesis XIV.** *The judgments of common sense are true.*

Proof. According to the principles that underlie inductive reasoning (No. 47), any constant, uniform, and unvarying effect produced by any class of objects must proceed from the very nature of those objects; but these judgments are constant, uniform, and unvarying in man; therefore they have for cause the very nature of man: in other words, it is natural or essential to man to form these judgments. Now, it cannot be natural or essential to man to form false judgments; else universal doubt would follow, which, however, has been proved to be absurd; therefore these judgments are not false, but true.

164. **Objections**: 1. Such judgments may have come from tradition, education, prejudices, human laws, etc. *Answer*. The effect cannot exceed the cause: all these causes are variable among men, except just so far as they can be traced to the very nature of man. Besides, mere traditions, etc., would not impose on the consciences of all so stern a sense of duty as belongs to the dictates of common sense.

2. These judgments might come from the passions of men. *Answer*. On the contrary, our passions would rather prompt us to deny these very judgments.

3. Huxley says that religion has been developed from men's instinctive belief in ghosts. *Answer*. Huxley's theory is, as usual with him, a mere theory unsupported by valid proof. The very fact that so determined and able an opponent of religion cannot adduce any more plausible theory to account for the conviction of mankind, is a strong presumption in favor of our thesis.

4. Ignorant men cannot reason well enough to form such judgments; therefore they only receive them from others. *Answer*. The reasoning in question is not difficult, but easy and obvious; though it is not pretended that every mind can give a philosophic account of its own reasonings.

5. Even great geniuses do not always see those conclusions. *Answer*. Geniuses often strive after originality of thought more than after truth, in order to make themselves a name; proud minds disdain to follow the beaten path, simply because it is the beaten path. (See further *Metaphysics*, No. 225.)

CHAPTER IV.

THE ULTIMATE CRITERION OF CERTAINTY.

165. The various sources of certainty, examined in the preceding chapter, furnish us *motives of certainty, i. e.*, reasons which move our intellect to elicit firm undoubting judgments. But these several sources do not give certainty except when properly applied to their proper objects; *e. g.*, our senses are not reliable except under the proper conditions. Hence, to have philosophic certainty in any given case, we must examine whether in that case all the necessary conditions have been complied with, and whether no reason remains to entertain any further doubt. For this purpose we need a rule or test by which to judge our very judgments; to ascertain beyond the possibility of error that they are conformable to the objective truth. This rule to judge by is called a **criterion** ($\varkappa \rho \iota \nu \omega$, I judge) of certainty.

166. We maintain that **the ultimate and universal criterion of certainty** is *the evidence of the objective truth.* By calling it *ultimate*, or *last*, we mean that, when this criterion is applied, it leaves no room for further inquiry concerning the existence of certainty; the ultimate criterion answers the last question that we can or need ask in examining the reliability of our knowledge. For instance, if I question myself how I know that bodies exist, I answer that I see and feel them, that by my senses I perceive their existence, and I cannot perceive that which does not exist as an object of perception; in other words, their existence is made evident

to me. If asked why I am certain that the Declaration of Independence occurred in the United States, I answer that I have learned it from reliable witnesses. And why do I believe these witnesses? Because my reason convinces me that their testimony is reliable. But why do I rely on my reason? Because it gives me evident conclusions from certain premises. I can question no further, because I can wish for nothing more evident than evidence.

By calling evidence the *universal* criterion of certainty, we mean that evidence is the crucial test in *all* cases of natural certainty; for it is with natural certainty alone, not with supernatural Faith, that Philosophy is concerned.

167. **What, then, is evidence?** It is important to understand it well, since all certainty is ultimately to be tested by this criterion. As stated above (No. 84), in the analysis of certainty we find that the firm adhesion of our mind to a truth, excluding all fear of error, is the *subjective* element of certainty; and the manifestation of the truth to the mind producing this firm adhesion, is the *objective* element. Now, such manifestation is the evidence of that truth. Evidence is to the mind what the visibility of a body is to the eye. That I may see a body, 1. It must exist; 2. It must give forth, or at least reflect, rays of light; 3. By that light it must impress itself on my eye. So, likewise, that a truth may be evident to me, 1. It must exist; 2. It must shine forth by its intelligibility, as all truth does, for ontological truth is the intelligibility of a thing; 3. Its light or intelligibility must be so presented as to force itself upon my intellect, making me see that the thing is so and must be so, cannot be otherwise. Hence a usual and correct **definition of evidence** is "such a manifestation of a truth as makes us see that the thing is so and cannot be otherwise," or, more briefly, "the manifest necessity of a truth." We do not mean here that the

objective truth is *absolutely* necessary, but only that, *if* I see it, it *must* be, else I could not see it; the truth is *hypothetically* necessary.

168. Before Descartes' time, the fact that evidence is the ultimate criterion of certainty was scarcely disputed; but this writer has so confused the question of certainty that many modern philosophers have assigned and defended false criteria. Descartes himself considers *clear ideas* as the great test or principle of certainty; while Reid, and the Scottish School generally, rely ultimately upon what they call *common sense*, by which they mean a blind instinct to consider a thing as true. But they should prove that such ideas or such an instinct is necessarily a pledge of the objective truth. In fact, these criteria are all internal; now, **no merely internal test** can settle the question whether the external things exist, since it is not necessarily connected with the objective truth.

Others look for the criterion in a merely external rule. Thus, De Lamennais, indignant that human reason had been adored in France during the Reign of Terror, strove to discredit reason and to show that we cannot trust our reason, but must test its reliability by comparing its judgments with the *common consent* of men. But how can we know that men are agreed upon any point, unless we can rely on our senses and our reason to ascertain whether men exist and what they say? **No merely external test** can be ultimate; for we need a further criterion to judge of its existence and its reliability.

169. **Thesis XV.** *The evidence of the objective truth is the ultimate and universal criterion of certainty.*

Proof. It is such if it fulfils the following conditions: 1. To be *a reliable test* of truth, the criterion must be inseparable from the truth, so that it cannot exist without the truth. 2. To be *ultimate*, it must leave no doubt to be removed by a further test. 3. To be *universal*, it must be applicable to every motive of natural certainty. Now, the evidence of the objective truth, and it alone, fulfils all these conditions: 1. It cannot exist without the truth, since it is the intelligibility of the truth itself made manifest to us. 2. It leaves no doubt to be removed by a further test, since it enables the mind to see the necessity of the truth manifested to it. 3. It is universal, for in no case have we real certainty unless we see that the truth is so and cannot be otherwise; but this supposes the evidence of the objective truth, and is nothing else than the perception of that evidence. Therefore this evidence is the ultimate and universal criterion of certainty.

170. **Objections**: 1. We cannot be certain of anything unless we know that others agree with us. *Answer.* We deny this. In fact, we could not know that others agree with us if our own faculties were not reliable, capable of seeing the evidence of that agreement.

2. We cannot know that we are not insane except by ascertaining that others agree with us. *Answer.* This, too, we deny. Besides, even an insane man cannot err when he has evidence; but he has not evidence in the matters wherein he is insane; for evidence is a manifestation of the truth. It must, besides, be remembered that we claim certainty for man in his normal state, not for crazy, drunken, or sleeping men; and the very reason why these cannot be certain is because they cannot reflect sufficiently to examine their judgments: they imagine that things are so, but they cannot *see* that things cannot be otherwise.

3. Evidence is only in our minds. *Answer.* True evidence is the light of objective truth perceived by our minds; that which is not cannot be perceived.

4. We cannot be certain that we have evidence. *Answer.* We can, as our consciousness testifies.

5. Every man is fallible. *Answer.* Not about matters that are evident.
6. We have no infallible knowledge except through Revelation. *Answer.* We have; and we could not rationally trust a Revelation if we had no evidence that it was made: those who attack the reliability of our reason thereby attack the foundation of Faith.
7. God is the ultimate motive of certainty. *Answer.* He is the first being existing and knowing, but not the first being known to me: His existence is first ontologically, not logically, with regard to me.
8. Consciousness is the ultimate criterion of certainty; for it answers the last question asked about the motives of certainty. *Answer.* We trust our consciousness because it is evidently reliable, thus evidence is the ultimate criterion.
9. Evidence itself requires attention and examination. *Answer.* As motives of assent, no; as necessary conditions for the existence of subjective evidence, yes.
10. Evidence does not reach all kinds of truth; for instance, we have no evidence of what we learn from witnesses. *Answer.* We have no intrinsic evidence of it, but extrinsic, *i. e*, we have evidence that the witnesses could not deceive us.
11. An evident conclusion may be false. *Answer.* Not if the whole reasoning is evident, premises and sequence.
12. It is the part of Protestantism to make one's own judgment the criterion of all certainty. *Answer.* Protestantism errs in making private judgment the criterion of supernatural certainty.
13. Many truths are certain, but not evident. *Answer.* Of natural truths all that are certain are either intrinsically or extrinsically, directly or indirectly, evident to man's natural powers.

MENTAL PHILOSOPHY.

TABLE OF CONTENTS.

	PAGE
INTRODUCTION,	5

MENTAL PHILOSOPHY.

BOOK I.—GENERAL METAPHYSICS, OR ONTOLOGY.

CHAPTER I. The Nature of Being:		7
Article I. Meaning of the Term "Being";		7
" II. Possible Being;		12
" III. Essence and Existence of Beings;		17
" IV. The First Principles Derived from Being.		20
CHAPTER II. The Transcendental Attributes of Being.		21
CHAPTER III. The Categories:		28
Article I. Substance;		29
" II. The Intrinsic Accidents;		32
" III. The Extrinsic Accidents.		36
CHAPTER IV. Cause and Effect.		42
CHAPTER V. The Chief Perfections of Being.		50

BOOK II.—COSMOLOGY.

CHAPTER I. The Origin of the World.	55
CHAPTER II. Purpose and Perfection of the World.	66
CHAPTER III. The Laws that Govern the World.	71
CHAPTER IV. The Constituent Elements of Matter.	79
CHAPTER V. The General Properties of Bodies.	85

BOOK III.—PSYCHOLOGY.

	PAGE
CHAPTER I. The Specific Nature of Plants and Animals.	90
CHAPTER II. Sensitive and Rational Cognition:	106
Article I. Sensitive Cognition;	106
" II. Rational Cognition.	112
CHAPTER III. Sensitive and Rational Appetite.	123
CHAPTER IV. The Nature of the Human Soul.	129
CHAPTER V. Origin and Destiny of the Human Soul.	136

BOOK IV.—NATURAL THEOLOGY.

CHAPTER I. The Existence of God.	145
CHAPTER II. The Essence of God:	154
Article I. Physical and Metaphysical Essence of God;	154
" II. The Perfect Simplicity of God.	158
CHAPTER III. The Quiescent Attributes of God.	162
CHAPTER IV. The Operative Attributes of God:	169
Article I. The Knowledge of God;	169
" II. The Will of God;	171
" III. The Power of God.	175

INTRODUCTION.

1. The word **Physics** means etymologically the study of nature (φύσις, nature); but even the ancient Greeks restricted the meaning of the term to the sensible or phenomenal properties of the material world. At present the meaning of Physics is still more limited: it now denotes that branch only of the Natural Sciences which explains the sensible properties of *bodies in general*, and the causes (such as gravitation, heat, light, magnetism, etc.) which modify those properties. It is thus distinguished from the sciences of Astronomy, Chemistry, Biology, etc., which deal specially with the sensible properties of only certain classes of bodies.

2. **Metaphysics** is the science of whatever is not sensible, of what lies beyond the reach of the senses, as far as it is cognoscible by human reason. It belongs to the *genus* science,—*i. e*, the certain and evident cognition of things by their causes; and it is the highest among the purely human sciences, for it traces its knowledge to the highest causes accessible to human reason. Its *specific difference* lies in dealing with whatever is beyond the reach of the senses, the non-sensible being its formal object; whether this be found in spiritual beings, totally beyond the reach of sense, or in material things in as far as these do not affect the senses.

3. What sensation cannot perceive is the formal object of our mind or intellect, the special functions of which are

abstraction and generalization; therefore *abstract and universal knowledge, as such,* is the **formal object of Metaphysics.** Hence this science, being distinctively intellectual, is also denominated 'Intellectual Philosophy,' or 'Mental Philosophy'; while the application of these abstract truths to the moral conduct of men is styled 'Ethics,' or 'Moral Philosophy.'

4. **Metaphysics is divided** into two parts: 1. **General Metaphysics** studies the non-sensible in general, its principal object is 'being,' as such; it is therefore called **Ontology,** or the science of being (ὄντα, beings). 2. **Special Metaphysics** studies what is peculiar to special classes of beings; it comprises *Cosmology*, which treats of the material world (κόσμος, the world); *Natural Theology*, which treats of the knowledge of God (Θεός, God), as far as He is knowable by merely natural means; and *Psychology*, which treats of living things (ψυχή, the vital principle), especially of the human soul. Metaphysics does not treat professedly of the Angels, because their existence is not known to us except by Revelation. Some modern Metaphysicians, confining Psychology to the study of the human soul, treat separately of organic bodies under the title of 'Organology,' or 'Biology' (βίος, life). Others consider all that is peculiar to man under the head of 'Anthropology.' The division which we have given above is the oldest and, even now, the most commonly adopted.

BOOK I.

GENERAL METAPHYSICS; OR ONTOLOGY.

5. **Ontology** is the science of 'being.' It examines: 1. The nature of being. 2. The transcendental attributes of being. 3. The Categories, or highest genera of beings. 4. The most important link that unites all classes of beings, viz., the relation of cause and effect. 5. The most important perfections of beings.

CHAPTER I.

THE NATURE OF BEING.

6. We shall consider: 1. The meaning of the term 'being.' 2. Possible being in particular. 3. The essence and the existence of beings. 4. The primary philosophical principles derived from the study of being.

ARTICLE I. THE MEANING OF THE TERM 'BEING.'

7. The term **being**, when used as a participle, is a synonyme of 'existing'; as a substantive it expresses the one mark or note common to all that can become the object of thought. It is not, then, confined to *actual* being, but it includes also *possible* being; for we can think, *e. g.*, of golden stars, and

other things only possible. It is not confined to substances, but is also applicable to accidents and relations; *e. g.*, we can think, not only of a tree, but also of its vitality, its color, its age, etc. Even a mere negation, *e. g.*, darkness, may be called being, because we can think of it. Yet, because we cannot think of it except by way of negation of something else—darkness denoting the absence of light—such an object of thought is not called a real being. But we call a **real being** whatever may be known or thought of positively and by itself, whether it is actually existing or only possible,—*i. e.*, capable of existing. That which is not a real being, but the absence of a real being, is a **mere figment of reason**, or *ens rationis*, as it is called by the Schoolmen. This same term is applied to whatever is intrinsically impossible, *e. g.*, a square circle.

8. Real being, viewed as such, is the **formal object of Metaphysics**. In English, the word 'thing' is used as an exact synonyme for real being, except when it is taken in a special sense as opposed to persons, as when we say ' persons and things.' Thus, we say a tree is a thing, its size is something, its fertility is something; blindness is not a real thing, but the absence of something real, etc.

9. Being is called a **transcendental**,* *i. e.*, a note common to all things, and thus transcending any genus or species. Still, it must be noticed that when we say ' a tree is a being,' ' its color is a being,' ' its age is a being,' etc., we evidently take the word ' being ' in senses somewhat different from one another; the term being is not taken *univocally* but *analogously*.

10. The **analogy** in this case is not that of mere *proportion* or resemblance; for there is more than resemblance

---

*Kant attached a new meaning to the term ' transcendental,' viz.: Whatever is beyond the reach of experience. He has thus created a confusion of ideas in many minds.

between the meanings of being; there is identity to a certain extent; it is the analogy of *attribution*. It is called *intrinsic*, because the note expressed by 'being' is contained in every being, and not merely attributed to one owing to some extrinsic relation with another being. But the mere *ens rationis* is called being by an analogy of proportion only, not of intrinsic attribution.

11. We must also distinguish between a *physical* and a *logical* being. Both may be real beings, but analogously. **Logical** being is being viewed as a mere object of knowledge, and therefore it can exist in the mind only, *e. g.*, all universals, all abstract ideas. **Physical** being can exist out of the mind, *e. g.*, this house, two houses. the Angel Gabriel, etc. Still the mind itself has also physical being, and so have its acts, viewed as modifications of the mind; but the terms of its acts, mental terms, have only logical being. All physical being is real being; a logical being is real when it is not an *ens rationis*.

Logical, as distinct from physical being, is the object of Logic.

12. A third distinction lies between *actual* and *possible* being; actual here means 'existing,' and possible means 'capable of existing.' Both actual being and possible being are real being, provided they be not negative.

13. **Thesis I.** *The term being does not express a genus of which the different classes of beings are the species.* Proof 1. A genus is univocally predicable of all its species; but being is not univocally predicable of all classes of beings, as we have explained (No. 9); therefore being is not a genus of which the different classes of beings are the species. *Proof* 2. If we examine with care how individuals are classified into species, and these into a genus, we shall perceive that the note which constitutes the difference between the

species is a something added to the genus, and not included in the notes which constitute that genus, *e. g.*, 'rational,' which marks the difference between rational and irrational animals, is not contained in the genus animal, but added to it in man and not added in the brute. Therefore, if 'being' were a genus, the difference that would be added to it in order to make a species would be something distinct from it, something not being. But there is nothing which is not being. Therefore no such difference can be added. Therefore being is not a genus; it may at most be called a *quasi-genus*, as bearing some resemblance to a genus.

14. Since being is not a genus, different classes of beings, *e. g.*, substance and accident, finite and infinite being, etc., are not species of beings; but they are called **determinations of being.**—*i. e.*, when I think of a substance, I do not think of a being with something else added to it, but of a being more clearly or less vaguely understood. As when a man looks through a telescope and vaguely discerns something, he knows not what; then, after focussing his instrument and looking again, he sees the same thing, recognizing it to be a ship, and such an individual ship; so when we see being as substance, we see no more than being, but we see it more distinctly; in short, being has not received an addition but a determination. (See this matter fully explained in the excellent work of Rev. Thomas Harper, S.J., *The Metaphysics of the Schools*, vol. i., Props. IV., V.)

15. **Thesis II.** *The idea of being in general is not the idea of the Infinite Being*

Explanation. This thesis is a most important application of the abstract truths so far considered. It strikes at the root of a philosophic system advocated by the Ontologists, whom we shall refute more directly in our treatise on Psychology (Nos. 187, 188).

Proof 1. The idea of being in general is very indefinite, that of the Infinite Being, or God, is very definite; for the former denotes any being, no matter how imperfect, the latter the union of all perfection in one Being.

Proof 2. Being in general is an abstraction, having only a logical entity; for no being can have physical existence except as a singular concrete being. Now, the Infinite Being has physical and concrete existence, existing not in general, but in an individual nature.

Proof 3. Being is not even predicated univocally of God and of any creature, but only analogically; because the being of all other things is distinct from their actual existence, for other beings may be actual or possible; whereas in God it is not distinct from existence, for a possible God would be no God at all.

True, the scholastic term *ens simpliciter*, 'simply being,' is predicated of God and of being in general, but in different significations; God is simply being, *i. e.*, being without any non-being; being in general is simply being, *i. e.*, being without specification.

How, then, do we get the idea of infinity? We perceive beings which have a certain amount of perfection and no more; we distinguish between perfection and limit, or the absence of further perfection; next, by our power of abstracting, we mentally remove all limit, and thus conceive abstractedly perfection without limit, *i. e.*, infinity.

16. **Objections**:
> 1. The idea of God is the first idea, but the idea of being in general is the first idea which our mind conceives; therefore, the idea of God and that of being in general are the same. *Answer*. Our idea of God is our idea of the first being, but it is not our first idea: God is first in the order of being or

ontologically, but He is not first revealed to our knowledge, not first logically.

2. God is the first truth. *Answer.* In Himself, yes; the first truth known to us, no.

3. From the finite we could never form the idea of the infinite: therefore we see the infinite directly. *Answer.* From the finite we could not form the intuitive perception of the infinite; but we can, by mentally removing all limits, form the abstract concept or idea of the infinite.

4. We could not understand what finite means unless we first understood the meaning of infinite; for the finite is only the negation of the infinite. *Answer.* The finite is not the negation of the infinite: it is the complex notion of 'being with limits'; now we see both 'being' and 'limits' all about us, we have only to conceive and unite those two notes in order to conceive the idea of finite.

5. If God is not admitted to be our first idea, we cannot prove the objective reality of our knowledge. *Answer.* In Critical Logic, the objective reality of our knowledge is proved without such admission.

ARTICLE II. POSSIBLE BEING.

17. A being is **possible** if it can exist. Possibility is twofold: *intrinsic* and *extrinsic*. A thing is **intrinsically** or internally possible if the notes of which it consists do not exclude one another; thus a mountain of jewels is possible, but a square triangle is impossible.

A thing is externally or **extrinsically** possible when there exists a power that can produce it; now, because the power of God is infinite, everything that is intrinsically possible is also extrinsically possible to God.

18. That which can be produced by no created power is said to be **physically** impossible. We call an act **morally** impossible when it might, indeed, be done by man, but, considering the uncommon difficulty of the act and the weakness of man, it would scarcely ever be done. Thus, it is morally impossible for a man to be always so careful as never to make any mistakes.

19. We get **our knowledge of what is possible** from the consideration of what is actual. Our imagination can combine various phantasms of material things perceived into new phantasms of things imaginable. Our intellect can combine notes of actual things which have become known to us, and form from them new concepts of merely possible things; but neither the imagination nor the intellect can combine elements that contradict each other; thus, we can neither imagine nor conceive a triangular circle.

20. **God's knowledge of possible creatures** is not derived from the consideration of actual creatures; but, understanding His own essence adequately, He saw from eternity how it could be imitated, or represented, by an endless variety of creatures. His infinite wisdom thus formed in itself the *exemplars* of all possible things, in a manner analogous to that in which an architect conceives the plans of various structures which he can erect. Thus, all things have not only their existence from God when they are created, but even their intelligible nature before creation; for God's intellect plans them.

21. **We do not intuitively behold the exemplars** as they are in the mind of God; but, when we conceive possible things, our concepts are conformable to those exemplars, except, of course, when our concepts imply a false judgment. The reason is that both God's concepts and ours are founded upon the same truth, viz.: that the notes which make up a possible

being can exist together. Various false views have been taken of these possibles by various philosophers, whom we shall now refute.

22. Thesis III. *The internal possibility of things does not formally depend on the power nor on the will of God.*

Proof. To say that the internal possibility of things depends formally on the power or on the will of God would mean that God's power as such, or His will as such, determined the difference between what is possible and what is impossible. But this cannot be.

1. God's *power* cannot determine the difference between possible and impossible; else certain things would be impossible simply and formally because the power of God did not extend to them, and thus the power of God would be limited.
2. God's *will* cannot determine this difference, else He could will the impossible to be possible; He could will that notes which contradict each other should nevertheless exist together, *e. g.*, that a circle should be square, that a truth should be false, that a thing could ' be and not be ' at the same time; thus all certainty would vanish and universal scepticism would result.

23. Objections:

1. If God cannot make the impossible possible, He cannot do all things. *Answer.* This we deny; *an absurdity* is not a thing, a real being; *e g.*, a triangular square would be a square that is not a square, but this is not thinkable, not intelligible, not a real being (No. 7).
2. Then God in creating would not be independent, He would depend on the possibles. *Answer.* The possibles themselves depend on His wisdom, and thus His dependence would not be on any existing being except Himself, for the possibles have no existence.

3. Then God would not create things out of nothing, but out of their possibility. *Answer.* He creates things out of nothing, actual or pre-existing; for the possibility is nothing actual, nothing existing.
4. If possibles have no existence, how can God know them? *Answer.* From eternity He knows His existing essence as capable of being imitated by beings which do not exist from eternity.
5. If it were not for the power and will of God, nothing were possible; therefore the possibles depend on His power and will. *Answer.* Nothing would then be *externally* possible; we grant that the external possibility of things depends on God's power and will.

24. **Thesis IV.** *The internal possibility of things depends on the intellect of God.*

Proof. The internal possibility of a thing consists in the agreement between its notes; not an actual agreement between actual or existing notes, but a merely logical agreement between notes considered as possible. Now, whatever is merely logical being depends on an intellect which conceives the notes and the agreement between them; therefore the internal possibility of a thing depends on an intellect; and since all things internally possible were so from eternity, their possibility depends on an eternal intellect, *i. e.*, on the intellect of God.

25. **Objections:**
   1. Even if we supposed that God did not exist, a round circle would still be internally possible. *Answer.* (*a*) From an absurd supposition it is no wonder if we get any consequence. (*b*) Nothing would be internally possible if there were no mind to conceive notes and associate them.
   2. We can think of possibles without thinking of God;

therefore they do not depend on God. *Answer.* We cannot fully understand them without referring them to the intellect of God. From the fact that we do not always think of them as dependent on God, it does not follow that they are not dependent on Him, but simply that we view them imperfectly.

26. **Thesis V.** *The internal possibility of things depends on the essence of God.*

Proof. God, being infinitely perfect, cannot be dependent for the knowledge of His intellect, except on Himself, on His own essence; but He knows all possible things; therefore, He must know them in His essence; but He does not know them as existing in His essence; therefore, He can only know them as having their source in His essence, as dependent on His essence; therefore, they depend on it.

Are, then, the possibles the Divine essence? No; the possibles, as such, or formally considered, have no actual entity, and therefore they cannot be the Divine essence, which has actual entity. But whatever foundation there was from eternity for the formation of these logical concepts, that foundation must have been something actual, and, therefore, identical with the essence of God.

27. **Objections:**
1. God must then have an infinite number of these concepts; but an infinite number of existing things is absurd. *Answer.* God understands all things by one concept, which embraces all that is knowable. Even we, in one concept of a line, embrace any number of parts into which it may be divided. The possibles are numberless (see No. 38); and they are not existing things, as the objection supposes them to be.
2. This explanation makes all things part of God's essence, and thus leads to Pantheism. *Answer.* It

makes all things finite imitations of God's infinite essence.

3. Knowledge supposes its objects and does not make them; hence the Divine intellect supposes the possibles and does not form them. *Answer.* The knowledge of the architect supposes his knowledge of the materials which he is to combine in his plans; thus, also, the intellect of God sees all perfections in His own essence, and understands how imitations of those perfections can be variously combined in finite beings.

ARTICLE III. ESSENCE AND EXISTENCE OF BEINGS.

28. The **essence** of a being is that collection of notes which must be conceived to understand that being, because they make it what it is and distinguish it from every being of another species: the essence (from *esse*, to be) answers the question, 'What is it?' '*Quid est?*' and is also called the 'quiddity.' For instance, the essence of a syllogism is "an argument consisting of three propositions so connected that from two of them the third follows." If any one of these notes is wanting, we have no syllogism, and if any of them is not apprehended, we do not apprehend the syllogism.

29. In its **widest sense,** the term essence is applied to anything, be it substance, property, or accident; for everything has notes which make it what it is, and about everything we can ask, 'What is it?' *e. g.*, What is color? what is figure? what is time? etc. But in a **stricter sense,** essence is said of substance only, and expresses the species to which that substance belongs; *e. g.*, the essence of man is rational animal, or a being composed of body and soul.

30. The essence of a substance may be viewed in two

ways: 1. The real or **physical essence** is the essence as it exists in the substance independently of our way of conceiving it. We conceive the physical essence when we conceive a being as composed of those elements which are really distinct in that being; and we express that physical essence by mentioning the parts really distinct, as body and soul in man. 2. The notional or **metaphysical essence** is the essence conceived as made up of parts which are not really, but only logically distinct. It is expressed by mentioning qualities which do not correspond to distinct parts; as when we call a man a rational animal. For we must not suppose that the animal and the rational are two distinct parts that make up man, as body and soul do, but the animal itself is rational; and if the rational part of man be taken away, there remains not an animal but an inanimate body.

31. **Are essences eternal and immutable?** In their physical existence, essences are not eternal, but created in time: but they may be called immutable, inasmuch as they remain while the substance lasts, for the accidents alone are changed. In their logical entity or intelligibility, essences are eternal and immutable, inasmuch as it ever is and ever was true, *e. g.*, that an intellect supposes a simple substance, that a part is less than the whole, etc.

32. It is clear that **we know the essences** of the things which we make or invent ourselves, as of a watch, a table, etc. We also know the essences of many things in nature, as of a fruit, a tree, an animal, the intellect, etc.; else, we could have no science about such things, since science treats not of singular things but of the essences of things. Still there are many natural agents of which we do not know the specific essences, *e. g.*, heat, electricity, magnetism, etc.; we know what they do, but not what they are. We define

such things by mentioning a genus to which they are known to belong, and, as the difference, we mention the effects which are peculiar to them; thus, we know that electricity has the power to produce certain effects, but we do not know whether it is a distinct substance or a modification of a substance; if it is a distinct substance, we do not know whether it is simple or compound.

33. **Existence** is a simple and primary concept, which, therefore, cannot be defined; the word is said to come from *ex-sistentia*, a standing forth out of its causes. By receiving existence, a possible being becomes actual; *e. g.*, Plato was possible and became actual. Are, then, existence and actual essence the same? This question is usually answered thus: "Between actual essence and its existence there is no real distinction, but only a logical distinction founded on reality." (See Harper's *Metaphysics of the Schools*, vol. i., Prop. XVI.)

34. The essence considered as the principle of actions is called the **nature** of a being. If, therefore, the actions of a being are sufficiently known, and are found to be uniform and constant, we can safely infer attributes belonging to the nature and essence of that being; thus, from the intellectual acts of man we infer the simplicity of his soul. The knowledge thus acquired is true and certain, for it rests on the evident principle that there must be a proportion between an effect and its cause. Therefore Locke and the positive philosophers are entirely mistaken when they teach that we know nothing but phenomena or sensible facts; we know that those facts can only proceed from proportionate causes, and thus from their effects we know something of the natures and essences of these causes.

Article IV. The First Principles Derived from Being.

35. From the very concept of being we derive analytically three primary judgments or **first principles of reason**, viz.:

1. The principle of *identity:* 'That which is, is,' or 'the being is.'
2. The principle of *contradiction:* 'A thing cannot be and yet not be,' or 'Being is not non-being.'
3. The principle of *the excluded middle:* 'A thing either is or is not.'

It is **a disputed question** whether the principle of identity or that of contradiction should be called the first principle. The two are inseparable, and, when properly understood, imply each other; for when we say, 'That which is, is,' we imply that it cannot not be, and when we say that being is not non-being we imply that it is being. There is no judgment prior in nature to these two, for every possible judgment contains these, and these imply no other judgments.

CHAPTER II.

THE TRANSCENDENTAL ATTRIBUTES OF BEING.

36. An **attribute** or **property**, *strictly* so called, is some note which is not the essence but still necessarily flows from the essence. Now, it is evident that from the essence 'being' nothing can flow which is not itself 'being'; therefore 'being' cannot have attributes or properties in the strict sense of these terms.

But in a **wider sense** we may, by analogy, give the name of attribute or property to any special view taken of being, provided such view can be taken of all and every being. Now, three such views are possible: (*a*) We may deny of every being that it is divided in itself; we do so by saying that it is *one;* oneness or **unity** is intrinsic to every being, and since it denies division it is a negative attribute. (*b*) Considering a being extrinsically, or as related to other beings, we may view it as conformable to knowledge, and call it *true;* **truth** is an extrinsic positive attribute. (*c*) We may also view every being as proportionate to an appetite or desire, and call it *good;* **goodness** is therefore also an extrinsic positive attribute. We shall find no other property which is common to all beings and is not identical with one of these three. These, then, are the only three transcendental properties of being; we shall examine them separately.

37. I. **Every being is one.** The term 'one' adds nothing positive to the being of which it is predicated, but it excludes the idea of many or of division into many; that therefore is called 'one' which is not many, which is not divided in itself.

It differs from 'alone,' which term has reference to something else, denying the existence of another being of the same kind. Still, unity is not always taken in its transcendental sense. When not taken in a transcendental meaning, but as a predicable, **unity may be differently considered.**

1. It is *metaphysical* when the being is not only undivided, but also incapable of division, as a spirit.
2. *Physical*, when nature unites real or separable parts into one whole, as in a tree, a man, a stone.
3. *Artificial*, when the parts are united by human skill, as a table, a clock, a book; this unity may be material or mental. Thus, a history in several volumes is an intellectual or mental unit.
4. *Moral*, when persons are united by a moral bond, as a family, a state.
5. *Accidental*, when the union is a mere aggregation without a bond, as a heap of stones. A being may have one of these unities without having the others. Metaphysical and physical unity make a being one in the proper sense of the word; the other unities make a thing one after a fashion, *secundum quid*.

38. The opposite of 'one' is 'many'; the opposite of unity is **multiplicity.** Many taken together constitute a multitude. A multitude measured by the unit is called a number. To number a multitude we must conceive three things: 1. *Oneness*, for number is formally a collection of units. 2. *Distinction*, or division between the units. 3. Some *similarity* between them. If that similarity is generic or specific, we have a **concrete number**, as five animals, twenty men, etc. If the similarity is only transcendental, we have an **abstract number**, as five, twenty, etc., *i. e.*, so many beings. Thus, also, five men, four plants, and five senses make fourteen things. When we have no definite unit to start with, we

can get no number; thus the arcs contained in a circumference are numberless. Since oneness, distinction, and similarity are conceived by means of abstraction, and abstraction requires an intellect, none but intelligent beings can count. Brutes may perceive many things, but they cannot perceive them as making a number.

39. The unity which a being has with itself or with another is called **identity** or **sameness**. When a being is viewed as the same with itself individually, it is said to be *numerically* identical; when as the same in species with another being, it is *specifically* identical; when as the same in genus, it is *generically* identical. Thus we say that two stone houses are of the same material (generically), two houses built of granite are of the same material (specifically), and when a house is taken down another may be built of the same material (individually).

When a thing ceases to be physically the same, but remains the same in the estimation of men, we denominate the sameness as *moral* identity; thus, a house might be called the same building, though all the parts one after another have been renewed.

40. To identity is opposed **distinction**, which means that one thing is not another. All distinction is either *real* or *logical*. 1. The **real distinction** is between the things themselves, independently of the manner in which the mind apprehends them. It is called a *major* or greater distinction when it is between species, as between man and brute; or between individual substances, as between Cæsar and Cicero; or between parts that can exist separately, as soul and body. The distinction between a substance and its accidents, as between a tree and its size; or between the accidents, as between the color and the taste of an apple, is by some called major, by others minor. The *minor*, or lesser distinction, also called

modal, exists between an entity and its mode. Now, by a mode we mean a manner of being that cannot possibly exist without something of which it is the mode; *e.g.*, figure, for there can be no figure without some quantity that has that figure. 2. The **logical** or mental distinction is between two ideas. It is *purely logical* when the ideas are exactly equivalent, as between a definition and the thing defined. The logical distinction is said to be *virtual*, or *to have a foundation in the reality*, when the concepts are not exactly equivalent, as when I distinguish the reason from the intellect of man, the mercy from the justice of God.

41. Under the head of unity we must also explain **individuality.** It is that unity of a being which makes it precisely this or that being. But what is it that thus individualizes a being? It is not the accidents; thus, a man, for instance, remains the same individual throughout his life, though his accidents are constantly changing, and two grains of sand exactly alike are yet not the same individual grain. St. Thomas puts the principle of individuation in matter, because " matter is incapable of being shared by several beings" (*De Ente et Ess.*, c. v.); and he adds that angels, or separated forms, as he calls them, are not individualized except by their specific notes, so that every Angel is a species by himself. Suarez, on the other hand, puts the principle of individuation in the form. Father Harper suggests that everything, be it matter or form, or compound of both, is intrinsically individualized by its own actual entity, and needs no other note; and thus that everything physically existing, or proximately apt to be brought into existence, is thereby individualized without needing any further principle to give it individuality. (Harper's *Metaph.*, vol. i. pp. 208 to 290.)

42. II. **Truth**, viewed as one of the transcendental properties of being, is metaphysical or ontological truth.

(*Crit. Log.*, c. i. a. i.) It means cognoscibility, or conformity of being to knowledge. As the form of a building is determined by the mind of the architect, so all creatures have their being and cognoscibility from God's intellect. The knowledge of God is therefore the *norma*, or *measure*, by which all created things are measured; while we derive our knowledge from creatures, and therefore these are the measure to which our knowledge must be compared in order to be true. Since God cannot fail of creating what He wants to create, the creature is conformable to His knowledge, and thus there can exist no metaphysical falsity. Things are called *false* only by analogy, inasmuch as some circumstance connected with them is apt to produce logical falsity in our mind. While truth is predicated both of knowledge and of being, still it must be primarily attributed to knowledge; in other words, logical truth is the principal analogue. But logical truth is not a transcendental, since many judgments are not true.

43. III. **Goodness** is being viewed in reference to some desire; it is that which is desired or may be desired. The goodness of a being is founded in its perfection. Now, a being is *perfect* when it has all the constituents that its nature requires, and all the power needed to act for the attainment of its end; if anything requisite be wanting, the being is imperfect. Its perfection is the reason of its goodness, and both are its very being; for anything is desirable in as far as it can perfect the being that desires it, and it can do so in as far as it has being; thus, every being is good inasmuch as it is a being. Still, perfection is logically distinct from goodness; for perfection regards the being itself, and goodness regards it in relation to the being that desires it.

44. Goodness is of **three kinds**:
 1. *Becoming, fit,* or *proper, i. e.*, conformable to right rea-

son. This, when taken in a stricter sense, is *moral good*, *i. e.*, conformity to reason as regulating free acts; in a wider sense, it also includes natural or *physical* good, *i. e.*, whatever perfects the nature of a subject, as health, knowledge, etc.
2. *Pleasurable*, *i. e.*, apt to give pleasure, to give satisfaction to an appetite.
3. *Useful*, *i. e.*, conducive to the attaining of some other good.

True good is that which meets the principal longing of a being, or which meets a secondary longing without injury to the principal; **apparent good** meets a secondary longing to the injury of the principal longing; thus, sensual delights, when they control a man's reason, are to him not true but only apparent good, since they withdraw him from the pursuit of duty and eternal happiness.

45. **Evil** consists in the privation of some due perfection; hence it is not real being, but the absence in a being of something which is due; no being can therefore be all evil or unmixed evil, for then it would be no being at all.

The privation of some physical good is *physical evil*, that of some moral good is *moral evil*, or sin; the latter supposes a free agent who departs from moral goodness. The absence of further perfection is called by Leibnitz *metaphysical evil;* incorrectly, for it may be no evil at all, since evil is a privation of some good that is due, and the perfection wanting may not be due to the creature. It may be asked what good there can be in physical suffering or pain. Pain can answer the purpose of punishment, of trial, of warning, etc., *e. g.*, if fire did not hurt animals it might destroy parts of their bodies without prompting them to protect themselves. Moral suffering, or grief, is chiefly an incentive to virtuous action, *e. g.*, grief for the sufferings of others prompts us to relieve them.

46. Among the good things that are of the agreeable or delectable kind, the most elevated is beauty. **Beauty** is the perfection of an object viewed as a source of pleasure to whoever beholds it. Since it is an object of desire, it is a kind of goodness; but taken in a stricter sense it is distinct from goodness; good things delight the possessor, beautiful things the beholder. We say the 'beholder,' because beauty is primarily predicated of objects seen or beheld: *quæ visa placent*, says St. Thomas. Still the word is also by analogy applied to the objects of other sense-perceptions, *e. g.*, to sound, and even to the objects of intellectual actions, *e. g.*, to virtue. *Physical beauty* is the perfection of natural objects, *intellectual* beauty is that displayed by the intellect, or exhibited by intellectual objects, *moral* beauty is that of virtue, *artistic* beauty that of art.

47. Since perfection as such cannot be perceived but by the intellect, beauty in its proper sense can be appreciated by none but intellectual beings. And because the perfection of an object implies a certain unity combining all its parts in proper proportion for the attaining of its one end, therefore many consider the very essence of beauty to consist in *proportion* or symmetry, and others in *unity amid variety;* but the essence of the beautiful is more correctly expressed by the terms 'manifest perfection,' 'striking excellence,' *splendor veri*, 'the brightness of truth.'

True perfection is **true beauty**; that false appearance of perfection which cannot stand the test of sound criticism is false beauty. The more perfect an object is, the more beautiful it is in itself, *i. e.*, the more capable it is of delighting the beholder; thus, God is infinitely beautiful; and, if He does not please us above all things, it is only because we know Him so imperfectly.

CHAPTER III.

THE CATEGORIES.

48. We have so far explained what is common to all being; we must next consider various classes of beings. Aristotle has pointed out ten highest classes under which all beings can find a place; these are known as the **categories** or **predicaments** (κατηγορεῖν, to predicate), because all that can be predicated of any being is found to belong to these ten categories. Such predicates are found in the answers to the following ten questions: What is the being? How great? What qualities has it? Whose is it? What does it do? What is done to it? Where is it? In what posture? When? How equipped?

49. When we ask what a thing is, the answer will be, either it is a **substance**, *i. e.*, something existing by or in itself, or it is something added to substance; it must be one or other. Substance is the first category. If a thing is not a substance, it is called an **accident**, *i. e.*, something added to a substance. Here accident is not taken in the same meaning in which it occurs in Logic. The logical accident is distinguished from the genus, species, difference, and attribute; the metaphysical accident now spoken of is a mere negation of that special manner of existence which belongs to substance. Accident does not constitute a genus of which the nine classes of accidents, *i. e.*, the nine remaining categories, would be the species; because the 'being' which is predicated of each accident is not taken univocally;—*e. g.*,

qualities, relations, time, place, etc., are accidents of substance, but so different from one another that they have nothing strictly in common which is not identical with that which is peculiar to each; and the mere negation of substantiality cannot constitute a genus; still, accident may be called a *quasi-genus.*

50. An **accident affects the substance** intrinsically or extrinsically:

1. *Intrinsically*, it may affect the substance absolutely or respectively. (*a*) Absolutely, it may affect the substance by reason of the matter, viz., *quantity;* or it may affect it by reason of the form, viz., *quality.* (*b*) Respectively, it affects one thing as connoting another, viz., *relation.*
2. *Extrinsically*, it may denominate the substance by reason of something else which affects it, viz.: its *action, passion, place, time, posture,* and *habiliment.* Each of the categories requires further explanation.

We shall treat: 1. Of substance. 2. Of the intrinsic accidents. 3. Of the extrinsic accidents.

ARTICLE I. SUBSTANCE.

51. By our senses we perceive things in the concrete, substance and accidents united. By our intellectual power of abstraction we, from the first dawn of reason, distinguish the quantity, the qualities, etc., of an object from the object itself, *e. g.*, the size and the color of an apple from the substance of the apple. We conceive the object as existing *in* or *by itself,* but the quantity, etc., as existing *in the object.* Philosophy is only the systematic teaching of common sense. Speaking philosophically, we say that a **substance** (*sub-stans*, standing under) is that which exists in or by itself,

and whatever does not thus exist we call an accident. An **accident**, therefore, is that which cannot exist in or by itself, but exists in some *substratum;* accidents are said to inhere in their subject.

52. When we say that **substances exist in or by themselves** (*per se*), we do not mean that they have no cause, that they exist by their own power (*a se*). This was a leading error of **Spinoza**, who, by making all substances thus self-existing, made them all necessary, and therefore identified all things with God.

53. **Hume** has fallen into another error, by teaching that we perceive nothing but qualities, and that what we call substance is only an unreal bond imagined as holding those qualities together; his theory contradicts the intuitions of all men, and leads directly to skepticism. **Leibnitz** makes substance a force or power; but a power is a quality of some being that has the power. **Locke** does not deny that qualities exist in something else, which he calls a *substratum*, but he adds: "Of this supposed something we have no clear, distinct idea at all" (*Human Underst.*, b. ii. c. 23, § 37). **McCosh**, on the other hand, appears to accept the Scholastic and common sense doctrine when he says: "Now I give up the idea of an unknown *substratum* behind the qualities. I stand up only for what I know. In consciousness we know self, and in sense-perception we know the external objects as existing things exercising qualities. In this is involved what we reckon the true idea of substance. We can as little know the qualities apart from an object exercising them, as we can an object apart from qualities. We know both in one concrete act, and we have the same evidence of the one as of the other" (*Agnosticism of Hume and Huxley*).

54. Substances are distinguished: 1. Into **simple**, *i. e.*,

such as have no parts, and **compound**, *i. e.*, such as have parts. 2. Into **complete** and **incomplete**. The incomplete is destined by nature to constitute with some other being a substantial unit; thus, the human soul needs the body to constitute man. The complete is not destined to such union, *e. g.*, an angel, a plant; it is therefore the complete principle of all its natural actions.

55. A complete substance is called a **supposit**; a supposit endowed with intellect is a **person**. As a human soul is not a complete substance, it is not a person. The Infinite Being, since it is complete and intelligent, is of course a personal being.

Since accidents exist in their substance, **actions**, which are accidents, belong to their supposit; the supposit it is which acts, *actiones sunt suppositorum;* the parts and powers of the supposit are not so properly said to act as to be the instruments by which the supposit acts. Thus we say 'A man walks,' not 'His feet walk'; 'I am thinking,' rather than 'My mind is thinking'; 'We see with our eyes, feel with our hands,' etc.

56. Since actions properly belong to the person, and the person who assumed human nature in the mystery of the **Redemption** is the Second Person of the Blessed Trinity, all the acts which He performed in His assumed human nature are really the acts of a Divine person, of God; they are Divine, and therefore of infinite merit. In becoming man He took upon Himself a complete individual human nature, *i. e.*, a soul and a body like ours, but not a human personality; He is not a human person, for person is the ultimate *substratum* of an intellectual nature. If, therefore, the ultimate *substratum* or person in Christ were human, then we could not say with truth what all Christians profess who recite the Apostles' Creed, viz., that the " only Son of God was born of the Virgin Mary, suffered, . . . was crucified; died, and was buried,"

etc., nor could St. John have written in his Gospel, "The Word was made flesh and dwelt amongst us."

57. **Personal identity** consists in the permanence of the intellectual supposit, not in the continuity of his consciousness; for even when we are totally unconscious we are still the same individual persons. Mankind has never believed that a man on losing consciousness ceases to be a person or becomes another person. On this point Locke, like many other philosophers, has written much that common sense does not support. He considers person to be merely a 'forensic term,' and personal identity to be nothing but consciousness. "It (person) is a forensic term appropriating actions and their merit. . . . This personality extends itself beyond the present existence to what is past only by consciousness, whereby it becomes concerned and accountable," etc. (*Human Underst.*, b. ii. c. 28, § 27). This doctrine would make us no longer accountable for acts which we have forgotten, of which we are no longer conscious.

Article II. The Intrinsic Accidents.

58. We have defined an **accident** as a being which cannot exist in or by itself, but needs a *substratum* or substance to exist in. By saying that accidents cannot exist by themselves we mean that they cannot do so as nature is now, or according to the actual physical laws. It is not, however, impossible for the Creator to maintain certain accidents in existence without a substance. God can do all that involves no contradiction; therefore He can keep in existence without inhesion in a substance such accidents as only imply a tendency, an exigency to inhere, and do not, in the very concept of them, imply the act of inhering, or actual inhesion in a subject. As a matter of fact, the Church teaches that

after the consecration of the bread and wine at Holy Mass the substances of the bread and wine cease to exist, and still their accidents of quantity, color, taste, etc., are preserved in existence by the supernatural action of the Divine will. In this doctrine there is nothing against reason. For the accidents have being or entity which is really distinct from the entity of the substance, since it may be changed while the substance remains the same. The substance supports that entity, but God can keep it in existence by His will directly without using the substance to produce that effect. For it is clear that whatever effects God can produce through second causes, *i. e.*, through His creatures, He can produce the same directly by His mere will whenever the effect is not of such a nature as to imply a created cause. Now, although the **accidents of bread and wine** naturally inhere in those substances, still human reason cannot see that quantity, color, taste, etc., essentially imply a substance to exist in. A full treatment of this question does not belong to a brief compendium of philosophy.

59. There are two classes of accidents which in their very concept involve inherence in something else, viz.: 1. **Vital acts**, such as those of will and intellect; and 2, **Modal accidents**, *i. e.*, accidents of accidents, *e. g.*, figure, which is a mode of quantity; for every quantity, by the very fact that it has limits, has necessarily some shape or figure, *i. e.*, some mode or manner of limitation. Those accidents which essentially imply only a tendency to inhere are often called **absolute accidents**, to distinguish them from modal accidents and vital acts. But, as explained above, the term 'absolute accident' is also used in contradistinction to the relative accident or relation.

60. The **intrinsic accidents** are three: *quantity, quality, and relation.*

I. **Quantity,** in its widest sense, is predicated of all that can be more or less. Thus taken, it is predicated:

1. Of *degrees of perfection*, as when we say that a man has a greater quantity of perfection than a plant. 2. Of *degrees of energy* or power, *e.g.*, a man has more intellect than a child. In a stricter sense, taken as one of the categories, quantity means the amount there is of a substance; it implies divisibility into parts of the same species as the whole, as of water into drops, not into gases. It is predicated: 1. Of *multitude*, which is called **discrete quantity,** because its parts are considered as separate from one another (*discretus*, viewed apart). 2. Of the *extension* of material substances, which is called **continuous quantity,** because its parts are considered as not separate (*continere*, to hold together), the end of one part being the beginning of another. The quantity of bodies has three dimensions: length, breadth, and depth; these, considered as existing in given bodies, are called **concrete quantities,** but when separately viewed, *i.e.*, only in their properties, as they are in mathematics, they are **abstract quantities.**

61. II. The term **quality** cannot be strictly defined, since it is a category, containing no genus and difference. It is that which denominates a substance as such or such and not otherwise; not as such a substance, say iron or gold, but such iron or such gold. Quality is often described as "any note that completes or perfects a substance in itself or in its action."

There are **four species** of qualities:

1. Those disposing the subject well or ill in itself or towards something else. Such qualities if transient are called dispositions, *e.g.*, well, ill, ready, unready, etc.; if permanent, they are called habits, *e.g.*, science, health, virtue, vice, etc.

2. Powers, *i.e.*, qualities which enable a subject to do

certain acts, whether such qualities belong to the very nature of the substance, *e. g.*, intellect, will, etc., which belong to every man; or are accidental to it, *e. g.*, talent to learn fast.

3. Sensible qualities, *i. e.*, those which affect the senses, *e. g.*, sweetness, sourness, warmth, cold, white, black, etc.

4. Figure, *i. e.*, qualities regarding the arrangement of material parts, *e. g.*, square, round, straight, etc.

A *passion*, when denoting a passing organic affection, such as anger, hunger, desire, etc., is not called a quality, but it is the accident or category called passion, for it means that a substance is acted upon; when denoting an abiding inclination to any affection, it is a quality of the first kind, *e. g.*, irascibility, gluttony, etc.

62 III. **Relation** is the accident denominating one thing as referred to another which it connotes, *e. g*, parent, greater, double, like, etc.; for there can be no parent unless there be a child, etc. Every relation supposes three things: (*a*) A *subject* which is related. (*b*) A *term* to which it is related. (*c*) A *foundation* of the relation; *e.g.*, when we say "virtue is more precious than gold," virtue is the subject of the relation, 'gold' is the term to which it is related, and 'precious' expresses the foundation of the relation, viz., price or value. A relation is *real, logical,* or *mixed:* (*a*) It is **real** when the foundation of the relation is in the things related, independently of our mind, *e. g.*, between cause and effect; if that foundation is found in each term, the relation is called *mutual*. (*b*) It is **logical** when its only foundation is in our mind, as when I say that the essence of God is the reason of His existence; for there is only a mental distinction, and therefore only a mental relation between His existence and His essence. (*c*) **It is mixed** when the relation is real in one of the things

related, and not real but only logical in the other; thus, a contingent being implies relation to the necessary being, but a necessary being can exist without a relation to a contingent being.

The **category of relation** is confined to the real relation; for all the categories express special manners in which things exist. It will be noticed that the mind cannot consider any relation without abstracting the foundation of that relation. Now, brutes have no power of abstracting, therefore they cannot apprehend relations, but only the things related.

ARTICLE III. THE EXTRINSIC ACCIDENTS.

63. The **extrinsic accidents** are six: *action, passion, the where, the when, posture,* and *habiliment.* They are **extrinsic** because in each of them we advert primarily to something distinct from the subject spoken of; *e. g.*, an action is denominated according to its term or effect, as 'to eat,' 'to walk,' 'to read,' etc.

64 I. **Action** signifies that accident which denotes a thing as proceeding from something else; thus, 'to think' denotes thought as proceeding from a thinking principle.

65. II. **Passion** is the receiving of an action. Action and passion are the two terms of the same motion; as when one strikes and the other is struck, one loves and the other is loved, etc.

An action is said to be **immanent** (*in-manere*, to remain in) if its term remains within the same faculty whence it proceeds; thus, 'to feel,' 'to know,' 'to will,' etc., are immanent acts. If the term does not remain within the eliciting faculty, the action is **transient** (*transire*, to pass over); as 'to push,' 'to pull,' 'to cut,' etc. The term 'transient,' *i. e.*, 'passing over,' should not lead us to imagine that a modification of the subject passes over to the object; but the subject by its action so affects the object as to make a new modification arise in it.

66. III. **The where** is the accident which determines material substances to a place. **A place** is the inner surface of the surrounding body considered as immovable; for bodies may move, but places remain. Thus, the place of a rock is the inner surface of the air or earth that surrounds it on all sides. Hence it is evident that the 'where' is an extrinsic accident. The distance between the surfaces of a body is called its intrinsic place. A body is naturally so related to place that each part of the body occupies a part of the place; this is meant by saying that a body is **circumscribed by the place**. A spirit, having no parts, cannot thus be circumscribed, but is whole and entire in the place and in every part of the place; it is said to be **limited to the place** to which its power is restricted. Spirits are not directly related to place by their own nature, but indirectly and accidentally, inasmuch as their power either is being exerted or may be exerted on certain bodies, and those bodies are in a place. Thus, a spirit is truly in a place; for where it is not, it cannot act; yet place does not belong to spirits in the same sense as to bodies.

67. **Thesis VI.** *Limitless vacant space is not a real being existing independently of our minds.*

Explanation. Space, as far as our observation goes, is not vacant, but filled with matter, at least with ether, *i. e.*, with some imponderable substance, the vibrations of which transmit light even from the most remote points of the universe. Probably there is no perfect void anywhere in the world But, outside of the material world, space is still imagined to extend; we also imagine that, before matter was created, there was a limitless vacant space. Now, we assert that this vacant space is nothing really existing out of the mind; we merely conceive a possible capacity, the absence of bodily substances.

Proof. If it were a real being existing out of the mind, it would have real quantity, for it has parts outside of parts; its quantity would be finite, or infinite, or indefinite. But it cannot be *finite*, else there would be other space around it; nor *indefinite*, for whatever exists really exists definitely, since indefinite means actually finite but capable of increase; nor *infinite*, for it will be proved hereafter that an infinite quantity actually existing is absurd (No. 93). Hence it is nothing real.

68. **It may be asked:** 1. Cannot space be the immensity of God? We answer, by no means; for space has parts outside of parts, and God's immensity has not; for it is God Himself, who is perfectly simple.

2. What is beyond the universe? Vacant space, *i. e.*, nothing actual.

3. What existed before the creation? Nothing but God.

4. If all substances in a vessel were removed, would there be space in it? Yes, there would be vacant space; vacant inasmuch as it contains no substance, yet real space inasmuch as the sides of the vessel are really related to each other.

5. How, then, is space defined? All space is conceived in reference to extension and relation between extended things. **Real or actual space** is the relation of place between real bodies, *e. g.*, between the sides of a vessel; **possible or imaginary space** is the imagined relation of place between possible bodies; **mathematical space** is extension considered in the abstract; **vacant space** is possible or imaginary space coupled

with the negation of a substance being there. Other authors designate as *physical space* all that we mean by actual and possible space united, and they define it as capacity to contain extended substances.

69. **Objections:** 1. If there were no bodies, space would still have real quantity out of our mind; for it would be really extended, having the dimensions of length, breadth, and depth. *Answer.* It would be only abstract or logical quantity; for it would be imagined as the possible quantity of possible bodies, and thus have only logical entity.

2. If all bodies but one were annihilated, and that one were moving, owing to its inertia it would keep on moving. But it could not move unless real space actually existed. *Answer.* It is enough for motion that there be possible space; real space is a relation between real bodies, and it is clear that this is neither necessary nor actual when there is only one body.

3. But it would really move, and real motion requires real space. *Answer.* We grant it would really move; but motion may be taken in two meanings: (*a*) As extrinsic to the moving body, *i. e.*, as a change of places, and such there could not be, since place supposes a surrounding body. (*b*) As intrinsic to that body, as a mode of its being, opposed to rest, and such motion has nothing to do with the relation which constitutes real space.

70 IV. **The when** is the accident which regards succession in time. To understand succession we must understand duration, *i. e.*, permanence in being. Now, a being can be permanent in three ways: (*a*) If it remains perfectly immutable, its duration is called **eternity.** (*b*) If its

nature is devoid of changes, but its accidents are susceptible of them, as is the case with the Angels, its duration is called **aevum** by the Schoolmen, for which term we have no English equivalent. (*c*) If its very nature is subject to changes, as is the nature of bodies, its duration is said to be in time. Such durations succeeding each other can be counted, and their number or measure constitutes **time**. In this kind of duration alone the 'when' of the categories finds its place.

71. **Time**, therefore, is the measure of succession in changeable beings; it is ever flowing, as the 'now,' or present moment, is ever moving onward, separating the past and the future. The 'now' is the indivisible limit between them. From this explanation of time it is clear:

1. That there was no time before the creation, as there were no changeable beings.
2. That some unit is needed in order to measure time; the apparent motion of the sun around the earth is a unit accepted by all nations.
3. Since time implies a relation between the measure and the measured, brutes cannot apprehend time as such (see No. 62); they apprehend the phenomena only, which happen in time.
4. Since the successions measured are objective realities, time exists outside of the mind; and it is absurd to maintain with Kant that time is merely a subjective concept, by which the mind puts order into the objects of its knowledge.

72. V. **Posture** is the manner in which the parts of a body are disposed with regard to an adjacent body; *e. g.*, when a man is standing on, lying on, leaning against a material object. Posture may remain the same though every part of

the space occupied should change, as when a person travels in a sitting or standing posture.

73. VI. **Habiliment** is the accident by which one bodily substance is furnished with another, as its dress, protection, ornament, etc.

The last two categories, just explained, are of minor importance; but they are needed by the philosopher in order that there may be no manner of being which cannot find its place under one of the highest genera.

CHAPTER IV.

CAUSE AND EFFECT.

74. A cause is anything which influences the existence of another thing; the latter is called the **effect.**

A **principle** or **principiant** is that from which a being proceeds or originates in any way. It may proceed from it:

1. *Logically*, as the conclusion does from the premises in reasoning.
2. *Physically*, by deriving physical being from the principiant. It may do so in two ways: (*a*) The principiant may produce it, *e. g.*, a tree producing fruit. (*b*) The principiant may be one of its constituent elements, as a wheel is of a clock.

A principiant is always **prior** to that which proceeds from it, in one of two ways: (*a*) In *time*, by existing sooner. (*b*) By *nature* only, when one being produces or constitutes another without existing before it; thus, flame is a principiant of light, roundness of a circle. These two ways of procession and priority do not embrace the peculiar procession by *origin* only, viz.: when the principiant and what proceeds from it are one identical being. This priority does not exist except in the Blessed Trinity, God the Father being the principiant of God the Son, and these two Persons together the principiant of the Holy Ghost.

75. It will be readily inferred from these definitions:
1. That the terms cause and effect always denote two distinct beings, while the term principiant may denote the same being with that which proceeds from it.

2. That procession does not necessarily denote succession in time.
3. That mere succession in time does not constitute procession; thus, the night succeeds the evening, but does not proceed from it.
4. That therefore the terms principiant and beginning are not synonymous; the principiant has an intrinsic and necessary connection with whatever proceeds from it, while the beginning may have only an extrinsic and accidental connection with what follows it.

76. When a cause is viewed as producing the effect, it is taken **formally** as a cause; else it is **materially** a cause. Thus, Columbus was from his boyhood the discoverer of the new world materially, not formally. This distinction between being materially and formally a cause should not be confounded with the other distinction which is next to be explained.

77. There are **five kinds of causes**: the *material* cause, the *formal*, the *final*, the *exemplary*, and the *efficient*.
  1. The **material cause** is the matter out of which a thing is made; thus, steel is the material cause of a watch-spring; the distinction between matter and form will be explained further on (No. 127). Speaking analogically, philosophers often apply the name of matter, or material cause, to anything out of which another is produced; thus, they call the faculty of the will the matter, and an act of the will a form.
  2. The form, or **formal cause,** is that which specifies the matter, *i. e.*, which makes the matter be of one species rather than another. The form is: (*a*) *Substantial*, if it goes to make the very nature of the substance and cannot be removed without changing that nature; *e. g.*, the vital principle in all plants and animals; for when

it ceases to be or departs, the substance or nature of the plant or animal is no more. (*b*) *Accidental*, if it can be destroyed without affecting the nature of the substance; *e. g.*, the shape of a hat.

3. The **final cause** is the end or purpose intended in an action; *e. g.*, when a man exerts himself to acquire riches, the acquisition of riches is a true cause of his exertion. The object itself aimed at, *i. e.*, riches, is the final cause materially considered; the acquisition of riches is the final cause formally considered.

78. **Thesis VII.** *All action is directed to some end or purpose.*
Proof. Every action is either done with intelligence or not; if done intelligently, the agent has some motive for his action; he is aiming at some result or other; he acts for an end. If an action is not done with intelligence in the agent, then it proceeds from an impulse of nature; it is then the effect of a physical cause. But physical causes act according to the laws by which the Creator governs the universe—*i. e.*, by which a wise God directs all things to proper ends. Therefore all action is directed to some end.

79. **Objections:** 1. A man often acts without a purpose. *Answer.* He then acts upon an impulse of his nature, and all such action is directed to some end by the Author of nature.

2. If he acted upon a natural impulse his action would be good, since it would come from God; but such actions are often evil. *Answer.* As far as his impulses are physical or purely natural they are not evil; but as far as he freely neglects to control his natural impulses according to the law of reason, they are evil.

3. Many actions are merely accidental. *Answer.* Every act proceeds from a cause, necessarily or freely, and therefore no action can be accidental; but an action

may have effects not intended by the agent, and these may be said to be accidental with regard to him, though they, too, have a definite cause, which acts for a definite end.

80. IV. The **exemplary cause** is the model conceived by an intelligent agent to the likeness of which he directs the effect of his work. It may be some pattern extrinsic to the agent which he wishes to imitate; thus, an artist sketches a real scene. Or it may be an original image intrinsic to the agent's mind, such as the plan conceived by a painter of the ideal scene which he wishes to represent.

81. V. The **efficient cause** is the agent that does the action. Every agent acts by its powers or faculties. The power itself is called, in the terminology of the Schoolmen, the *actus primus*, or potential act; the exercise of the power is the *actus secundus*, or elicited act. The potentiality itself is *remote*, or *proximate*; *e. g.*, an infant, from the very fact that it is a human being, has the power of reasoning, but remotely, *i. e.*, not in a condition fit for use; a grown person has the same power proximately, *i. e.*, fit for use.

82. The requisites for the exercise of a power are called **conditions**; these are not properly causes, since they do not bring about an action, but only remove what might prevent action. For instance, citizenship is usually a condition required for voting, but it does not as such induce one to vote.

A circumstance which is apt to induce an agent to act, though he might also act without it, is called an **occasion**; thus, a time of political excitement is an occasion apt to induce many to vote. If occasions influence actions they are real causes.

83. Several **further distinctions** apply to the efficient cause:
    1. If it depends on no other cause, it is called the **first cause**: such is God alone; all others are **second causes**.

2. It is **properly** (*per se*) the cause of the effect intended and of such other effects as are natural consequences of the action done; thus, the surgeon is properly the cause of the pain he inflicts and of the cure he works. It is **accidentally** the cause of effects which were neither intended nor naturally to be expected, as when the surgeon causes death.

3. A **principal** cause is that to which the effect is chiefly attributable; an **instrumental** cause is that used by a principal cause; as when a lancet is used by a surgeon to open a sore with. The instrumental cause is always made to extend, by him who uses it, to some effect beyond its own competency; *e. g.*, the lancet could not cut *skillfully* without the skill of the surgeon.

4. A **free** cause can determine its own actions, a **necessary** cause cannot do so.

5. A **moral** cause is one to which an effect is justly imputed, because it induces another agent to act; it does so by command, advice, threats, provocation, etc., as when a naughty boy provokes a man to anger.

84. Since a cause is that which produces an effect, it is evident that it must in some manner contain the effect; for as the axiom expresses it, *Nemo dat quod non habet*—" No one gives what he has not." Now, **a cause may contain an effect**, or rather the perfection which it communicates to the effect, in three ways:

1. *Formally*, when the cause and effect are of the same species; thus, a plant produces a plant, clouds bring rain, etc.

2. *Eminently*, when the cause is specifically superior to the effect and contains the perfection of the effect in a higher manner of existence; thus, God contains all the perfection of creatures.

3. *Virtually* or *equivalently*, when the cause possesses a superior perfection which can produce the effect; thus, an artist may produce a painting much fairer than himself; he does not possess its beauty eminently, but he possesses an intellect which can conceive and a skillful hand which can express ideal beauty.

When a cause contains an effect formally, it is called a **univocal cause;** else it is an **equivocal** cause.

Since an effect is contained in its cause, it is evident that **no effect can be more perfect than its cause.**

85. We must notice two important **limits to causality:**

1. A finite cause can only modify an existing subject, but not produce a substance from nothing.
2. No cause can **act at a distance,** *i. e.*, where it is in no way present; for where it is not, there it is nothing, and nothing can do nothing. Still it suffices that the cause be mediately present to its effect, as when the sun, by the vibrations of ether, gives light and heat to the earth.

Sceptics have denied the **reality of causes and effects**; but it is evident: (*a*) That all men distinguish the relation of cause and effect from that of mere succession in time. (*b*) That all men judge causes and effects to be realities, on which all legislation, all commercial and professional pursuits, as well as all trades, are based. (*c*) That all languages proclaim this reality, *e. g.*, in the use of such verbs as 'to make,' 'to produce,' 'to push,' 'to pull,' etc., and of such particles as 'why,' 'because,' 'therefore,' etc. (*d*) That we are conscious of exercising effects, *e. g.*, of raising our hands at will, of speaking, walking, etc.

86. The study of principiants and causes obviously suggests two important principles of certain knowledge, viz.: (*a*) **The principle of the sufficient reason,** expressed thus: "There is

nothing without a sufficient reason for it." (*b*) **The principle of causality**, expressed thus: " Nothing is made or begins to exist but by a cause."

87. **Thesis VIII.** *The principle of the sufficient reason and that of causality are absolutely certain.*

Proof. 1. The principle of the sufficient reason is an analytical judgment so obviously evident that we cannot rationally deny or even doubt it without thereby implicitly affirming it; for rationally to deny or doubt it we should see some reason for so doing; and thus we admit the validity of the principle, denying it because we see a reason for so doing.

2. *The principle of causality* flows from the preceding; for when anything begins to exist, there must be a sufficient reason for this beginning. That reason must be either in the object itself that begins to exist or in something else. It cannot be in the object itself; neither in the acts of that object, for it cannot act before it exists; nor in its nature, for then the object would be necessary, but a necessary being is so from eternity and has no beginning. Therefore, the reason of its beginning to exist must be in another being; but this means that it has a cause.

88. **Objection**: All our knowledge comes through our senses; now, causality does not come to us through our senses; we see facts only as succeeding one another, not as causing one another. *Answer.* This objection refutes itself; we know what causality means, yet, it says, this knowledge is not conveyed to us by sensation; therefore, it follows we do not get all our knowledge by sense only. It is, however, correct to say that all our knowledge begins in sensation. The relation of cause and effect is not perceived by sense, but by the intellect on occasion of sense-perception (see Nos. 178, etc.);

e. g., I understand that my sensations are caused by myself as the eliciting subject, and by the bodies perceived as the determining object of my perceptions.

89. **Corollaries.** From all these explanations it is evident: 1. That nothing can be its own cause. 2. That two things cannot cause each other. 3. That the principle of causality is not acquired by induction, but is *a priori*, and only verified by experience. Children show that they have begun to reason when they ask, "Why is this?" (what is the sufficient reason?) "Who made this?" (what is its cause?), etc.

CHAPTER V.

THE CHIEF PERFECTIONS OF BEING.

90. The **chief perfections of being** are *simplicity, infinity, necessity,* and *immutability*.

I. **Simplicity** is that perfection which makes a being identical with everything that constitutes it; it is a positive perfection, but it is conceived by us in a negative way, viz.: by the exclusion of all composition. A being is *absolutely simple* if it excludes all manner of composition.

91. **Composition** implies a want of identity among the parts of a whole or unit. The whole and its divisions are called **actual**, if there is outside of the mind a true junction or combination of parts. If the parts can exist separately, *e.g.*, 'soul' and 'body,' the actual unit is called **physical**: if they cannot, it is **metaphysical.** Thus man's 'animality' and 'rationality' are metaphysical parts of a metaphysical whole, for they cannot exist separately; take away from a man the principle of his rationality, the soul, and you have left, not an animal, but a dead body. It will be noticed the metaphysical division regards the *comprehension of an idea*. The whole and the division are called **potential** when the parts are not united outside the mind, but are capable of being classed together as realizing the same idea. For instance, 'animal' expresses a potential whole if we consider its extension—*i.e.*, the class of individuals to which it is applicable. This is often called the *whole of extension*, and also a *logical whole*, because the union of the individuals is not in nature but

in the mind only, which apprehends them all by their common nature, and forms of them a mental unit. The latter division is the one which logic properly deals with; for it breaks up larger classes into smaller, and these into smaller again.

92. II. The **Infinite** is the perfection which contains all entity so that none be wanting; it is a most positive perfection, though conceived in a negative way, viz.: by denying all limitation. But, since limitation is itself a negation of further perfection, the absence of limitation in a being, *i. e.*, its infinity, is a negation of a negation, and therefore an affirmation.

The **Potential Infinite** is the finite conceived as capable of constant increase; it is, therefore, not truly infinite but indefinite, though in mathematics it is usually called infinite. The infinite cannot be measured or counted; because measure and number express a limit, and the infinite has no limit. It is also to be observed that no amount of finite additions can ever make the finite become infinite.

93. **Thesis IX.** *No existing quantity can be infinite.*

Proof. Since the essence of quantity implies divisibility, any existing quantity may be divided, at least mentally. Let us, then, cut off a small portion from the quantity which was supposed to be infinite; what remains will be finite; and that finite remainder increased by the small portion cut off will be infinite. But this is absurd, viz., that a finite quantity should differ from the infinite by a small portion. Besides, suppose we add to the finite remainder a portion greater than that cut off; we should then have a quantity greater than infinite, which is impossible. An infinite body would measure an infinite number of yards, and more than an infinite number of feet.

94. **Objections:** 1. The multitude of possibles is infinite;

for there is no limit to the things that God can create. *Answer.* The possibles are not existing; the thesis regards existing quantity.

2. The acts of creatures will go on increasing in multitude for ever. *Answer.* The number of past acts will always be actually finite, though capable of constant increase—*i. e.*, the multitude of future acts is indefinite.

3. It cannot be indefinite; for God knows all future acts of His creatures distinctly, and therefore definitely. *Answer.* God's knowledge is conformable to the reality—*i. e.*, to the object of that knowledge; now, that object is a series of acts, all distinct from one another, ever continuing, but never being an existing infinite series. Besides, distinctness of knowledge is opposed to vagueness of knowledge, and need not imply limitation of the things known.

4. Any extended body contains an infinite multitude of parts. *Answer.* The number of ultimate particles into which a body can physically be divided is finite; but the extension of the body can be mathematically divided without end—*i. e.*, it is potentially, not really, infinite in its divisibility.

95. It may be asked **how we acquire the idea of the infinite.** We do so, not by intuition of the Infinite Being, or God, nor by mentally adding perfections to perfections, for finite things added together can never give the infinite; but seeing finite things we distinguish in them, by abstraction, perfection and limitation; next, by denying limitation we form the abstract concept of unlimited perfection, *i. e.*, of the Infinite Being. The idea thus formed is of a positive object; objectively considered, it is not negative, but most positive; but subjectively considered, it implies affirmation and negation. The idea of the finite, on the other hand, is not a mere

negation; for it is the affirmation of something and no more —*i. e.*, it affirms one thing and denies anything beyond.

96. III. **A necessary being** is one whose non-existence is impossible. It is *hypothetically* necessary, if its non-existence is impossible under a certain hypothesis or supposition; it is *absolutely* necessary, if its non-existence is impossible under any supposition. Now, this cannot be the case unless its very nature implies existence, unless the being be self-existent. If such a being exists it must have always existed, and cannot cease to exist, else its non-existence would not be absolutely impossible; it is therefore eternal—*i. e.*, without beginning and without end.

97. Any being which is not absolutely necessary is said to be **contingent**—*i. e.*, it may be or not be, it is not self-existing. If it exists and yet has not in itself the reason of its existence, it must then have that reason in another being; but to have the reason of one's existence in another is to have a cause; therefore every contingent being, if it exists, must have a cause.

98. IV. **Immutability** is the necessity of remaining the self-same, the impossibility of changing. A **change** is a transition from one state of being to another. It implies three things: (*a*) A former state which is abandoned. (*b*) A latter state which is assumed. (*c*) A subject that abandons the one state and assumes the other.

99. **The change may occur variously:** 1. A substance may be changed from one species to another by losing an old and acquiring a new substantial form, as when metals are oxidized. 2. The subject may acquire or lose some substance without change of its species, as when a sand-bank grows larger or smaller. 3. It may acquire or lose a quality, as when iron gets hot or cold. 4. It may pass from local motion to rest, or from rest to local motion. 5. It may assume a new arrangement of parts, as when water freezes. 6. Supernatu-

rally, one substance may be substituted for another while the accidents remain, as when the bread and wine are changed into the body and blood of Christ. But in this case the word change is taken analogically for *transubstantiation*. A change of relation between one being and another is called an **extrinsic change**. This may occur though one of the two beings remains absolutely immutable, as when God became a Creator without undergoing any intrinsic change, simply because the creatures began to exist, and thus a new relation was established toward God which had not existed before.

BOOK II.

COSMOLOGY.

100. **Cosmology** is the first part of *Special Metaphysics* (No. 4); it is the study of the visible world in connection with its highest causes. We mean by the **world**, or the **universe**, the total collection of all material objects knowable by mankind.

In studying the visible world, we are to consider: 1. Its origin. 2. Its purpose and its perfection. 3. The laws that govern it. 4. The constituent elements of matter. 5. The general properties of bodies.

CHAPTER I.

THE ORIGIN OF THE WORLD.

101. The origin of the world is obviously one of the most important questions discussed in Philosophy. The ancients were divided among **various opinions** on the subject. 1. Plato maintained that the matter which composes the world was necessary, and therefore eternal, but that it was properly arranged by an intelligent Being, who is God. 2. Aristotle supposed that both the matter and the order of the

universe were necessary and independent of any cause. 3. Pythagoras held the theory, revived in the Middle Ages by the eccentric Scotus Erigena, that the world has come forth from the Divine Substance by an outward emanation, an outpouring or outputting of the Divinity. 4. Another explanation, not unknown to the ancients, was scientifically developed in the seventeenth century by the Jewish philosopher Spinoza, who taught that there exists only one substance, necessary, self-existent and infinite, endowed with the two attributes of extension and thought. These attributes he supposed to be necessarily in constant action; the evolutions of its extension producing the various bodies of the world, and the different series of its thoughts being the minds of men; thus, the whole universe would be nothing but a succession of constantly varying phases assumed by the infinite substance. This system has been called an internal emanation of the Infinite Being; it is really Pantheism (πᾶν θεος, everything God), for it makes all things mere modifications of the Divine nature.

102. **Idealism** is a modern system of Philosophy, taught chiefly by Fichte, which, instead of explaining the origin of the material universe, prefers to deny the existence of all bodies, and to maintain that there exists nothing but the *Ego*, whose ever-changing phantasms, like a sick man's dreams, are mistaken for objective realities. This vagary is refuted in Critical Logic, because it denies the reliability of sense-perceptions. The true doctrine, conformable alike to reason and to Revelation, is that "In the beginning God created heaven and earth " (Gen. i. 1).

103. **Pantheism**, if not expressly taught, is at least implied in the speculations of many modern infidels; the Agnostic school inculcates the same error in a milder form, teaching that, for all we know, the visible world may be the

sum total of actual being, the existence of a God distinct from this world being classed among unknowables.

Thesis I. *Pantheism and Agnosticism are systems destructive of all religion, of morality, and of human society.*

Proof. If Pantheism or Agnosticism were true, each of us would be, or at least might be, for all we know, a part of the infinite substance; in fact, the worst men in the world would or might be self-existent, and therefore independent of a Maker and Supreme Master, a part of God, as Divine and necessary as God Himself. If so, no one could or should worship a Superior Being, hence no religion; no one need obey a higher law-giver that would bind his conscience, hence no morality; without morality no restraint on man's selfishness, a mere struggle of might, whence would soon result a state of mere barbarism, the destruction of society.

104. **Thesis II.** *Neither the world nor the matter of which it is composed can possibly be self-existent.*

Proof 1. A self-existent being is immutable; for, if it must necessarily exist, it must also necessarily be such as it is; else why is it such as it is? If it was necessarily a certain thing, no other being could make it anything else. In other words, whatever gives an object existence gives it a definite existence; for it could not give it an indefinite existence. Now, the world and the matter of which it consists are not immutable, but subject to constant changes, as is evident to our senses. Therefore they are not self-existent.

Proof 2. The world and all matter are finite, for all matter is divisible, and as such has quantity; but whatever has quantity cannot be infinite, as was proved in *Ontology* (No. 93). Therefore both matter and a world consisting of matter are finite. Now, a self-existent being cannot be finite, it cannot have limits, for those limits would be self-imposed, but no being can impose limits on its own nature: (*a*) Not *freely*, for a being must first exist in a definite nature before it can act freely. (*b*) Not *necessarily*, for this would mean that the perfections of that being exclude all further perfections; but no perfection can be exclusive of any further perfection, since all perfection is positive, and there can be no contradiction except between a negative and a positive. Hence a self-existent being has no limits; it is infinite, and therefore neither the world nor its matter is self-existent.

Proof 3. (*A*) The world is not self-existent, for whatever is such must have existed from eternity, without a beginning, since nothing can begin to exist without a cause (No. 87). But the world cannot have existed without a beginning (see Thesis IV., No. 109). (*B*) Matter is not self-existent.

Who would persuade himself that every particle of dust is a necessary being, having the reason of its existence in its own nature? Every particle of matter bears, as it were, the trademark of a manufactured article. The proof may be thus proposed:

If the elements of matter were self-existent, they would constitute a finite or an infinite multitude, but they could do neither. *We prove the major:* (*a*) They would constitute a multitude, for any definite collection of units constitutes a multitude. Now, the elements of matter would be a collection of units, for each of them is a unit. (*b*) This multitude would be finite or infinite, for nothing can exist indefinitely; when, for instance, we speak of an indefinite quantity, we mean a quantity actually finite, but capable of further increase—finite as far as it exists. Hence the elements would constitute a multitude, and that multitude would be finite or infinite.

We prove the minor: The elements of matter cannot constitute a finite nor an infinite multitude: 1. Not an infinite multitude, for no existing quantity can be infinite, as proved before (No. 93). 2. Nor can it be a finite multitude; for if a million particles, say of gold, existed necessarily, then it would be either by accident or for some sufficient reason that there should be just a million, and not one more or less; but it can be neither: (*a*) Not by accident, for accident means a result without a reason for it, and there is nothing without a reason for it, therefore the number of particles cannot be determined by accident. (*b*) Nor can there be a sufficient reason in the particles why they are just one million in number, since the fact that a million exist cannot be a reason why there could not be one more, for there is no more contradiction in a million and one than in a million particles.

105. **Objections:** 1. Matter is indestructible, therefore it is necessary. *Answer.* It is not indestructible by the power of God.

2. The substance of matter might be immutable, though its accidents are known to be changeable. *Answer.* (*A*) Not only its accidents, but its very substance is changeable, *e. g.*, when a plant dies, when iron rusts, etc. (*B*) If matter being unchangeable, its accidents were changeable, they would have been changing from eternity, since necessary matter would have existed from eternity; and thus there would either (*a*) have been, by this time, an infinite quantity of changes; but an infinite series can never be gone through, and so the most recent change could never have been arrived at; (*b*) or if the number of changes were finite, then the matter must at first have been changeless; and if so, the first change could never have begun, for it was not necessary, and nothing begins by accident, *i. e.*, without a cause, and thus matter motionless from eternity could never have begun to move.

3. Though the elements be singly unnecessary, the wnole

collection of them may be necessary. *Answer.* By no means; a collection of unnecessary things is not and cannot be an absolutely necessary collection, for a collection is nothing else than the sum total of the things collected.

4. The world is infinite, for it fills all space, and space is infinite. *Answer.* It does not fill all possible space, but only all actual or real space, and this is finite (No. 68).

106. **Thesis III.** *Matter could not have originated but by creation.*

Explanation. By creation we understand the making of a substance out of nothing. Now, we maintain that, though some species of matter may arise from other species of matter, *e. g.*, water from the chemical combination of oxygen and hydrogen, still ultimately the first matter in existence must have been made out of nothing, *i. e.*, by creation.

Proof. To be created is to be made out of nothing; but matter was made out of nothing; hence it was created. *We prove the minor:* 1. ' *It was made*,' *i. e.*, it received its existence from another being, for there is nothing without a sufficient reason. This reason must be either in the being itself or in another being. Now, the sufficient reason of matter is not in matter itself, else matter would be self-existent, and we have just proved that it is not so. Therefore the reason of its existence must be in another being, *i. e.*, it is made. 2. ' *Out of nothing*,' for if it were made out of something pre-existing, that something would be mutable, else nothing new could have been made out of it; but what is mutable is not self-existent (No. 103); hence it, too, must have been made, either out of something else or out of nothing. If out of nothing, then our proposition is proved; if out of something else, the same difficulty will always return, until we arrive at some matter that was not made out of anything else. The only way to evade this argument is to suppose an infinite series of transformations that matter has undergone; but an infinite series could never have been passed through; besides, it would be infinite and still not infinite, but increasing; therefore there was, or is, a first matter made out of nothing.

107. **Objections:** 1. Scientists object that it is unscientific to trace natural effects to a supernatural cause. *Answer.* Scientists do say so, but the only scientific way is to trace effects to their true causes by whatever name you call these. Now, the only true, the only possible cause of matter is creation, as we have proved.

2. But creation is impossible, for out of nothing nothing can be made. *Answer.* It is true that nothingness cannot become a material out of which things are made. But that is not the meaning of creation; it means simply that God, by His Almighty will, without using any material, has made that to exist which would not exist, either in its present state, or in its elements, or in any way whatever, but for the mere fact that He wills it to exist.

3. But the cause must contain the effect, and God did not contain matter. *Answer.* God contained all perfection of matter without its imperfections—*i. e.*, He contains matter *eminently*. For instance, matter is something that can exercise certain powers. God can exercise all those powers—*i. e.*, He can produce all those effects; and thus there is nothing in matter that does not find its prototype in God. He also contains matter *virtually*—*i. e.*, He can produce it, for He is Almighty.

4. The very idea of matter contains extension, but there

is no extension in God. *Answer.* It contains extension in the object of the idea, not in the subjective idea. As to the minor, extension is not formally in God, but eminently—*i. e.*, as far as it implies no imperfections.

108. **A further question** is often discussed with regard to the origin of the world, viz.: Is it certain that its creation could not absolutely have been from eternity, that the world must have had a beginning, that matter itself must have had a beginning? Though it would seem that the very essence of creation implies a transition from non-existence to existence, and therefore a beginning of the creature, still St. Thomas, and many of the most distinguished philosophers, say that a creation from eternity cannot be conclusively proved to be absurd, because it is not so: (*a*) On the part of the Creator, Who was from eternity Almighty. (*b*) Nor on the part of the creature, which was from eternity capable of being created. (*c*) Nor on account of the necessary subordination of creature to Creator, for that, too, would be secured. But though creation, as such, may perhaps be possible without a beginning, there is something special in the nature of the world which shows that it cannot have existed from eternity.

109. **Thesis IV.** *The world cannot have existed from eternity.*

Proof. The world contains a series of changes. If it had existed from eternity, there would have been an infinite series of changes before any particular change could have taken place, *e. g.*, before vegetation began; but an infinite series can never be passed, nor can anything infinite be further extended. Therefore the world cannot have existed from eternity.

110. **Objections:** 1. St. Thomas and many others admit the possibility of creation from eternity. *Answer.* St. Thomas admits that the proofs of this proposition are

not absolutely conclusive; many other great minds think they are conclusive, and they are certainly very powerful, far more so than any objection brought against them. St. Thomas did not wish to rest our belief in creation on a mere reasoning about which logicians might quibble, because it rests on the firmer basis of Divine Revelation. (*Summa*, i. q. 46, art. ii.)

2. The world might have been changeless at first. *Answer.* A material creation absolutely at rest would be useless.

3. The creative act was from eternity, therefore its effect also. *Answer.* It was eternal subjectively, *i. e.*, in God; not objectively, *i. e.*, on the part of the creature.

4. When the cause exists the effect must exist. *Answer.* If the cause acts necessarily, yes; not if it acts freely and by one single act which extends from eternity to eternity (see Nos. 243, 244).

5. But God is a necessary cause. *Answer.* He is a necessary being, but a free cause.

6. The act of creation would have produced a change in God. *Answer.* Yes, if it were not subjectively eternal.

7. From not being a Creator He would have become a Creator. *Answer.* The change was extrinsic to Him and intrinsic to the world, leaving Him as He was.

8. God always does what is best, but to create from eternity is best. *Answer.* God can never do for a creature what is absolutely best, for He could always do better still; the finite cannot exhaust the infinite fund of power and goodness.

9. Motion cannot have had a beginning, for every motion must come from a preceding motion. *Answer.*

Philosophers often call any *act* motion, and it is true that there must have been activity of some kind without a beginning. But the first activity is not in material things; it is in God, Who is all activity from eternity, not by a succession of acts, but He is one infinite act, or, as it is technically called, a pure act, *actus purus*.

111. As to the question **how long the world has really existed**, we are left in considerable darkness. The extrinsic argument of authority is that of the **Mosaic Revelation**. It gives the ages at which the patriarchs begot their oldest sons; whence we calculate that mankind did not exist on earth more than 6,000 years before the birth of Christ. But how long did the material universe exist before the creation of man? The inspired account of Moses, evidently not intended to teach us chronology, is capable of various interpretations, and has been, from remote periods of the Christian era, variously understood by the learned. Some suppose that an unknown period of time, which may have been of any length, elapsed before the first day began; and this appears to be the obvious meaning of the second verse of Genesis. Some interpret the six days as six periods of unknown duration. Others prefer to understand the Mosaic account in the most literal and most restricted sense; these must suppose that the Lord created the earth with many marks of old age upon it. This is indeed possible, but there is no proof of it.

It is the part of Philosophy to trace effects to appropriate causes, and therefore physical effects to physical causes, whenever it can do so without contradicting any certain teaching of Revelation. By *a priori* reasoning we cannot prove either the recent or the remote period of the creation. Reasoning *a posteriori*, Geology, though still most imperfect as a science, makes it appear probable that the earth had been in existence for a long period of time before the creation of man. [See both the theological and the scientific arguments treated with much learning and logical accuracy in *Geology and Revelation*, by Rev. Gerald Molloy (Part II.); also, Cardinal Mazzella's *De Deo Creante* (Disp. III., art. iv.) and Schanz's *Christian Apology* (vol. i. c. xv.)]

CHAPTER II.

THE END OR PURPOSE AND THE PERFECTION OF THE WORLD.

112. To understand the end or purpose for which anything has been made, we must distinguish between the **purpose of a work** and the **purpose of the workman** who produced the work. For instance, the purpose of a watch is to show the time, the purpose of the watch-maker may be to earn money. We must, therefore, consider two questions with regard to the world: 1. What purpose did God intend in His own creative act? 2. What purpose is the world to accomplish?

113. **What purpose did God intend in His creative act?** He cannot be said to have acted without any purpose; for it is the part of wisdom to act for an end and even for a worthy end. Now, God alone is worthy of Himself: therefore He created for Himself.

Had God, then, anything to gain by creating? He had, of course, to exercise His free will; but He could do this equally well by choosing to create or by choosing not to create. Why did He prefer to create? He had nothing to gain for Himself; for He possessed all perfection. But He could benefit others by creating, and thus exercise His goodness or bounty. It was not necessary for Him to do good to others; yet it was worthy of Him. In this double sense, therefore, God created for Himself, viz.: to exercise His liberty and His bounty. This purpose of God cannot, however, be called the **final cause** of His action; for a cause produces an effect which is really distinct from itself, while in God there is no real distinction of any kind; His bounty is His will, not the cause of His will; yet it may be called the *reason* or *motive* of His choice. Inasmuch as God wished to exercise His bounty, He created in order to bestow happiness on His creatures; but He intends this end as worthy of Himself, and thus the happiness of the creatures is subordinate to the exercise of His bounty, which is truly God's ultimate purpose.

114. **What is the purpose of the work?** Or what purpose is the world meant to accomplish? Since it was created to exercise God's bounty, the world is certainly intended to make creatures happy, especially the chief creatures, *i. e.*, rational creatures. But this is not its ultimate purpose. For to know the ultimate end for which anything is intended by a wise maker, we have only to consider the highest good which it is capable of accomplishing, and not some inferior good which it may also attain. Thus, a watch may indeed be used as a mere toy or an ornament of dress; but it is fit for something better, viz.: to indicate the time, and this is its primary end. Now, the world is capable of doing more than making creatures happy; it can *glorify the Creator;* and this is, therefore, its ultimate or primary purpose.

115. **Glory** is the recognition of exalted excellence. God recognizes all excellence in Himself, and this recognition constitutes God's *intrinsic glory*. The world manifests to intelligent creatures the goodness, power, wisdom, etc., of the Creator; their recognition of God's perfection constitutes His *extrinsic glory*. It is the highest purpose that this world can answer; it is therefore the primary purpose for which the world exists, the happiness of men being subordinate to

it, as an inferior end must ever be subordinate to a superior end.

While the happiness of men is truly and proximately intended by the Creator, it is fitting that the happiness of intelligent creatures should be made to depend on their own free choice. Therefore men are left free to work out their own happiness; and, as a natural consequence, they are free to fail in that choice by preferring something else; thus moral evil is possible, though not intended by the Creator. But it is not fit that the work of an all-wise God should fail to attain the primary purpose that it was created to accomplish, which is the extrinsic glory of God. Therefore free creatures cannot deprive God of His extrinsic glory. Man can only choose his own manner of glorifying God; either he can reach happiness, and thus *glorify His bounty*, as God invites him to do; or he may spurn this invitation and command of his Master, and, by incurring deserved punishment, *glorify the justice* of the Creator.

116. Hence it is evident that God's will to punish a guilty creature is consequent on the free acts of that creature; it is therefore called God's **consequent will**; but His will to make all men happy is antecedent to their free choice, and is called His **antecedent will**. Hence it is also clear that the doctrine which maintains that God predestines some men to eternal loss is as directly opposed to Philosophy as it is to Revelation.

117. **Thesis V.** *The world is not absolutely but relatively perfect.*

Proof. 1st Part. Not absolutely perfect. A thing is absolutely perfect if it attains perfectly the best possible end; but the end which the world attains is not the best possible; for it manifests God's perfections in a finite degree, and its end would be better if it manifested those perfections in a higher degree. Therefore it is not absolutely perfect.

2d Part. Relatively perfect. A thing is relatively perfect if it attains perfectly the exact end for which it is intended; but God must make the world do so; for a wise being makes his works as suitable to their ends as he can, and God, Who is infinitely wise and powerful, must therefore make all His works attain exactly the end for which He intended them.

118. **Objections**: 1. The work of the absolutely perfect Being must be absolutely perfect. *Answer.* No creature can be such that an infinite Creator could not produce a better one.

2. At least an infinitely wise and good God could have produced a much better world than this; therefore this world is not relatively perfect. *Answer.* He could have made one suited to procure a much higher manifestation of His perfections, but not one better suited than this to procure just such an amount of that manifestation as He wishes; relatively to this end the world is perfect.

3. The end of the world is the happiness of men. *Answer.* The happiness of men is their own intrinsic end—*i. e.*, their end as far as their own tendencies are concerned; but it is not their extrinsic end, which is the glory of God.

4. To be relatively perfect the world should manifest the goodness of God; but a world in which most creatures are ultimately unhappy does not manifest His goodness. *Answer.* If this reasoning were correct, it would only follow that most of God's free creatures will ultimately be happy, which we do not deny, because reason and Revelation leave us in ignorance on this matter; for all we know, men may be a small portion of free creatures. Still, it is clear

that the reasoning of the objection is not conclusive, for the minor proposition is not capable of proof.

5. God does not attain the extrinsic glory intended; for many men, instead of honoring, dishonor Him. *Answer.* God will draw good out of evil; the creature will either repent and glorify His mercy, or be punished and glorify His justice for ever. St. Thomas writes: "The defect of doing is made up by suffering, inasmuch as they (the wicked) suffer what the eternal law prescribes for them to the extent to which they fail to do what accords with the eternal law" (1ᵃ, 2æ, q. 93, art. vi.). And St. Anselm: "God cannot possibly lose His honor; for either the sinner spontaneously pays what he owes, or God exacts it of him against his will. Thus, if a man chooses to fly from under the will of God commanding, he falls under the same will punishing" (*Cur Deus Homo*, Nos. 14, 15).

CHAPTER III.

THE LAWS THAT GOVERN THE WORLD.

119. It is evident *a priori* that a wise Creator cannot produce a world that should be perpetually a mass of wild disorder; and we know *a posteriori* that the world displays the most wonderful unity amid variety, both in the structure and in the operations of its parts. In particular, we observe that all material things have well-defined and constant modes of action, which we call **the physical or natural laws.** The word *law* is here used analogically; it strictly means a rule of action for moral beings.

120. Now, some important questions on this subject present themselves to the philosopher:

1. What is the **nature of those laws?** or whence are those constant and uniform modes of action? There is no effect without a cause; what, then, are the causes of the physical laws? Since all things act according to their natures, the obvious answer is that the natures of things are the causes of their modes of action; and the Author of all nature is the Author of those laws. The physical laws themselves are the uniform modes of action of created natures or essences.

121. 2. Are the modes of action so necessarily constant that **departures from them** are impossible? It is evident that nothing can act except in conformity with its nature, and therefore departures from the physical laws are *physically* impossible, *i.e.*, no created power can produce them; but they are not *absolutely* impossible, for nothing created exists except as

dependent on the power and will of the Creator, and therefore the Author of nature can affect the action of created things, suspending and otherwise controlling it for wise purposes of His own. He may either suspend the action of a physical law, or make a creature for the time being follow other modes of action; for He can change the very natures of created things and therefore all their powers. Or He may let every law continue in action, but neutralize or counteract a force by a stronger force in a different direction. An evident interference of God with the workings of physical agents is called a **miracle.**

122. Thesis VI. *The laws of nature are not absolutely immutable, and therefore miracles are possible.*

Proof. That is not absolutely immutable to which God can make exceptions; but God can make exceptions to the laws of nature, for He can do all that involves no contradiction; but that God should make exceptions to the laws of nature involves no contradiction. If it did, the reason of it would be either, (*a*) That the natures of material things are absolutely necessary beings, existing and acting independently of God's will; or, (*b*) That making exceptions to general laws would suppose a change of mind in God with regard to the permanence of His own laws; or, (*c*) That such exceptions would be unworthy of God's wisdom. But these reasons are invalid; because, (*a*) The natures of material things exist and act only in as far as God gives them existence and action; He may, therefore, suspend their action or produce effects that shall neutralize their action, and that shall cause even opposite results. (*b*) When God wills an exception, He wills it from eternity. (*c*) It is wise, on the part of God, to reserve to Himself means of evidently controlling His creation, and thus manifesting His will to man. Now, miracles are such means of Divine manifestations, and are therefore possible to God.

123. Objections: 1. Hume and others have learnedly proved *a priori* that miracles are impossible. *Answer.* All their arguments are easily refuted; even Huxley acknowledges the possibility of miracles, saying: "No one is entitled to say *a priori* that any given so-called miraculous event is impossible, and no one is entitled to say *a priori* that prayer for some change in the ordinary course of nature cannot possibly avail." ("Science and the Bishops," *Nineteenth Century*, Nov., 1887.)

2. An all-wise Creator should have made the world so that it needed not His interference. *Answer.* The material world does not need God's miraculous interference; but God cannot deprive Himself of the power to interfere with it when He sees fit to do so; for instance, when He manifests His will supernaturally to His intelligent creatures.

3. God could manifest His will by affecting directly the intellects of men. *Answer.* He could do so, and does so frequently; but it is natural to man to obtain his knowledge by sense and reasoning.

4. The physical laws flow from the very natures of things, therefore they cannot be suspended while their causes exist. *Answer.* The physical laws need not cease to exist during the miracle, but a stronger power may prevent their effects; thus, our hands do not cease to be heavy bodies while our will raises them up.

5. Miracles only complicate the economy of nature, and thus destroy the beauty of order. *Answer.* They introduce into the world a higher beauty than that of mere physical regularity.

6. It is an analytical principle that the order of nature is constant. *Answer.* We deny this; unvarying constancy is not contained in the idea of order. It is an analytical

judgment that there must be order in the works of a wise Creator; but order does not, as we have seen, exclude all exceptions. It is the adaptation of means to ends; now, miracles are well suited to the ends for which they are wrought.

7. If there could be miracles, the physical sciences would cease to give certainty. *Answer.* If miracles were of such frequent occurrence that we could not distinguish their effects from natural effects, we grant; else we deny.

8. Miracles are, at least, opposed to physical certainty. *Answer.* Not at all: we have physical certainty regarding what must happen when no miracle interferes, but we have no physical certainty that no miracle ever happens; on the contrary, we have physical certainty of the miraculous facts when we witness them.

9. We have physical certainty that a given miracle did not happen, and only moral certainty that it did happen; now, physical certainty is stronger than moral. *Answer.* We have no physical certainty that a miracle did not happen, but only that a certain effect could not proceed from natural causes; we have moral certainty that the miracle did happen, *e. g.*, that Christ raised Lazarus from the dead: both physical and moral certainty are true in their own lines.

10. Miracles could answer no wise purpose unless they could be known to be miracles; but they cannot be known; for any strange fact may come from some unknown law of nature. *Answer.* An objection that proves too much must be unsound; now, this objection proves too much; for, if it were valid, we could form no scientific induction whatever until we knew all the

natural laws, else what we attribute to one law might be due to another, hidden law. We could then never predict any fact with physical certainty. With regard to miracles, we need not know all the laws of nature to form, *e. g.*, the certain judgment that a dead man cannot return to life by any power of nature.

11. We do not know the full power of the devil; therefore we never know whether God works the wonder. *Answer.* Some facts are evidently the work of the Creator, *e. g.*, the restoration of life to the dead; for this implies supreme dominion over the noblest beings of this world. Besides, the circumstances of the miracle are often such that, if it could be from evil spirits, mankind would be invincibly led into error, and all means would be taken away by which the action of God could be outwardly manifested to the world: thus God would unwisely deprive Himself of what is evidently His sole right. For instance, if the miracles of Christ and His followers as a body could be diabolical deceits, then God Himself would be accountable for the deception of the best portion of mankind.

12. The moral laws are immutable; therefore the physical laws too must be so. *Answer.* There is no parity; it is unholy to violate the moral law; but to oppose the action of a physical law implies nothing that is unworthy of God.

13. The mesmeric fluid is capable of wonderful effects; it may produce many so-called miracles. *Answer.* Effects which may be produced by a mesmeric fluid must not be called miracles; but many things are falsely claimed for a mesmeric fluid—*e. g.*, it is not possible that any material fluid should produce acts of

intelligence, as when the medium is made to speak a language never learned by the person, and to know secrets unknown to all other men; often an invisible intellectual agent is present, distinct from all men concerned. (See Nos. 172–174.)

124. Besides, both with regard to the power of the devil and the strange effects claimed for mesmerism, hypnotism, etc., in many cases it can be clearly found out from the circumstances of the concrete fact in question whether it is the work of God or of the devil, or may be within the power of material nature; and in all cases where this cannot be discovered we must suspend our judgment and not pronounce the fact to be miraculous.

To discern whether a certain effect may proceed from mere physical or material causes, we must observe whether the effect is always the same while the circumstances remain identical. If not, then the causes are not material, since the same physical causes must ever produce the same physical effects in the same physical circumstances.

Since a miracle is a *manifest* interference of God with the working of physical agents, it is evident that we should not call an astonishing event a miracle, unless we know for certain that it is due to God's interference. Now, God may interfere in two ways: either directly, by Himself, or indirectly, through the ministry of His good Angels. When the wonderful event produced implies the action of creative power, it comes from God directly; for no finite being can create, or be the total cause of a new substance. Such acts are said to be **miracles of the first class**; while **miracles of the second class** are those that can be produced by the instrumentality of the good Angels acting as ministers of God. This supposes that the Angels have certain powers over matter. Now, the devils are of the same nature as the good Angels, and they, likewise, have certain powers over bodily substances, which, however, they cannot exercise independently of God's permission.

125. How shall we know whether, in a given case, the effects produced are not owing to the action of the demon? Evidently, we must have some test or criterion to distinguish true miracles of the second class from mere prodigies of Satan. If we had no test, a miracle of this class could not be known to be from God, and, therefore, could not be an undoubted sign of His will. And, since men cannot readily discern in most cases what wonders require creative power and what others do not, God would deprive Himself of the power of exhibiting His interference to men, if we had no means whatever, no reliable test, whereby true miracles can be discerned from diabolical deceits.

The criterion is this: That everything concerned in the wonderful event be worthy of the holiness and the wisdom of the Creator and His blessed Angels. Hence, we know that an evil spirit is at work if:

1. The preternatural effect is produced in favor of a doctrine or principle which is certainly known to be false, as being either self-contradictory, or against morality, or against a well-established point of Revelation.
2. If the prodigy can answer no purpose worthy of God; for instance, if it were chiefly intended for the gratification of idle curiosity, or for money-making, etc.
3. If the human agent who claims to be the wonder-worker were actuated in such performances by unworthy motives; for instance, by the love of human glory or any inordinate passion.

When the application of this criterion leaves a reasonable doubt as to the genuineness of the miracle, we should not pronounce the effect to be miraculous. For while, before a court of justice, a man is accounted innocent until his guilt be proved, the presumption being in his favor, we claim no such presumption in favor of miracles; on the contrary, we accept none as certain unless it be demonstrated beyond a doubt that the wonderful event cannot be due to any natural agent, nor to the preternatural agencies of the evil spirits.

CHAPTER IV.

THE CONSTITUENT ELEMENTS OF MATTER.

126. We may consider matter as extended substance possessed of different powers according to its different species; or we may consider it as to its further constituent elements of potentiality and activity, whatever be its species. Considered in the former way, matter is divisible into *homogeneous* particles, *i. e.*, into particles of the same nature as the entire mass. Many species of matter can be further dissolved into chemical particles, which are *heterogeneous, i. e.*, of different natures; thus, water can be decomposed into oxygen and hydrogen. Oxygen, hydrogen, etc., are not known to be further resolvable into other particles; they are called *simple elements*, not as if their particles had no extension, but to distinguish them from the molecules of chemical compounds.

127. We are now to investigate the **ultimate composition** of bodies, even of molecules of matter, whether they be chemically simple or compound. The following is the explanation given by Plato, Aristotle, St. Thomas, and by the Schoolmen generally; it is called the **system of matter and form.**

Every one of the smallest particles into which a non-living body may be divided possesses, just like the whole mass, certain powers or energies, *e. g.*, affinities, attractions, etc.; for matter without powers would be a useless being, and a wise God creates nothing useless. The source of these powers, the active principle in matter, is called its **form**; by it a substance is constituted such a substance, and different from every other;

it is therefore its substantial form. In living bodies the source of their energies is not in each separate particle, but in the one life principle which determines the species of each plant or animal; of the vital form we shall treat in *Psychology* (Nos. 139, etc.).

Besides the forms, which differ for the different species of bodies, there is something which is the same in all material substances, viz., the principle of extension; it is matter in its first abstract entity, and may be called the *potential principle*, the prime matter, or *materia prima* of the Schoolmen. It cannot exist by itself without some form, for all matter is some kind of matter. This potential principle thus informed by the active principle is, in its ultimate particle which we are now considering, a natural or **physical unit**; it naturally occupies some space which has extension in length, breadth, and thickness. But being a physical unit, though extended, the ultimate particle is not physically divisible into smaller parts. The space, however, which each particle occupies is indefinitely divisible. For instance, when hydrogen and oxygen unite to constitute a molecule of water, their potential principle remains, but their active principles cease to exist as such and are succeeded by a new active principle, that of water.

128. This form of water is said to be **educed out of the potentiality of matter**—*i. e.*, that same prime matter which before was of the nature of oxygen and hydrogen now becomes of the nature of water; before the change it was in **potentiality** to become water, now it is *actually* water; somewhat as a cubic block of wax can become a ball of wax. The change of a square block to a ball of wax is a change of an accidental form, that of one substance into another is a change of the substantial form. The active principles of the simple elements do not, as such, or formally, remain in the compound, yet they may be said not to have perished altogether; they exist still

in the power or virtue of the compound, which can reproduce them, just as the ball of wax can become a square lump again.*

129. If from a mass of non-living matter any physical particle be detached, it remains of the same nature as the mass, and has its own potential and active principle, its matter and form; but in a living mass, an organized body, be it plant or animal, while the potential principle of all the particles remains, all the forms which may have informed the single particles, before being taken into the organism, have ceased to exist as such, and are replaced by the one active principle or form which is the **vital principle** of the plant or animal. It is the form that constitutes any material substance in its species; from the form proceed all its powers of action; the properties which a body derives from the potential principle are extension, divisibility, and, in general, whatever is common to all matter. In a **crystal** there appears to be one principle of action pervading and thus unifying the whole mass, building up the structure on one plan; in this crystals appear to agree with living beings, though, as we shall explain in *Psychology*, they differ from them in many essential respects. (See No. 140.)

130. **Two other systems** of explaining the constituent elements of matter are advocated by other schools of philosophy. The **dynamic theory**, not unknown to the ancients, after being remodeled by Leibnitz, owed its first popularity to the further improvements made in it by Roger Boscowich, S.J., and later by Kant. It teaches that the ultimate elements of matter are *simple unextended particles*, called *monads* ($\mu o \nu \alpha$'s, unit), all of

---

* Chemists claim, besides, that some of the properties of the simple substances are preserved in the compounds, in particular their chemical affinities; so that in a molecule or atom of water the affinities of hydrogen and oxygen continue in a manner to exist. They add that spectral analysis shows that the 'spectra' of the simples do not altogether vanish from the 'spectra' of the compounds. (See Pesch, *Institutiones Philosophiæ Naturalis*, No. 132.)

which are homogeneous, and endowed with powers of attraction and repulsion. As each of them occupies only a mathematical point, no number of them could ever make up any bulk, or produce extension, except for their mutual repulsion; and they are kept together by mutual attraction.

131. The **atomic theory** teaches, as its fundamental truth, that the ultimate particles are extended and yet indivisible; they are called *atoms* (ἄτομος, indivisible). This system agrees with the scholastic in affirming that there are ultimate particles of matter which are extended and yet cannot be physically or chemically divided into smaller particles. But it differs from the scholastic theory in denying that the atoms consist of a potential and an active principle, the active principle constituting the specific difference of bodies. It gives no satisfactory reason why the extended atoms are not divisible, since it supposes that they are not constituted as units by a simple form which demands a definite size as well as it demands definite powers. Nor does that theory explain satisfactorily the specific powers of bodies, *e. g.*, of iron and gold. Some writers suppose that the atoms differ specifically, but attempt no explanation; others suppose that the difference consists only in the figure, size, or motion of the atoms.

132. **Thesis VII.** *There are in matter two substantial principles, that of extension and that of specific action.*

Proof. Bodies can undergo substantial changes; but they could not do so if there were not two substantial principles, that of extension and that of specific action; therefore these exist.

We prove the major: Bodies can undergo substantial changes—*e. g.*, water is not a mere mixture of hydrogen and oxygen, but it is a new substance into which the elements are changed. This truth is proclaimed by common sense, by the languages of all nations, and even by the manner of speaking of those very philosophers who implicitly deny this fact; few will attempt to deny it explicitly. In fact, all draw a distinction between a mere mixture, *e. g.*, the atmospheric air, and a chemical compound.

We prove the minor: No substantial change of matter is possible unless there be two substantial principles. For in a substantial change something substantial must remain, else there would be a creation of the new substance, not a change from the old; and something substantial must go and come, or be exchanged; for if what is exchanged is only accidental, *e. g.*, figure, arrangement of parts, etc., then the change is accidental and not really substantial. Now, it is noticed that extension always remains, and the specific powers are changed; therefore there are in matter two substantial principles, that of extension and that of specification.

133. It will be noticed, on careful consideration, that neither the **dynamic** nor the **atomic** theory can satisfactorily account for truly substantial changes; for both admit only one substantial principle, which the dynamic calls simple and the atomic extended, but which both theories suppose to be permanent; so that what is changed in the formation of new substances is only the accidents of quantity, figure, motion, etc. If such were the fact, the new bodies would not differ substantially from their elements.

Besides, the **dynamic theory** does not account for extension; for no number of simple monads can fill a space; and the supposition that those monads possess attraction and repulsion does only attribute to one principle two contrary effects, which is anything but scientific. On the other hand, the **atomic theory** does not explain how the atoms can be extended and have certain figures, and yet cannot be separated into parts; nor does it account scientifically for the specific differences.

It belongs to **Chemistry** to study the phenomenal properties of the simple elements, but to Metaphysics to go back of the phenomenal and study the inmost essences of things material and immaterial. In doing so, the metaphysician must take into account all that the phenomenal can teach him. If he is mistaken about the effects, he is apt to misunderstand the nature of the causes. It is, therefore, not a little remarkable that the theory of matter and form, laid down in ages when the physical phenomena were so little understood, should still to-day account more plausibly than any other for all the facts which Chemistry, Biology, and other modern sciences have discovered. And yet such is the case, as is proved by Father Harper in his *Metaphysics of the Schools* (vol. ii. b. v. c. ii. § 4).

CHAPTER V.

THE GENERAL PROPERTIES OF BODIES.

134. The principal **properties common to all bodies** and to no other substances are *extension, impenetrability, figure, local motion,* and *inertia.*

I. **Extension** is continuous quantity, or that property of a body by which it has parts outside of each other and so united by a common bond as to constitute a physical unit. That this property really exists in bodies we know for certain by the testimony of our senses. Still, the essence of bodies does not consist in extension, as Descartes supposed; for space, too, has extension, and yet it is not a body. Extension is natural to bodies, but it is not, therefore, essential to them. True, every body has parts distinct from each other; besides, quantity gives parts a tendency to be outside of one another; next, this tendency is actuated if not divinely impeded. But it may be divinely impeded; and when this happens, as it does with regard to the Body of our Lord in the Holy Eucharist, the parts of the body are not outside of each other; but the sacred Body of Christ is present, after the manner of a spirit, being whole in every part of the species.

135. II. **Impenetrability** is the property by which one body excludes another from the place it occupies. It is natural to bodies, and the tendency thus to exclude other bodies is even essential to bodies; still, its effects can be suspended by the Almighty, as can all action of any created substance. In such a case two or more bodies could occupy the same place, as

when the risen Saviour entered the Upper Room, though the doors were closed. On the other hand, it is not absolutely impossible, because not self-contradictory, that one body should, by **reduplication** of its relations, be in two or more places at the same time.

136. III. **Figure** is an accident of continuous quantity which results directly from its limitations; for whatever is limited must have definite limits; these definite limits to extension constitute figure. The natural figure of a body is determined by its substantial form; for the form gives to the body every determination that belongs to such a species, though its effects in individual beings are influenced by present circumstances. Thus, the forms of metals determine the figures of their crystals; so with plants and animals; still, circumstances may favor or impede the action of the form in each individual case, as when a plant is dwarfed in a cold climate.

137. IV. **Local motion** is the successive transition of a thing from one place to another. It supposes a *subject*, a *term* to which the subject tends, a *force* impelling it to that term. If only one body existed, there would be no such a term, and therefore no motion in the strict meaning of that word, though an impelling force might exist, and cause in that body a mode which might analogically be called motion. Local motion, then, implies a change of place; but **spirits** are not in a place, in the same sense that bodies are in a place, and therefore motion is not predicated of them in the same sense. Spirits, as such, have no necessary relation to matter, and may have been created before matter; but place and local motion are properly accidents of matter only, and therefore cannot affect spirits except indirectly, inasmuch as spirits may be in union with a body, either substantially, as the soul of a living man, or virtually, as when an Angel protects a child. (See St. Thomas, *Summa*, i. q. lx. 4, 1um) In this latter case he

exhibits his presence in space and acts in space, but is not limited by space.

138. **V. Inertia** does not mean that bodies, as such, have no powers to act, but that they cannot of their own accord begin to act or cease to act, or make any change in their mode of acting. The reason of this impotence lies in the fact that bodies, as such, *i. e.*, as mere material substances not informed by a vital principle, have no perceptions, and therefore no motives to determine their actions in one way rather than another; therefore they can only act uniformly and without spontaneity or power of self-determination. Intelligent and sentient beings, on the contrary, can know a term to which they may tend, and therefore determine themselves to motion or rest, or to one motion rather than another. Intelligent beings may do so freely, because they apprehend the term as unnecessary; but those that are merely sentient, as brutes are, act necessarily upon the stronger attraction; still, their actions, unlike those of non-sentient things, are determined by their instinct, which is a principle intrinsic to themselves.

BOOK III.

PSYCHOLOGY.

139. **Psychology** is the study of living things (ψυχή, the vital principle). Now, life consists in the power of immanent action—*i. e.*, in action that affects the agent alone; its effect is self-evolution and self-perfection.

There are **three degrees of life**: vegetative, sensitive, and intellectual life. These rise in dignity above one another as they become more independent of matter:

1. **Vegetative** life needs material organs and assumes into itself material food; still, it is so far above mere matter that it controls the physical and chemical powers of such food, which it converts into its own substance.
2. **Sensitive life** also needs material organs, and perceives only material things; but it assumes into itself the images only of the objects, not the gross matter, in its action of sense-perception.
3. **Intellectual life**, as such, needs no material organs, nor even material images: the soul can understand things entirely immaterial, and material things in an immaterial manner, though, as long as it is substantially one being with the body, it understands its objects in connection with bodily phantasms. We distinguish,

therefore, all living creatures to which our natural knowledge extends into three classes or genera, viz.: plants, which have only vegetable life; animals, which have vegetable and sensitive life; and man, who has vegetable, sensitive, and intellectual life.

We shall consider: 1. The specific nature of plants and animals. 2. Sensitive and rational cognition. 3. Sensitive and rational appetite. 4. The nature of the human soul. 5. The origin and the destiny of the human soul.

CHAPTER I.

THE SPECIFIC NATURE OF PLANTS AND ANIMALS.

140. **Thesis I.** *Living bodies cannot originate from non-living bodies.*

Proof. The effect cannot be superior to the cause; now, there is something in the vital principle superior to all the powers of non-living bodies, no matter how these be combined with one another; viz., it gives living bodies essences superior to the essences of all inorganic bodies. For the essences of things are known by observing their properties and operations; now, all living bodies are observed to have certain properties and operations most of which are superior to those found in any non-living bodies; therefore, all living bodies have natures or essences superior to those of non-living bodies.

The two classes differ:

- 1. *In structure.* All living bodies, and they alone, are furnished with organs—*i. e.*, with parts of peculiar structure suited to perform vital acts.
- 2. *In figure.* All living bodies have determined figures proper to each species, and these figures are bounded by curved lines; while non-living bodies have no determined figures, except crystals, and these are bounded by straight lines.
- 3. *In growth.* Living bodies begin with a cell, from the evolution or multiplication of which the whole organism gradually arises; this development proceeds by

Specific Nature of Plants and Animals. 91

means of nutrition, or intussusception of food which is transformed into the living substance. Non-living bodies do not arise from a cell; and they increase by juxtaposition of particles from without.

4. *In origin.* Living bodies never come but from germs produced by other living bodies; for the cells cannot be formed by mere chemical combinations, though all the simple elements be present in the proper proportions.

5. *In chemical action.* The vital principle of plants enables them to decompose carbonic acid into its simple elements of carbon and oxygen, absorbing the carbon by their leaves, thus overcoming its strong affinity for oxygen; while animals, inhaling oxygen, which so readily destroys dead matter, use it to support their animal life.

6. *In unity.* All the elements composing any plant or animal obey the vital principle which directs them to procure the preservation of the individual and of the species.

7. *In duration.* Living bodies have a limited period of existence, while non-living ones are independent of time.

Objection. Fungi and maggots are generated by dead matter. *Answer.* They come from living germs floating in the air; the leading scientists are agreed that there is no spontaneous generation, but that, as nature is now, all living plants and animals come from living germs. As to the question whether the Creator could possibly establish spontaneous generation, see No. 158.

141. **Thesis II.** *All plants differ essentially from all animals.*

Proof. The essences of things are known by observing

their properties and operations. Now, all plants are confined to these three functions: nutrition, growth, and reproduction; while all animals exhibit, in addition to these, the power of sensation, and, as a consequence of sensation, an appetite for sensible good, and a shrinking from sensible evil. There is, besides, in all animals an appropriate power of motion, which enables them to move instinctively upon the apprehension of good or evil. Therefore all plants differ essentially from all animals.

142. **Objections**: 1. Of some living things—*e. g.*, of sponges—it is not certainly known whether they are plants or animals; therefore, the difference between them is but slight and cannot be essential. *Answer.* The difference between plants and animals is the power of sensation; though but slightly manifested, it constitutes an essential difference; so that if sponges possess it, as they seem to do, they are animals; if not, they are plants.

2. The sensitive plant has sensation, as its name indicates, and still it is not an animal. *Answer.* It has no sensation; its scientific name is "mimosa," because it mimics sensation; its leaves are mechanically contracted by outside influences, not by its own immanent action.

3. The sunflower turns its face to the sun, the tulip closes its petals at night, etc.; therefore they perceive the sun, the night, etc. *Answer.* The physical action of the sun and of the damp air upon those plants produces these mechanical effects.

4. But many plants grow towards the light, and growth is not mechanical action. *Answer.* The growth comes from the life-principle in the plant, but its effects are modified by favorable influences on the side of the

light, and by unfavorable influences on the opposite side; this argues no power of sensation in the plant.

5. It cannot be proved either *a priori* or *a posteriori* that animals feel and plants do not. *Answer.* (*a*) It is known by the judgment of common sense. (*b*) It is proved scientifically by observing that all animals, even the lowest species which are certainly known to be animals, have organs of sense, while no plants, even the highest, possess these. Besides, animals have motions which cannot be explained except as consequent on the power of sensation, and they give signs, by cries, etc., of pleasure and pain, which no plants ever do.

143. **Thesis III.** *All the vital acts of an animal flow from one vital principle.*

Proof 1. Nutrition, growth, and reproduction in plants are not attributed to three distinct principles, but to one, the vegetative principle; because the effects are subordinated to one another, and thereby show a unity in the cause. *A pari*, since all the functions of life in an animal are subordinate to one another, and co-operate harmoniously to one common end, there must be unity in the cause; *i. e.*, there must be but one principle from which proceed all the vital acts of animals.

Proof 2. If the animal were composed of two vital principles, it would be two beings; for the vegetable would not be the animal, nor the animal the vegetable, but all men judge the animal to be one being endowed with vegetative action, yet not a vegetable.

144. **Thesis IV.** *The vital principle in any living body is truly the form of the body.*

Proof. The form of a body is that principle which makes it be such a body and not a body of another kind, which gives it such powers and actions and not other powers and actions; in a word, which constitutes the body in its species.

Now, such is the vital principle of any living body. For, 1. If the vital principle ceases to animate the matter, as it does in death, all the specific powers and actions of that body cease. 2. The mere matter, as separate from the vital principle, may become successively the food and the very substance of different plants and animals, its specific nature ever changing with the vital principles that successively inform it. But this supposes that the vital principle constitutes it in its species, or is its form.

145. Objection. The substantial form of a body is simple, and therefore indivisible; but the vital principle of some plants is divisible; *e. g.*, a twig may be cut off and continue to live by its own life, the vital principle of the tree being divided. *Answer.* Simplicity has different meanings. We grant that all forms, as such, are simple; they are simple in two senses: 1, Inasmuch as they are not composed of matter and form; 2, inasmuch as they are not aggregates of parts quantitatively distinct, as bodies are. Just in the same senses is the vital principle simple, for it cannot be divided into matter and form, nor into parts quantitatively distinct. As to the curious question whether the principle of life is ever divided, we say that it exists whole and entire in the body and in every part of the body, so, however, that it can neither act, nor even exist, but in an extended body, excepting only the soul of man. To animate a body, the life principle requires a complete organism; therefore, when the organism is destroyed, the vital form ceases to be. Now, in many plants, and in a few of the lower animals, the organism is so simple and uniform throughout in its structure that, when divided, the several parts may still be suited to the functions of life. In such a case the principle of life may continue to animate the several parts; but it is not properly said to be divided; rather the body is divided; for the vital principle is whole and entire in both parts, which now become two plants. It was before whole and entire in all portions of one body; it is now whole and entire in all portions of two bodies, and in this sense it is rather said to be multiplied than divided; or, better still, it is neither; but the animal or plant is divided. (See upon "Simplicity," *Inst. Phil. Nat.*, by Tilmann Pesch, S.J., No. 211.—Compare St. Thomas's *Summa*, p. 1, q. lxxvi., a. 8.) Thus the twig may become a distinct plant; thus, too, the segments of annulated worms, when severed from the rest of their bodies, become individual worms, this result being accomplished by the division of the matter and the multiplication, if you will, of the form. Other philosophers maintain that the principle of life is really divided in such cases; perhaps it is a mere dispute on words.

146. Theses **V.** and **VI.** *The brute soul is irrational and therefore ceases to exist when the organism is destroyed.*

Proof 1. It is a judgment of common sense that brutes are irrational or incapable of reasoning, and that their vital principles do not outlive their bodies.

Proof 2. I. **That the brute soul is irrational** is proved scientifically, (*a*) *By induction.* For it is found, by an endless variety of observations, that all the acts of brutes can be accounted for without supposing in them the power of reasoning, of drawing conclusions from premises; in other words, they give no signs of reasoning, and it would be unscientific to ascribe to them a faculty of which they give no indications. This becomes the more evident if we compare their actions with those of rational man. All men, in the full possession of their faculties, can grasp the abstract relation between means and ends, inventing and making new and various means, *e. g.*, tools, to accomplish their designs; brute animals never do so; they can only follow the one beaten track to which their specific nature determines them. Hence, too, a man can improve himself by study, by exertions of his own talents; brutes cannot do this; they may be taught various actions by man, but they cannot improve *themselves*. Hence, too, a race of men may increase in knowledge and civilization; brutes act now as they were always known to act; and when, by the training of man or the change of physical surroundings, new ways of acting are brought about in some brute animals, it is found by experiment that all brutes of the same species would act in about the same way under those peculiar circumstances. Therefore the effects can be accounted for by reference to phantasms and organic modifications, without attributing to the brute the abstract perception of the relation between means and ends.

That brutes are irrational is proved scientifically, (*b*) *From the nature of reasoning*. Reasoning is absolutely impossible without universal concepts; for in all reasoning the middle term must be at least once distributed or taken universally. Now, brutes never give signs of having universal ideas: all their actions can be accounted for by means of sense-perceptions, phantasms, and instinctive action, which will be explained further on (No. 149).

II. **The brute soul ceases to exist when the organism is destroyed.** For it would be unwise to keep anything in existence which can answer no purpose; but the brute soul, when its organism is destroyed, can answer no purpose; therefore the Creator does not keep it in existence.

The *minor* is clear from the fact that all the functions of the brute soul—*i. e.*, nutrition, growth, reproduction, sensation, and motion—require bodily organs. Besides, it is an obvious principle that the nature of a being is of the same kind as its actions; now, the actions of the brute soul are all bound up in matter, therefore the brute soul is so too; and, therefore, it cannot exist without matter.

147. Some obvious corollaries follow from this: 1. That the brute soul, unlike the soul of man, cannot exist by itself; it is only the substantial form of the brute body. 2. That it needs no creation to bring it into existence; it is educed out of the potentiality of matter, as are the forms of inorganic bodies; with this difference, that the brute soul, unlike those forms, is not educed from matter except by the action of a living agent of the same species.

148. **Objections:** 1. Many actions of brutes manifest design, the intelligent adaptation of means to ends; *e. g.*, when a bird builds its nest. *Answer.* This is true; but the design is not in the animal, but in Him who made the animal such that it must act in that manner— *i. e.*, in the Creator; just as the intelligence that guides the hands of a watch is not in the watch, but in its maker.

2. The watch does not perceive, while the brute does; there is no parity. *Answer.* There are many cases in which the brute acts for a remote end of which it has no more knowledge at the time of its action than the machine has of the purposes of its maker; as when the bird builds a nest for its future offspring, the bee stores up honey in summer for its support in winter. The intelligence thus displayed is certainly not in the brute animal.

3. But the brute displays intelligence in directing means to proximate ends which it presently apprehends, as when it eats to satisfy its hunger and prolong its life. *Answer.* The future prolongation of life is not intended by brutes; they merely apprehend by sense the sensible good of food to satisfy their sensible appetite. The

brute apprehends things in the concrete; there is no abstraction, and therefore no reasoning.

4. If a dog is called by his master, he will run around by a gate or by a staircase, just as a rational man would do; here he displays reason as well as man does. *Answer.* We know from other sources that man has reason. Such actions as the dog performs can all be explained by the sense-perceptions and the phantasms of the brute, together with its appetites and instincts, which we shall explain further on (No. 149).

5. Some brutes can understand language; they must therefore have abstract ideas. *Answer.* They merely associate certain familiar sounds with familiar phantasms. The parrot can even be taught to utter articulate sounds associated with his sensible appetites.

6. Darwin shows that some brute animals have improved themselves; for instance, that the dog has six different barks to express six different feelings. *Answer.* Darwin does not prove that dogs have not always possessed the same accomplishment, but have invented it; if dogs may always have used the same barks, their progress is not proved.

7. Some brutes learn to avoid traps, and one rat, for instance, will avoid them more skillfully than others. *Answer.* The association of phantasms suffices to produce this skill; and one rat may have acquired more of such experience than another. Besides, animals of the same species may have a more or less perfect organism, and, therefore, more skill in animal actions.

149. While brute animals have not the faculty of reason, they have a power or aptitude for the proper guidance of their actions which supplies for them the place of reason; it is called

instinct. It may be defined as the natural impulse that prompts animals to do what is useful to the individual and to the species. It is not something superadded to the animal, but it is the sensitive tendency of its sensitive nature—for instance, its inclination to eat when hungry, to rest when fatigued, etc.

150. Instinct prompts animals, not only to embrace what they sensibly apprehend as present good, and to shun what they apprehend as present evil for themselves; but also to do those **preparatory actions** which are naturally and sensibly connected with the gratification of animal appetites, such as looking for food, retiring to their lair, and even excavating a hole, spinning a web, storing up food, building a nest, etc.

151. In all instinctive actions there is an adaptation of means to ends, proximate and remote. The brute animal organically apprehends the nearer sensible ends, and such connection between means and ends as can be represented by phantasms; for instance, it perceives the sensible satisfaction of eating and resting, and the material relations between itself and its food and lair; but it does not apprehend the more remote ends, such as the future prolongation of life, the future propagation of its species, etc. The entire adaptation of means to ends, manifested in the workings of animal instinct, is the work of the Creator, who made the nature, the powers, and the tendencies of animals such as we find them at present.

152. We can the more easily understand the workings of instinct, because we experience them in ourselves. In brutes, however, they are far more perfect than in man, for they are intended by the Creator to be the sole guides of their actions. In man they are to be supplemented by the nobler faculty of reason, to which instinct is intended to be subservient. On many occasions we have nothing but instinct to guide us, as

in early infancy and in many animal functions throughout life, such as breathing, swallowing, sleeping, closing our eyelids at the approach of danger, withdrawing our tongue before the closing teeth, etc. In all such adaptations of means to ends we know that reason has usually no part. On many other occasions we are conscious that we are drawn one way by our sensible appetites and another way by our reason; the latter ought then to be obeyed.

153. **Thesis VII.** *Plants and brute animals are intended for the use of man.*

Proof 1. The purpose for which an object is intended, especially when it is of a complicated and delicately adapted structure, can be known by examining its fitness to accomplish a certain end or purpose; else we should have to grant that the striking adaptation of means to ends is an effect without a proportionate cause. Now, plants and animals are most delicate contrivances of intricate structure, and they are admirably adapted to the use of man. Therefore they are made for it.

Proof 2. All things are created for the extrinsic glory of God (Nos. 113 to 115); now, irrational things cannot by themselves glorify God, but only through man, being in some way of use to man; hence they are intended for the use of man.

154. **Irrational creatures may be of use to man**, and thus glorify God through man, in various ways: 1. By displaying to the eyes of man the power, wisdom, goodness of their Maker, and thus prompting man to love and praise God. 2. By supplying the bodily wants of man, and thus aiding him to serve God. 3. By administering aids to his rational pleasures, thus inducing him to love his God, and to serve him cheerfully. 4. Even things which molest man, such as the inclemencies of the seasons, beasts of prey, troublesome insects, etc.;

render service to man, making him more industrious, cleanly, provident, etc., and enabling him to bear the ills of life in the spirit of dutiful submission to the sovereign will of God.

155. **Objections:** 1. Many creatures are absolutely useless or even injurious to man. *Answer.* There are creatures of which we do not know the use; but it does not follow that they are of no use. From the fact that the vast majority of creatures are known to be very useful, we should rather conclude by induction that the others also answer a useful purpose.

2. Some plants and animals are known to be injurious. *Answer.* They may be injurious in some respects, and yet be very beneficial in other respects; thus, poisons become medicines in the hands of science.

156. **Thesis VIII.** *The species of plants and animals are fixed—i. e., incapable of transformation.*

Explanation. By a species we mean a class of plants or animals which have characteristic properties in common and can be indefinitely propagated without changing those characteristics. A species may indeed produce a variety—*i. e.,* one or more individual plants or animals marked by some striking peculiarity not common to the species generally. A race is a variety perpetuated through several generations. Thus, in the canine species, we have many races that differ considerably from one another; still, all have certain characteristics in common, which mark them as belonging to the canine species. By saying that the species of plants and animals are fixed, we do not mean that no new races may arise and be propagated; but we here assert that the changes will never result in the evolution of new species. The **crucial test,** by which the distinction of species is known, is this: if animals can be paired together and thus propagate an indefinitely fertile offspring, they are of the same species; else they are not. Thus horses and asses are known to be different species, because, although they can by crossing generate the mule, still this hybrid is incapable of continued propagation. It is also important to notice that those scientists who maintain the evolution or transformation of species as a theory pretend that the new organisms evolved are usually more perfect than the antecedent species.

Proof 1. There can be no effect without a proportionate cause; but if higher species were evolved from lower, the improved new species would be without a proportionate cause. For inasmuch as the new species is more perfect than the old, it has no cause in the old. The new offspring of plants and animals may, at the most, have some accidental superiority over the parent stock, being born and raised under more favorable circumstances, but accidental changes constitute no specific difference.

Proof 2. By induction. Though scientists have now been at work for many years in exploring lands and seas, in examining the fossil remains of countless species of plants and animals, and in applying all the inventive genius of man to obtain and perpetuate new varieties and races, they have never yet been able to exhibit a single decisive proof that a transformation of species has ever taken place. Animals are now as they are represented on the pyramids or found mummified in the tombs of Egypt, as they were before they left their fossil forms in the rocks. Many species have become extinct, others are found now of which no very ancient specimens have been discovered; but it cannot be proved that any species was ever evolved from any other.

Proof 3. That the test of indefinitely continued fertility in the species is the crucial test by which the theory of evolution must be judged, and that the theory cannot stand this test, is acknowledged by its ablest advocates. "Without verification," says Tyndall, "a theoretic conception is a mere figment of the intellect" (*Fragments of Science*, p. 469). "Our acceptance of the Darwinian hypothesis," says Huxley, "must be provisional as long as one link in the chain of evidence is wanting; and as long as all the animals and plants certainly produced by selective breeding from a common stock are fertile, and their progeny are fertile with one another, one link will be wanting" (*Man's Place in Nature*, p. 107). Therefore, the theory which contradicts our thesis is a mere figment of the intellect. (See No. 209.)

157. *Objections:* 1. Paleontology shows that the fossils found in the higher strata of the earth belong to more perfect species of plants and animals than those in the lower strata; there must have been an evolution of less perfect into more perfect species. *Answer.* The fact stated is not found to be true in all cases; but even if true, it would only show that there is order in the works of the Creator, not that the higher species are evolved from the lower. *Post hoc, ergo propter hoc*, is a sophism.

2. Anatomy proves that all the forms of life are constructed according to a uniform type or plan, so as to constitute a regular system. *Answer.* This, too, shows that there is symmetry in the works of God, but not that there is evolution of species in nature; you might as well say that all Gothic buildings are evolved from one another.

3. Anatomy also reveals the fact that the more perfect animals retain certain rudimentary organs which are of no present use, and which are mere remnants of a former useful structure; therefore evolution has taken place. *Answer.* Anatomy does not prove that the so-called rudimentary structures are of no use to those higher animals; they serve, at least, for ornament, and

give symmetry to the creation. Darwin classes our sense of smell and our external ear among these useless remnants, while it is certain that they are very useful; such pleadings exhibit much weakness in the theory.

4. Geography shows that certain species of plants and animals are peculiar to certain climates; therefore the influence of the climate must have produced them. *Answer.* The wisdom of God has provided for each climate its appropriate fauna and flora, usually by the natural process of variety of races, never by the evolution of new species.

5. Physiology has discovered that the embryo of a higher animal species passes through the forms of all the lower species in its process of evolution. *Answer.* The development of an individual animal is one thing, and that of species from species is quite another; the one fact does not prove the other. Besides, the statement itself is inexact, and the order of embryonic evolutions is different in different species.

6. A worm becomes a butterfly; therefore a less perfect animal may be developed into one more perfect. *Answer.* Only those worms become butterflies which come from the eggs of butterflies; the species remains unchanged.

7. Even the Schoolmen admitted the possibility of spontaneous generation—*i. e.*, of the generation of an animal from brute matter only, without a living germ. *Answer.* They admitted it as possible in connection with a higher influence proceeding from a heavenly body, but not as resulting from the combination of merely material elements; this higher influence might, in their opinion, replace the living germ, thus showing that they felt convinced that life cannot proceed from lower elements

only, no matter how combined. (Pesch, *Inst. Phil. Nat.*, No. 190.)

158. It may be asked whether the Creator could have established a series of **evolutions from less perfect to more perfect species.**

Reason answers that God can do all that is not self-contradictory. Now, such a series, taken in one sense, would be self-contradictory, but not in another sense. It is absurd that a superior effect should proceed entirely from an inferior cause, but not that God should supply by His own action whatever perfection is added to the effect—*i. e.*, to the new generation. Nor is it evidently impossible that the Creator should direct the evolution of a lower into a higher species by the agency of second causes, wisely combined for that purpose. But it is metaphysically impossible that a merely fortuitous combination of causes, without a wise designer to direct the work, should build up a most wonderful system of development, running through the whole vegetable and animal kingdoms, such as scientists claim that evolution has accomplished. To say that merely blind forces produce so much beauty and harmony, is fully as absurd as to pretend that a man can compose a grand and harmonious poem without knowing a word of the language in which it is written. A system that ascribes effects to totally inadequate causes is unscientific.

CHAPTER II.

SENSITIVE AND RATIONAL COGNITION.

159. In our treatise on Critical Logic we have devoted a whole chapter (Ch. III.) to the explanation of the means by which certainty is obtained, entering into considerable detail on the subject of sensitive and on that of rational cognition. We have now to examine **the nature and the workings of those two faculties** in themselves; and we, therefore, add in this place such further details as were omitted before because they did not affect the certainty of human knowledge.

ARTICLE I. OF SENSITIVE COGNITION.

160. Speaking in *Critical Logic* (*Logic*, No. 142) of the outward senses, we remarked: "Two very different questions present themselves on this subject: 1. How far is the testimony of our external senses reliable? 2 How do the senses work so as to give us reliable testimony?" We then examined the first question; we are now to present the **Scholastic theory**, which answers the second query.

161. **How, then, is sense-perception effected,** whether it be considered in man or in the irrational animal? All animals have at least the sense of touch; perfect animals have the same five outer senses as man: the sight, hearing, taste, smell, and touch; they have also the inner senses, viz.: the common sense, imagination, sensile memory, and power of appreciation (*Logic*, No. 102). These are not mere instruments of

a most delicate structure, but they are living organs in which and by which the animal exercises its faculties. The purpose for which they are intended by the all-wise Creator is to enable the animal in different ways to acquire cognition of the material objects with which it comes into immediate or mediate contact. Now, cognition implies that an object impresses some likeness of itself upon the cognitive subject, and that the subject, reacting, expresses the object thus impressed, apprehending it vitally. Thus the cognitive subject perceives, not indeed a likeness of the object but, by means of the likeness, *the object itself*. This process is observed both in all sensitive and in our intellectual cognition.

162. Confining our attention, for the present, to sense-cognition, we notice two distinct steps in the act of perception. 1. The object perceived must act upon the subject perceiving, by impressing on it—whether directly, as in touch, or through a medium, as in vision—some likeness, image, or species of itself. This image is called by the Schoolmen the **species impressed,** *species impressa.* Hence it is clear that sense-cognition begins with the action of the object; and, as the object cannot give forth an image of what it is not, but only of what it is, therefore it tends essentially to beget true cognition in the subject.

2. The subject perceiving must not be merely passive; for then it could not be said to elicit the act of perception or sensation; it must, therefore, react vitally on the impression received. And since all cognition is an immanent act, the sentient subject must reproduce in itself a vital image of the object. This vital image is styled the **species expressed,** *species expressa;* and the subject's immanent act of forming this vital image is its apprehension or cognition of the object.

163. The species impressed and expressed in sense-perception are, of course, **the images of material objects existing in the concrete.** Those objects are directly perceived by sense;

the species are no more noticed by the sentient subject than the picture formed on the retina of the eye is noticed by us in our acts of vision.

164. If it be asked **where the sensation takes place**, in the sense-organ, say the eye, or in the brain, we answer that both brain and eye and connecting nerves co-operate in the act of seeing; all these together constitute the complex organ of sight; but the act of seeing should be said to be accomplished in the eye, the act of hearing in the ear, etc.; for thus only can it be properly said that we see and hear the outward object, and not the image of the object, or a modification of our senses.

165. The **imagination**, on the contrary, does not act in the organ of the outer senses; but its organ is the brain. It exists in perfect animals, and may perhaps be wanting in lower species of sentient life, some of which appear to have no senses but those of touch and taste. The imagination is the faculty by which animals form to themselves organic images, called phantasms, either of sensible objects perceived, or, in man at least, of other objects never perceived. In the latter case the images result from the combination of former phantasms, which themselves have been ultimately derived from objects of sensation.

166. The **sensile memory** performs a threefold office: (*a*) It directly brings back former phantasms; (*b*) Indirectly—*i. e.*, through the phantasms reproduced—it represents objects formerly perceived; (*c*) It represents them as having been formerly perceived.

167. There is one sensible power of cognition to which it was not necessary to advert in Critical Logic since it is not one of the means by which men acquire certainty; we mean the **power of appreciation**, the *vis æstimativa*, of the Schoolmen. It is the highest of merely organic faculties, because

it approaches the nearest to the intellectual power of judgment. Its action consists in apprehending certain concrete relations which sensible objects bear to the sentient animal. By it the lamb, even the first time that it sees a wolf, apprehends him as dangerous to itself; by it the bird apprehends a straw as just then suitable for its nest. Such apprehensions are often called *sensible judgments*. They differ from intellectual judgments: (*a*) In always dealing with concrete material things; (*b*) In apprehending by mere organic action the relations existing between such things and the animal subject; (*c*) In absolutely excluding all abstraction.

168. In connection with the imagination, referred to above, it is appropriate to give here a brief explanation both of *dreams*, which are chiefly the work of the imagination, and of *sleep*, which occasions dreams. **Sleep** is a natural interruption of the equilibrium between the various faculties of man; for we shall confine our remarks to the sleep of man. It arises from the exhaustion of the animal organism, and is ordained by nature to restore that organism to its former freshness. It differs from disease, which is an unnatural disturbance of the same equilibrium.

169. We should not, then, imagine that sleep is a cessation of vital action, but rather it is **a special mode of vitality**. In sleep, 1. All the vegetative powers continue to act, but more gently and with more uniform motion than before. 2. The action of the senses is more or less suspended. 3. The sensible appetites are much relaxed. 4. The intellect may act, but it is not fully conscious of its operations. 5. The will may act, but not freely; hence we are not accountable for its actions when we are fully asleep, and not fully accountable when we are half-asleep. Sleep is really a time of repairs to the body, during it the machinery of the organism is out of gear.

170. **Dreams** are series of phantasms, reproduced and combined anew by the fancy, accompanied at times by some intellectual activity, while the nerves of the body are relaxed in sleep. Dreams are often started by actual impressions on the slumbering senses—for instance, by some sounds or feelings—and they are greatly influenced by any abnormal condition of the nerves and the blood. Our phantasms are not isolated, but variously associated with each other by similarity, by congeniality, by having been formed contemporaneously, etc.; and thus, when one phantasm is aroused, others are thereby excited, whether we are awake or asleep. When awake, we can to a great extent regulate the workings of our imagination by our will, and we are inclined to do so in connection with our sense-perceptions; but when we are asleep, our fancy has full play, and may, for all we know, be constantly moving, though it may leave no traces of its vagaries. From the nature of dreams just explained it is evident how foolish it is to attach any signification to them as foretelling future events, unless on special occasions they should be preternaturally produced by Providence for worthy and important purposes.

171. **Somnambulism is a dream giving rise to corresponding external actions.** Somnambulists act outwardly in conformity with their imaginations, but in a strange manner. 1. They proceed as if they saw, while their eyes are closed or rigid; thus they will avoid obstacles in their way, yet they really do not see, but are guided by their mere imagining of the familiar places, and therefore they will strike against obstacles to which they are not accustomed. 2. They do bolder and sometimes more ingenious things than when awake; for they do not reflect on danger, and all their faculties are concentrated on one purpose. 3. On awaking, they have no recollection of their wanderings.

172. Phenomena similar to those of somnambulism are produced by the **mesmeric sleep**. Mesmer (A.D. 1733–1815) boasted of having invented an art of healing diseases by means of magnetism, which he excited by touching the sick with a firm will to restore their health. One of the means employed in that process is the artificial or magnetic sleep. Seeing that sleep is merely a natural disturbance of the vital powers, we find nothing astonishing in the production of an artificial sleep by natural means. Nor is it absurd to suppose that the mesmerizer may affect the slumbering faculties of the sleeper or medium, usually a nervous woman, and so influence her imagination as to direct, to some extent, her feelings and her outward motions. But the magnetizer cannot do this directly by his will or his intellect; these faculties are essentially incapable of acting outside of the soul, and the soul is not outside its living body.

173. Induction proves that the souls of men cannot, in our present condition, communicate or act upon each other except by means of the body, and therefore by means of matter. As long, therefore, as the effects claimed to be produced upon the medium can be the results of material influence, those effects may be natural; but many phenomena of mesmerism are beyond the reach of material causes, and therefore they are **preternatural**. For instance, it is claimed that the person magnetized may become possessed of new intellectual powers, such as mind-reading and the power of seeing what is beyond the reach of the senses; or the medium suddenly possesses knowledge of things never learned, as of the latent causes and the remedies of diseases, or exhibits familiarity with foreign languages, etc. It is the part of Philosophy to trace effects to adequate causes. Now, some of the effects attributed to mesmerism, when they are really such as they pretend to be and not mere jugglery, cannot have any adequate causes in

man, but only in spirits distinct from the souls of all those visibly present on such occasions.

174. The same test will apply to the phenomena of **spiritism**; namely, all clear exhibition of knowledge or intellectual action must be ascribed to an intellect as its source. If this cannot be the intellect of living men, then the effects must be ascribed, both in spiritism and mesmerism, to the agency of the evil spirits. For neither God, nor His good Angels, nor the souls in bliss could be supposed to put themselves at the disposal of spiritists or mesmerists, especially if we consider the unworthy and often immoral means employed by such men in their trades. Nor can a man claim control over the souls of the condemned; and, even if he could, it would be unholy and unwise for any one to make these his advisers and helpers. But it is perfectly conformable to the teachings both of reason and of Revelation to conclude that the evil spirits, or demons, are the agents of all such effects in spiritism and mesmerism as cannot be attributed to human power. Spiritism is explicitly forbidden in Holy Writ: "Neither let there be found any one among you that seeketh the truth from the dead. For the Lord abhorreth all such things." (Deut. XVIII. 12. See further Jouin's *Evidences of Religion*, pp 74, etc.)

ARTICLE II. RATIONAL COGNITION.

175. From the explanation given in the preceding article it is clear that sense-perception consists in the formation, by the sentient being, of vital images representing the material objects perceived. Now, a similar process must be followed by rational or intellectual cognition: it too consists in producing an image of the object known; not, however, an organic, a material, but an intellectual image. For truth in the mind, logical truth, supposes that the mind is made conformable

to the object known; and it can acquire this conformity in no other way than by conceiving an image of that object. This point, then, is **common to sensitive and to rational cognition**, that both are accomplished by the formation, in the subject, of vital images representing the objects. Another point must be common, viz., both must derive the image from the object which it represents; else the cognition would not be certainly true, or conformable to the object known.

176. **But a difference between sensitive and intellectual knowledge** arises from the fact that, in sensitive knowledge, a material object impresses a material image of itself upon the material organ of sense; but it cannot impress a material image upon the immaterial intellect. The intellect cannot receive such an image into itself. It takes, **abstracts** from the material objects presented, or rather from the sensible phantasms of them, the intelligible notes of the objects; these are the immaterial images, impressed on the intellect as the *species impressed;* and re-acting, eliciting the vital act of cognition, the intellect forms the *species expressed*, thus completing the act of intellectual apprehension. The result or term of this process is an *idea:* here, then, we have the Scholastic theory which accounts for the **origin of ideas**.

177. The Schoolmen, always careful to give names to every step discernible in the analysis of any process, gave the name of **intellect in action**, *intellectus agens*, to the intellect when viewed as abstracting from the phantasms and producing the immaterial image, and the name of **receptive intellect**, *intellectus possibilis*, to the same faculty viewed as vitally receiving that image.

178. It may be asked whether all our ideas are obtained by a like process; and if so, how can we have ideas of things immaterial? Many philosophers have supposed that we have some **innate ideas**, ideas born in us, such as those of

truth, virtue, vice, etc. Others have gone so far as to maintain that all our ideas are inborn, and only awakened, not acquired, under favorable circumstances. These are idle suppositions, devoid of all proof and, moreover, liable to the serious objection that, if our ideas are not derived from the objective reality, they may be merely subjective, and our knowledge may be an illusion. But our ideas are truly derived by way of likeness from the objects themselves; and therefore our knowledge is objective and reliable.

179. Another false theory is that of the **Traditionalists**, who pretend that all our knowledge comes to us by tradition, —*i. e.*, by the teaching of other men. This is a most unsatisfactory theory: other men can only use signs corresponding to our ideas, but not put ideas into our minds. If they give us a sign to which none of our ideas corresponds, the sign is unintelligible to us: thus, no amount of explanation can make a man born blind understand the nature of color, or the formal difference between one color and another. There remains a last false theory, that of the **Ontologists**, which we shall later on refute with more detail. (See Nos. 187, 188.)

180. We must first consider how we get ideas of things immaterial, inaccessible to the senses. We have no intuitions of such objects—for instance, of virtue, vice, justice, truth, etc., nor of spirits, of God, of our own soul, etc. How do we get our ideas of all such things? The Schoolmen, in accord as usual with the ancient Peripatetics, or followers of Aristotle, clearly lay it down as a maxim that **there are no ideas in our intellect which we have not derived from sense-perception**, *nihil est in intellectu quod prius non fuerat in sensu.* This principle is true, but it needs explanation.

181. At first sight the saying appears absurd: we have an **idea of spirit**, but we have never beheld a spirit; how, then, can we be said to have derived this idea from sense-perception?

Let us consider what we mean by a spirit: we mean an immaterial substance capable of thinking and willing. Now, by our senses we perceive material substances. By our power of abstraction we look at substance only; we strip substance of all that is material in or about it. In conceiving a spirit, we affirm substance and deny matter: our idea of an immaterial substance is partly affirmative and partly negative; but all its elements are derived by abstraction from sense-perception. But how do we get the ideas of 'thought' and 'will'? We perceive acts of thought and will in ourselves by our consciousness. But how is consciousness connected with sense? We could not be conscious of our mental acts, if these acts did not exist; and they would not exist, if sense-perception did not prompt our minds to act. For no thought, and of course no volition, would arise in the human soul, if sensation did not call forth the exercise of our faculties. Thus we see that all the elements contained in our idea of spirit are traceable to sense-perception; the same holds for all our other ideas. In fact, if we were to examine all the ideas expressed in so intellectual a poem as Milton's "Paradise Lost," we should find in it no concept the elements of which have not ultimately arisen from sensation. Many of those concepts are not conformable to an objective reality, because they are not directly formed from objects represented by them; but inasmuch as their elements are derived from real objects, all ideas have a foundation in the reality. Such are, for instance, the concepts of Death and Sin, as Milton describes those creations of his poetic mind.

182. We are now prepared to give a connected and, as it were, an historical account of the origin of our ideas according to the system of those Schoolmen who follow St. Thomas most closely. We start with the maxim, explained above, that all natural knowledge originates in sense-perception. The

mind of the child is at first like a clean tablet, *tabula rasa*, on which nothing as yet has been written : it has no inborn ideas. Its avenues to knowledge are its senses. If these should be so clogged by disease as to be unfit for action, the intellectual powers will never be set to work ; in fact, we find that persons born deaf and blind are apt to remain idiotic. When the senses of any child first open to the outward world, it begins to have sense-perceptions, as brute animals have ; there is for a considerable time no sign of intellectual action. When the brain, the organ of the imagination, becomes sufficiently perfected to elaborate phantasms suitable for intellectual use, the intellect becomes aroused to its specific activity. It sets to work abstracting what is intelligible in the object, and forming an image of the object's nature. It impresses this abstract species upon the receptive intellect, which in turn seizes upon or expresses the image in itself, and thus intellectually apprehends or cognizes the object. For instance, the hand seizes an orange, the eye sees it, the palate tastes it, etc. ; the phantasms formed by the imagination represent all that is sensible in the fruit. The intellect goes deeper; it reads within the reality, as its Latin name signifies (*intus legere*, to read within) ; it abstracts and conceives the ideas of 'being,' 'substance,' 'accidents,' in particular of 'size,' 'taste,' 'smell,' 'color,' of 'cause,' 'effect,' 'food,' 'pleasure,' etc., etc. All the senses, interior and exterior, are constantly bringing new phantasms to the brain; the intellect is constantly abstracting and comparing, conceiving and judging; inductive reasoning, now fairly aroused, contributes its share to develop knowledge ; and thus all our ideas are gradually formed, having a foundation in objects of sense-perception.

183. At first these ideas are not considered by us as representing whole classes of things : the ideas are **direct**, representing the notes 'being,' 'substance,' 'cause,' etc., which

exist identically in each individual object considered; but we do not yet reflect on the fact that the objects are generically or specifically identical. For instance, when I see a rock, a fruit, a man, etc., I apprehend each as a substance; this apprehension gives me the **direct universal** concept 'substance.' By observation I notice the identity of the objects; but it may be a long time before I reflect sufficiently upon my direct universal concepts to perceive distinctly that they are universal—*i. e.*, that they represent one thing common to a whole class of things. When I do so at last, I have a **reflex universal** idea.

184. Philosophers have warmly discussed the nature of reflex universals. The question is a radical one; errors on this subject strike at the root of all our knowledge. The **Nominalists**, such as Bain and J. S. Mill, maintain that universals are mere names assigned to a whole class of things, because we choose to fix our attention on some attributes which resemble each other in different objects; they do not suppose that anything is common to such objects, but only that we give the same name to things similarly marked. They would deny that there is anything identical in all men, in all substances, etc.; simply, we classify things by an arbitrary grouping, and we assign names to the groups. The **Conceptualists** admit more than identity in the name; but still, they admit nothing identical in the things—*e. g.*, in animals, in plants, etc. They admit similarities so close that we imagine them identical, and thus we conceive, say a lion, by a sort of vague or blurred phantasm, which will sufficiently represent any lion in general. This is not an idea at all, but merely a phantasm; besides, it is essentially relative, since the word *animal* will not call up the same phantasm in every mind; thus conceptualism has led to the modern theory of relativity of all human thought. " It is," remarks Rev. R. F. Clarke, S.J.,

"the central error of modern Logic, but it has a twin brother in Metaphysics no less subversive of truth. The radical and fundamental mistake of modern metaphysicians consists in the supposition that it is possible for two objects to resemble each other without having some *fundamentum in re*, something truly and really common to both of them in which this resemblance has its origin." (See *Amer. Cath. Quart. Review,* 1888, pp. 52, etc.)

185. **Thesis IX.** *The reflex universals are not mental images derived from universal objects physically existing, nor are they mere names, nor mere fictions of the mind; but they have a foundation in the reality of individual objects.*

First part. *Not images of existing universal objects,* as the exaggerated Realists maintain. *Proof.* Every object physically existing is a concrete and singular object, while universals are neither concrete nor singular. For instance, there is no concrete physically existing being which is a universal "body," a body that is neither large nor small nor middle-sized, neither white nor black, nor cold nor hot, etc. The universal has no definite accidents, but everything physically existing has definite accidents. Therefore there exist no physical universals.

Second part. *Universals are not mere names,* as the Nominalists pretend. *Proof.* A *mere* name, or oral term, has no mental term, or concept, corresponding to it; but universal names have each a concept corresponding to them and signified by them. If they had not, all the common nouns and the verbs of a language, and most other parts of speech, would be without any certain signification; for most words express universals, and the Nominalists suppose that universals are mere names to which no definite concepts correspond. But it is subversive of all certainty to maintain that nothing definite in meaning corresponds to most of the words of men.

Third part. Universals are not mere fictions of the mind, but they have a foundation in the reality of individual things. It is here maintained that universals express some one thing which is the same in many things; while the Conceptualists maintain that there is nothing the same, but only something similar, in all the individuals of a class.

Proof 1. Similarity is impossible without something that is one in the things similar. For similarity is, as Aristotle defines it, "unity in some quality"; things are similar inasmuch as, to a certain extent, they agree or are the same. Therefore, if all things of a class are said to be similar, they are really one to a certain extent; now, the universal signifies things by that in which they are the same—*e. g.*, animals, plants, etc.

Proof 2. If there were not some one thing common to all the individuals of a species, then the concept could not represent the nature of that species, but only something which is not the species, but is mistaken for it; and thus all our apprehensions of universals would be founded upon mistakes; all the words of a language would have a meaning, but a false meaning. Now, this leads to universal Scepticism. Therefore universals express some one thing which is found in all the individuals of a species or genus; therefore they have a foundation in the reality of individual things.

186. The now antiquated mysticism, taught formerly by Plato, consisted in a very peculiar theory on the origin of ideas. He supposed that the souls of men, before being united with their bodies, were in another state of existence in which they saw truths intuitively; afterwards, when united with their bodies, the souls retain the truths formerly perceived, but they are unconscious of their knowledge till sense-perception comes to awaken it anew. Plato could give no proof of his conjectures; his only reason for them was that he

could not in any other way account for the origin of our ideas.

187. **Ontologists teach:** 1. That the human soul has not in virtue of its own essence the power of knowing truth; 2. That this power must be supplied by a principle extrinsic to it; 3. That this extrinsic principle must be immediately present to the soul and directly intelligible, and must be of such a nature that in it all other things can be made intelligible to us; 4. That there can be no such being except God; 5. That our ideas, even our universal ideas, are not psychological, *i. e.*, formed by our souls, but ontological, *i. e.*, having objective existence, being the objects known to us. Still, many Ontologists allow that our mind can, by means of reflection, form to itself psychological ideas, which it can then compare with the ontological, thus knowing them to be conformable to the objective truth.

188. **Thesis X.** *Ontologism does not properly account for the origin of our ideas.*

Proof. That theory does not properly account for the origin of our ideas, 1. Which does not give a good explanation of known facts; 2. Which makes gratuitous and even false suppositions; 3. Which leads to false conclusions. But such is Ontologism.

1. *It fails to give a good explanation of known facts:* (a) It is a certain fact that our knowledge is intimately dependent on sense-perception; why is this so, if we see truth in God? (b) We know all things in connection with phantasms: bodily things by their own images, and things immaterial by reference to images borrowed from matter; why is this? The very terms applied to immaterial things are taken from material objects, *e. g.*, incomprehensible, immaterial; an acute, sharp, dull, clear intellect, etc. (c) We have no consciousness, even on reflection, that we see God; why is this, if we see Him?

2. *It makes gratuitous and even false suppositions:* (*a*) That actual finite beings are not cognoscible in themselves; why are they not cognoscible in themselves, if they have their own entity? (*b*) That we see things in God, and still we do not see God; why is this? (*c*) That we know God by species taken directly from Him, and other things by species taken from God; the opposite is evidently the case.

3. *It leads to false conclusions*; for, as entity and intelligibility are convertible terms, if finite things have not their own intelligibility, it will follow that they have not their own entity distinct from God's entity, that they are one with God; thus Pantheism is arrived at as a logical conclusion from Ontologism. In striving to refute this argument, Ontologists contradict and refute each other, and are divided into a number of schools: Malebranche claims that all things become intelligible to us by means of their archetypes, which we see in the Divine essence; Gioberti maintains that we do not behold the essence of God, but His creative act, *Ens creans existentias;* Rothenflue supposes that we see God "merely as being," *esse simpliciter*, etc. Therefore Ontologism does not explain the matter properly.

189. In connection with the study of ideas we must speak briefly of the expression of our ideas by words or **articulate language**. A word is an arbitrary articulate sign of an idea; therefore the same word has not the same meaning in different languages. Hence words cannot of their own force communicate our ideas to other men; but they are readily associated with ideas so as to become their inseparable companions. It would be incorrect to say that we cannot think without words: in fact, we often form ideas, judgments, trains of reasoning, and we experience feelings which we have no words to express, and deaf-mutes have no articulate signs at all. Still, thought without articulate language would be far less distinct,

more embarrassed in its process; and the minds of children would develop much more slowly and imperfectly if it were not for the use of speech.

190. As to the **origin of language**, it need not be to us a subject of vague speculation. We know from the historical account of Genesis that man had a language from the beginning, which he to a certain extent elaborated under the direction of the Creator (Gen. xix. 20); but he was then, before his fall, in a state of higher mental and bodily perfection than he is now. The question has often been discussed whether, with none but his present mental powers, man could have invented a language. No one doubts that it would have been difficult to do; it is even difficult now to make any decided improvement upon any nation's tongue. Still, there appears to be no conclusive reason to deny that it might, perhaps, have been gradually effected. To give a history of the supposed development of language, as Evolutionists sometimes attempt to do, is an idle task, always most unsatisfactory and never scientific.

CHAPTER III.

SENSIBLE AND RATIONAL APPETITE.

191. **Appetite**, in its widest sense, was, in the language of the Schoolmen, any tendency of a being towards a good suitable to its nature: (*a*) If the being does not apprehend the good to which its nature inclines it, its appetite was by them called *natural;* such is the tendency of a stone to fall down to the ground, of a plant to grow and produce fruit, the result being intended by the Creator. (*b*) If it apprehends the good by sense, the appetite is *sensible*. (*c*) If by reason, it is *rational* appetite or will. In English we never use the term *appetite* except for the tendency to sensible or to rational good.

192. The natural appetite of a being tends to what is essentially good for that being as a whole, and for the species; the **sensible and rational appetites** tend to the special good of sense and of reason; they are two distinct faculties, differing by their formal objects, viz., sensible and intellectual good.

193. An act is called **spontaneous** whenever the principle giving rise to it is in the agent; thus, all vital acts are spontaneous. In a stricter sense, however, only the acts of sensible appetite are called spontaneous; the acts of the rational appetite or will are termed **voluntary**. Now, voluntary is not the same as *free;* thus we voluntarily desire happiness, but we are not free to desire it or not.

194. **Freedom** is the absence of constraint. The absence of extrinsic constraint is *liberty from coercion;* even brutes may enjoy this. The absence of intrinsic constraint is

freedom from necessary action. This last is freedom or liberty properly so called: it enables our will to choose for itself between two alternatives; it is also styled *liberty of indifference.*

195. Sensible appetite as such, whether in man or brute, is not truly free; it is, indeed, free from extrinsic constraint, but not from intrinsic necessity. The reason is that its action is organic, the heart probably being its organ; and all organic action is subject to the physical laws of the material creation. When, therefore, an object is apprehended by sense as good, or delectable, or when the phantasm of such an object is aroused in the animal, the sensible appetite must, by a physical necessity, tend to that delectable good. Brutes, therefore, are entirely irresponsible for their appetites.

196. But man has an indirect power of controlling, to a certain extent, the workings of his sensible appetites; and he is in duty bound to regulate them by the law of reason. For good order requires that the superior faculty shall rule the inferior. Now, **man can indirectly control his animal appetites in various ways:** 1. He can avoid such external objects as would excite his appetites. 2. He can use in their stead objects that will affect him differently. 3. Even when he cannot change his material surroundings, he can recall phantasms of a different tendency. 4. He can withdraw his attention from any particular objects or phantasms. 5. He can often, by a powerful effort of his will, compel his sensible appetites to a reluctant obedience. 6. He can control his members so as not to yield obedience to his animal appetites.

197. The <u>**essence of liberty**</u> consists in this, that, when everything is ready for action, the will has still a choice of its own with regard to the action. Man can exercise that choice in various ways: he may choose to act or not to act,

to take one thing or its contrary, or to select between things not opposite to each other; technically he has liberty of *contradiction*, liberty of *contrariety*, and liberty of *specification*.

198. **Thesis XI.** *The will of man is free, not only from coercion, but also from necessary action.*

Explanation. We do not maintain that we are always free in every respect—for instance, we cannot help desiring our own happiness—but we are free with regard to particular means of seeking our happiness. The liberty of man is true liberty, in the meaning explained in the preceding paragraph.

Proof 1. We have a clear and invincible consciousness that we often will things when we could restrain ourselves from willing them, or could will something different or the contrary of them. We experience this consciousness: (*a*) Before we make our choice, when we notice that we could delay our choice and take longer time to consider, or act at once without further delay; even when we are going to act, we know that we can take one thing or another. (*b*) In the act of choosing we distinguish between necessity and free choice; when we choose freely, we are conscious that our decision is our own, of which we assume the responsibility, and that we could, if we would, choose differently. (*c*) After our choice, we are conscious that we have done morally well or ill, that we have reasons for self-reproach or for self-approbation. Now, consciousness is an infallible motive of certainty. (*Logic*, No. 116.)

Proof 2. We judge without any fear of error that others also are responsible for their choice. All men agree with these judgments—witness the laws, tribunals, histories, etc., of all nations.

Proof 3. When we submit one of our free acts to a scientific analysis, we understand that it must be free. For the will is presented by the intellect with the choice between things which the intellect proposes as desirable in some respects and not desirable in other respects, and not necessary just now. Our intellect does not then compel the assent of the will to any particular choice; still, our choice is made; the reason, therefore, of the choice must be in the will itself.

199. **Objections:** 1. "The essence of that which is improperly called the free-will doctrine is that, occasionally at any rate, human volition is self-caused—that is to say, not caused at all" (Huxley, "Science and Morals"). *Answer.* We deny it. This is a play on the word *self-caused:* the act of volition is not caused by the act of volition, which it would be if it were self-caused; but the act of volition is caused by the faculty of the free will. It is true that matter cannot determine the nature of its action; but it does not follow that a spirit cannot do so. Rather, from the fact that matter cannot determine its action, and our soul can, it follows that our soul is not matter; to avoid granting this logical conclusion, Huxley finds it necessary to deny the liberty of the will.

2. Consciousness testifies to the existence of our acts, not to the manner nor the causes of our acts, therefore not to their liberty. *Answer.* Consciousness often testifies to the manner of the act as well. Besides, we are conscious of our acts by which we decide between different courses of conduct; *i. e.*, the direct object of our consciousness is the exercise of our liberty: we are conscious that we make a free choice.

3. We mistake spontaneous action for free action. *Answer.* We clearly distinguish between *free* and *not free;* thus, we do not call the pleasure free which we find in food, though our perceiving it is spontaneous.

4. We cannot help choosing what we like best; therefore we are not free. *Answer.* If this means that we cannot help preferring what we prefer, we cannot choose and yet not choose a thing, it is true, but not to the point. But if it means that we cannot help choosing that which holds out the stronger attraction, it is false; if it were true, no one would be accountable for his action, all mankind would be in error about moral good and evil, our own consciousness would deceive us, etc.
5. If we could choose what holds out the weaker attraction, that choice would be without a reason, but there is nothing without a reason for it; therefore we always choose what is more attractive. *Answer.* The reason for choosing what is less attractive is not that it is less attractive, but it is reason enough that it is attractive at all, and therefore capable of exciting our appetite.
6. Our will always obeys our last practical judgment; but our judgment is not free. *Answer.* Our judgment may be influenced by our free will, as when we make ourselves believe that a thing is right because we like it; in this case our judgment is free. But if the objection means that our will always obeys our last practical judgment, which is entirely independent of our will, the statement is false. We know that, when our intellect tells us we ought to do one thing, we can still do another; we can also choose what we judge to be less useful or less agreeable.
7. God knows what I shall do to-morrow; therefore I must do it. I am not free. *Answer.* God knows it, because I will freely do it: knowledge is by nature consequent on the fact known and does not in the least influence the fact.

8. Statistics show that the same average of crimes occurs each year, therefore such things obey a necessary law. *Answer.* Statistics may show some remote proportion between temptation and crime; but no more than can be explained by the fact that men, even though free in any single case, are more inclined habitually one way than another, and that there is a certain uniformity in the circumstances which tempt men to the commission of crimes.

CHAPTER IV.

THE NATURE OF THE HUMAN SOUL.

200. **Thesis XII.** *The soul of man is essentially a simple being.*

Proof. Our soul takes in simple ideas; for instance, those of truth, holiness, justice, infinity, being, etc.; but a principle that can take in or conceive a simple idea is simple. For if it were composed of parts, then either, 1, *Each part would take in the whole idea;* each part would be a soul, and every man would be not *I* but *we*, which is against the testimony of consciousness and of common sense; or, 2, *Each part would take in a part of a simple idea;* but a simple idea is not an aggregate of parts; or, 3, *Only one part would take in the whole idea*, the other parts not apprehending it; then the part apprehending the simple idea would be the soul. If this part is simple, the soul is simple, as we maintain it is. But if that part is itself compound, the same reasoning must again be applied to it; and the absurdities arising cannot be avoided except by granting that the principle which conceives simple ideas is simple, or that the soul is simple.

201. **Objections:** 1. A simple soul is unthinkable, *i. e.*, cannot be thought of, says Huxley. *Answer.* It is unimaginable, not unthinkable; if we could not think of it, we could not point out the essential notes by which it is distinguished from all other beings.

2. Our intellect is affected by our bodily ailments; it may be disorganized, deranged, enfeebled, excited, etc.;

therefore it consists of parts. *Answer.* The intellect itself cannot be deranged, but its co-natural objects are presented to it by the phantasms of our imagination. Now, our imagination can be deranged, for it is an organic power; and in reality all mental derangement, enfeeblement, excitement, etc., can be traced to affections of the imagination.

3. Phrenology shows that all action of the soul is modified according to the modifications of the brain; therefore the soul is identified with the brain. *Answer.* Phrenology is not founded upon certain principles; therefore it is not a science and cannot draw scientific conclusions. Elevations in the brain do not always correspond to elevations in the cranium, nor do mental dispositions always correspond to special modifications of the brain. Even if they did, it would only prove that the action of the soul is modified when its organ is affected; for the brain is the organ of the imagination; and the imagination exerts an extrinsic influence on the understanding, presenting to it the images that assist thought.

202. **Thesis XIII.** *The soul of man is spiritual.*

Explanation. Spirituality expresses more than simplicity; every spirit is simple, but a thing may be simple without being spiritual; such is the soul of the brute. (See No. 145.) A being is spiritual when it can act and exist without material organs.

Proof 1. The soul will actually survive the body, as will be proved further on (Nos. 213, 214); this supposes that it can exist and act without the body; therefore, that it is spiritual.

Proof 2. The soul, even now, performs acts in which matter cannot have an *intrinsic* share; for instance, when we conceive such ideas as virtue, holy, honest, will, intellect, God, angel, spirit, etc.; also when we love spiritual good, which cannot affect any organism. In fact, all abstract, all universal ideas are beyond the reach of matter; for matter being essentially concrete and singular cannot represent any but concrete and singular objects. Likewise all judgments, reasonings, volitions, every act that is distinctively intellectual, is inorganic in its essence; the imagination does furnish it with materials extrinsically, but cannot enter into its specific action. Now, it is evident that a being acts according to its nature; therefore the nature of the intellect is spiritual, distinct from matter, independent of matter in its own specific sphere of activity; therefore intrinsically capable of acting and existing without a body. The argument may be stated thus: An organic faculty—*i. e.*, a faculty which has matter as a con-cause of its operations—can only perceive such objects as can make a material impression upon it; but our intellect perceives objects which cannot make a material impression upon it; therefore our intellect is not an organic but a spiritual faculty. But a faculty is necessarily proportioned to the subject in which it resides; therefore the soul is spiritual.

Proof 3. No being can tend to a good which is above its nature; but the soul tends to spiritual goods, essentially above all material natures; therefore its nature is spiritual.

Proof 4. Matter cannot act freely, as materialists grant; but our soul acts freely, as proved above (No. 198); therefore our soul is not matter.

Proof 5. Our soul is conscious of its own acts; but consciousness supposes inorganic action and inorganic being. For an organ cannot inspect itself, a being dependent intrinsically on matter cannot double itself back on its own acts; therefore the acts of consciousness and the nature of a conscious soul are spiritual.

203 **Objections**: 1. All intellectual action begins in

sense, therefore the soul is dependent on the body for all its acts. *Answer.* The soul is, in our present state of existence, extrinsically dependent on the body in more than one way viz.: for its communication with the visible world, for its phantasms, and for the exercise of its faculties generally; but since matter does not intrinsically co-operate in its intellectual acts, there is nothing impossible in the separate existence and action of the soul, without the extrinsic aid of the body.

2. The soul is the form of the body; therefore its very being is the being of the body. *Answer.* Though it makes one being with the body, still its being is not exhausted by the being of the body; in other words, it is the form of the body, but it is not only the form of the body; it is more.

3. Whether the aid of organs in the acts of the intellect be called intrinsic or extrinsic, it is necessary for intellectual action; therefore the soul cannot act without the body. *Answer.* The aid of phantasms is now necessary, because every being acts dependently on the circumstances in which it is placed; thus, when we are in a room, we depend on the window to see objects outside. The soul, therefore, being at present one being with its body, must now act in union with that body, using the aid of that body as far as it can aid the act of intelligence. Therefore we now think of all things in connection with phantasms. When, however, the body will be no more one with the soul, the latter can retain all its intellectual species formerly acquired; it can know its own essence directly, and, by reasoning on all this, know its Creator; besides, it can receive divinely infused knowledge, and knowl-

edge communicated to it by other intelligences in manners suitable to its new condition.

204. Thesis XIV. *The intellectual soul is the only principle of life in man, and is therefore the form of the human body.*

Explanation. It was proved above (Thesis V.) that the vital principle of any living body is truly the form of that body; if, then, we prove here that the intellectual soul is the only vital principle in man, we thereby establish the fact that the soul is the form of the body. Now, the intellectual soul is really the only vital principle in man.

Proof 1. Every man is conscious of being a unit, which he signifies by the term 'I'; he is conscious, moreover, that the same 'I' feels, and thinks, and wills. Now, if there were more than one vital principle in man, the intellectual soul could not be conscious of all this; for vital principles perform immanent actions, and one principle cannot be conscious to itself of performing the immanent act of another principle, conscious of doing what it does not do.

Proof 2. The more the intellect works, the more the inferior vitality of a man is relaxed; on the other hand, when the lower functions of life are most energetically exercised, the mind is less fit for its own activity. Thus, while wrapped in deep thought, a man scarcely sees or hears; he digests imperfectly. Now, all this cannot be explained except by supposing that the same principle performs the higher and the lower functions of human life.

Proof 3. Anatomy shows that the entire organism of the human body is one unit, combining the organs of vegetable and animal action into one harmonious whole.

    205. Corollaries. 1. The soul is in every part of the body, acting in every organ with a vitality appropriate to such organ; seeing in the eye, hearing in the ear, breathing in the lungs, digesting in the stomach, moving in the muscles, etc.

2. All organic action in man is the action of the compound soul and body; for matter can do nothing except in virtue of its form.

3. The soul is directly united with the prime matter or potential principle, being itself the active principle: it gives to the body all its powers and its very nature of a body, and such a body. Still, when the soul departs at death, the body cannot cease to be a body of some kind; for the potential principle of matter cannot exist without a form. Whether this new form be one form for the whole corpse, a form supplied for the purpose by the laws of nature, or whether the flesh, bone, sinew, etc., have each its own form, existing before death under the control of the life principle and now acting independently, matters very little. (Pesch, *Inst. Phil. Nat.*, No. 210.)

206. Those who do not understand the Peripatetic system of matter and form are greatly embarrassed to explain **how body and soul act on each other.** Various theories have been imagined, all of them unscientific. Plato supposed that the soul is *seated in the brain*, whence it rules the body as the rider does his horse. The *assistance* theory of Descartes maintains that soul and body do not act on each other, but God acts on either one of them whenever a modification occurs in the other. Leibnitz's theory of *pre-established harmony* teaches that God, foreseeing all that any soul would do in the course of life, has in his wisdom given to each soul a body so constructed that it will automatically act just when and as the soul wills, though the soul does not influence it in the least. The theory of *physical influence* makes the soul and the body act on each other as two distinct beings.

Günther imagined a principle of animal life, called by him *psyche*, which he supposed to be substantially united with the intellectual soul. No system can be scientific which makes man to be, not one but two beings, each having its own activity; the only theory in harmony with man's essential unity is that which views the soul as the form of the body. The form is not acted upon by the body, nor does it act on the body; but it is itself the active principle of the body. Thus, the soul is not acted upon by the eye or the ear, but the living eye, the living ear acts, perceiving color and sound. The whole question about the interaction of body and soul thus ceases to be a question at all; for there can be no interaction where there are not two agents each having its own action, but the action is common to both.

CHAPTER V.

ORIGIN AND DESTINY OF THE HUMAN SOUL.

207. Many ancient philosophers, finding the soul of man so evidently and immeasurably elevated above the entire material creation, erroneously conjectured that it, in some way or other, must have **emanated** from the very substance of the Divinity. To-day a very different error has not a few advocates among the votaries of the physical sciences: they imagine that man may be a mere **evolution** of the brute, and the highest step in a universal movement of evolution.

208. The most popular shape in which this vagary has found favor with the modern public is the **Darwinian theory**, which may be stated thus: All plants and animals, man included, are evolved from inferior species, and, as many of Darwin's disciples add, ultimately from unorganized matter, by means of *natural selection.* The process of natural selection is as follows: All plants and animals tend to increase their numbers in a geometrical progression; hence arises a severe *struggle for existence,* in which contest nature causes the weakest individuals and species to perish, and the best-constructed to multiply, thus producing the *survival of the fittest.* Consequently, organic life must ever be ascending in perfection, and lower species have thus been developed into higher species. (See Mivart's *Genesis of Species,* pp. 17, 18.) This theory is interesting and ingenious; but its disastrous consequences to morality, to religion, to social life, and to individual happiness for time and eternity are so obvious, that noth-

ing but the most convincing evidence of its truth could possibly excuse those who love to disseminate its noxious principles.

209. And yet the Darwinian theory, far from being established beyond a doubt, is totally devoid of demonstration, and is a **mere figment of the intellect.** Charles Elam, M.D., after an accurate analysis of facts in three articles of the *Contemporary Review*, continues thus (Dec., 1876, p. 132): " The conclusions which necessarily follow from the foregoing observations may be briefly summed up in one syllogism, embracing not only Natural Selection, but also the larger theme of Organic Evolution generally:

"'Without verification a theoretic conception is a mere figment of the intellect' (Tyndall's *Fragments of Science*, p. 469).

" But the theory of Organic Evolution is an unverified conception.

" Therefore Organic Evolution is a mere figment of the intellect."

To prove the minor, we may quote the rule laid down by Huxley, that the only way in which any hypothesis of progressive modification can be demonstrated is " by observation and experience upon the existing forms of life." Now, he grants in the same paragraph that the Darwinian hypothesis has not yet received such demonstration. (*Lay Sermons*, p. 226. See further Mazzella's *De Deo Creante*, Disput. iii. art. i. § 3.)

210. We have proved above (Thesis VIII.) that the species of plants and animals are fixed, incapable of transformation. With regard to the evolution of man, in particular from a lower animal species, and of the intellectual from the sensitive soul—the main point with which we are here concerned—we add the following:

Thesis XV. *The gulf between brute and man is absolutely impassable by any process of evolution.*

Proof. The brute animal is entirely material: though it is animated by a simple soul, still that soul is only the substantial form of the body, the principle of bodily action and nothing more; it can neither exist nor act except in matter, so that all its life, all its activity consists in material modifications of a material organism. This much is admitted by modern philosophers and scientists generally, as well as by the Schoolmen. Now, what is merely material can never be developed, whether by the Darwinian process or by any system of evolution, into a spiritual being; or, which is the same thing, matter cannot possibly be evolved into a thinking, a reasoning being. For all evolution is merely a modification of matter; but matter in all its modifications remains matter; therefore evolution of matter cannot produce anything but matter. Now, matter cannot possibly reason; for reasoning implies universal ideas, since at least its middle term must be distributed (*Logic*, No. 32); and matter cannot conceive a universal idea. For an idea is an image of the object, and every image in matter can only be a concrete image of a concrete and singular thing; while a universal idea is an abstract image of what is neither concrete nor singular, and therefore cannot possibly be imaged in matter. Therefore matter can never become capable of reasoning. But our soul reasons; hence a material being can never be evolved into the human soul; or, the gulf between brute and man is absolutely impassable by any process of evolution.

As a fact, evolutionists find it impossible to account, in their theories, for the spirituality of the human soul; hence they either deny this spirituality, believe in nothing but matter, and become Materialists; or they refuse to draw the logical conclusions which flow from their false principles, and, to veil their inconsistency, they assume the sceptical position of Agnostics.

211. **Thesis XVI.** *The soul of man cannot originate except by creation,* i. e., *by being made out of nothing.*

Proof. If it were made out of anything, this would be material or spiritual. It can be neither: 1. *Not material;* for, as we have just proved, no change in matter can fit it for the acts of thinking. 2. *Not spiritual;* for it cannot be made out of a part of that spirit, since a spirit has no parts: nor out of the whole of that spirit, which would then cease to be when the soul begins to be. Among all the wanderings of genius, no philosopher has ever maintained that the soul is made out of a previous spirit which then ceases to exist. The human soul, therefore, cannot be made out of another being; hence it is created, made out of nothing.

212. As to the question **when the souls of men are created**, Plato supposed that all human souls lived before in the stars, whence they were banished for crime; others have taught the transmigration of souls from one body into another, even into brutes, as a punishment for their moral degradation; Leibnitz and Wolf pretended that all human souls were created in the beginning of the world, but remained without intelligence till united to their destined human bodies. All such theories are destitute of proof and even of plausibility. Why should a soul exist before it can do work suited to its nature? **The scientific answer** is that which is derived by careful reasoning from known facts. The soul of each man must begin to exist when its work begins. Before biology became a science, it was supposed that the human soul was not created till the body was sufficiently organized—first by a previous vegetative, and next by a merely animal soul—to become the fit organism of that higher principle which was to build it up into a distinctively human body. That principle was the intellectual soul. At present it is far more probable that the rational soul is created, and made the substantial form of the

body, from the very moment of conception: the infant of a day has already an immortal soul; hence the wilful destruction of its life is murder.

213. **Thesis XVII.** *The human soul does not perish with the body.*

Proof 1. This is one of the most universal judgments of common sense.

Proof 2. The justice and the wisdom of God require that there shall be a sufficient sanction for the moral law—*i. e.*, that there shall be such rewards for virtue and punishments for vice as shall make the good ultimately much happier than the wicked. But such a sanction does not exist in this world, where the virtuous are often oppressed, despised, persecuted unto death; therefore it must exist in a future life.

214. **Thesis XVIII.** *The human soul is immortal.*

Proof 1. The Creator has given us a longing for a never-ending existence, an endless happiness; but He could not have done so if our souls were not really destined for an endless life. For it would be unworthy of His goodness to give us a longing after a great good, which we could not possibly attain; and it would conflict with His truthfulness to give us, in such natural desires, an implicit promise of immortality, if He did not enable us to attain it.

Proof 2. A spiritual being is capable of acting and existing for ever; in fact, immortality is natural to it, because, having no parts, it cannot be dissolved or corrupted as to its substance. Therefore it is natural for it to exist till it be annihilated by its Maker. But the Creator can have no reason to annihilate it, as long as it can answer the purpose of its existence; now, it can answer that purpose for ever, by showing forth the justice, the power, and the goodness of God, and thus contributing to His external glory. God makes nothing useless; but the natural indestructibility of the soul would be useless if God should annihilate it, no matter after how long a period.

215. Can we prove that **the souls of the wicked shall suffer for ever,** that the pains of the lost are eternal? We can certainly prove by reason: 1. That it is natural for all spirits to exist for ever; 2. That God is not bound to destroy those who He intended should glorify Him throughout eternity; 3. That a being which freely fails to attain its destined happiness must naturally expect to be disappointed for ever, and can only blame itself for its unhappiness; 4. That God is not bound to give new chances to a free creature which has with full deliberation rejected His sincere offers of beatitude; 5. That it is proper for every immortal being not to be in a provisionary state for ever, but to come sooner or later to a definite and final condition, and to remain in the same for eternity; 6. That there would be no complete sanction of the moral order, if the punishment of such as will persevere in their wickedness till the end would not last for ever; 7. That no motive but the dread of eternal punishment is under all circumstances sufficient to restrain man's passions. Hence it is abundantly proved that reason itself appears to demand eternal punishment for those who die in a state of rebellion against their Maker.

216. Those who deny the spirituality and, consequently, the immortality of the soul are called *Materialists*, since they admit nothing but matter in the world. Many recent writers, anxious to disclaim this odious title, have invented the less unpopular appellation of **Agnostics.** "I called myself an Agnostic," writes Huxley. "Surely no denomination could be more modest and appropriate" (*Lay Sermons*, p. 294). These strive to evade the arguments of all sound philosophers by pretending that such questions as concern the existence of God, the nature of the soul, its future destiny, etc.,

are too deep for our investigations. Still, while pretending to keep aloof from such matters, they are constantly alluding to them, arguing against the great truths of philosophy in a covert manner. They do not prove their thesis, but they take it for granted, calling God the Unknown, as if no man knew anything about the necessity and the greatness of the Creator, sneering at the spirituality of the soul, as if it were a self-contradiction, etc., etc.

217. **Thesis XIX.** *Agnosticism is destructive of all sound Philosophy.*

Proof. That system is destructive of Philosophy which renders all the most important inquiries impossible: in particular, which denies that we can know anything certain about the existence of the soul as distinct from the body, of a future state, of a wise and personal God, the rewarder of good and evil; and which, consequently, makes it doubtful whether there is anything worth living for beyond the gratification of the passions. For Huxley himself admits that "The question of questions for mankind, the problem which underlies all others, and is more deeply interesting than any other, is the ascertainment of the place man occupies in nature, and of his relation to the universe of things. Whence our race has come, . . . to what goal we are tending, are the problems which present themselves anew, and with undiminished interest, to every man born into this world" (*Man's Place in Nature*, p. 57).

Now, Agnosticism renders all such inquiries futile and such questions incapable of satisfactory settlement. The same writer acknowledges this: "Why trouble ourselves about matters of which, however important they may be, we do know nothing and we can know nothing?" (*Lay Sermons*, p. 145).

The Mental Philosophy of the Schoolmen, so far briefly

outlined, answers all these questions clearly and without hesitation. Its voice comes to us from the most distant past, strengthened by the approving accents of all intervening generations.

The advancement of true science, so far from having weakened its teaching, has strikingly confirmed, and daily confirms more and more, the truth of its doctrines. It alone satisfies the reason and the heart of man.

BOOK IV.

NATURAL THEOLOGY.

218. Natural Theology is our study of God by the light of reason, without the direct influence of supernatural Revelation. We exclude the direct, but not the indirect, guidance of Revelation; for no earnest investigator of truth will close his eyes to the bright light of Divine teaching, and prefer to grope his way by the faint glimmer of unaided reason. We live in the full blaze of Christian civilization, which it were folly to ignore. We set out, therefore, in the pursuit of wisdom, not as pagan sceptics in quest of the unknown cause of this world, if perhaps there be such a cause, but as enlightened Christians, who wish reverently to investigate what our reason can understand about a matter so far above us, viz.: the nature and the perfections of the Creator, and the relations in which He stands to His creatures.

We shall consider: 1. The existence of God. 2. His essence. 3. His quiescent attributes. 4. His operative attributes.

CHAPTER I.

THE EXISTENCE OF GOD.

219. We shall begin by considering God as He is most obviously conceived by man, viz., *as the first and intelligent Cause of the universe, and the Supreme Lord to whom we are all responsible for our moral conduct.* Those who refuse to acknowledge the existence of God are called **Atheists**: *practical* Atheists deny Him by their conduct, and *theoretical* Atheists in their speculations. Unfortunately there have been many practical Atheists; but those of the theoretic kind have been comparatively few, and none of them conspicuous for virtue. The **Agnostics** are a very recent school of physical scientists, rather than of intellectual philosophers, who do not deny that God exists, but pretend that His existence cannot be validly demonstrated.

We are to prove in this chapter that the existence of God, such as He is most obviously conceived by man, is absolutely certain. Various proofs may be given; we select the following, which we present in bare outline:

220. **Thesis I.** *The existence of God can be demonstrated by metaphysical, physical, and moral arguments.*

Proof 1. The **metaphysical argument** considers God as the first efficient cause of this world; it may be thus proposed: the world is a system of contingent beings; but no contingent being can exist without a necessary being which is its first efficient cause; therefore a necessary being exists which is the first efficient cause of the world.

We prove the major: A contingent being is one that may exist or not exist as far as its own nature is concerned—in other words, a being that is not self-existent. But the world is not self-existent, as was proved in *Cosmology* (No. 103). Therefore the world is a contingent being.

We prove the minor: There can be nothing without a sufficient reason; hence a contingent being must have a reason for its existence. But that reason is not in the contingent being itself; therefore it must be in another being. This is its cause; for a cause is a being that influences the existence of another being. Now, if that cause is a necessary being, then our proposition is proved; if it be not a necessary being, then it is contingent, and therefore must have a cause, as we have just proved. Thus we must go on reasoning, till we come to a first cause which is not contingent but necessary; or we must suppose that there has been an infinite series of contingent causes without any necessary cause. But besides the fact that such a series is absurd (because an infinite series in the past could never have come to a particular effect, since the infinite can never be passed through or left behind), even if it were not absurd, it would be inadequate to produce such an effect. For a multitude of contingent beings without a necessary cause could not have a sufficient reason for existence; since contingency is the want of an intrinsic reason for existence. Therefore no contingent being can exist unless there exists a necessary being which is its first cause.

221. *Proof 2.* **The physical argument,** supposing it proved that the world is contingent (No. 103), views God as its intelligent cause, and proves His existence from the physical order conspicuous in the world; it is this: There exists in the world a most wonderful order, or adaptation of means to ends: (*a*) to particular ends, as of the eyes to see, of the ears to hear, of the tongue to suit various purposes, etc.;

(*b*) of all the parts to a common end, viz., to the preservation of the whole. Now, such adaptation, visible in the world, requires intelligence in its cause, and even an amount of intelligence proportionate to the vastness, the variety, and the perfection of the order produced; therefore the first Cause of the world must be intelligent beyond all our conception.

The *minor*, viz.: order in the effect requires intelligence in the cause: (*a*) It is analytically certain; for a disposing of means for an end implies the intellectual perception of the relation existing between means and end, and therefore it requires intellect in the cause. (*b*) It is attested by the common consent of mankind; for no one could believe, *e. g.*, that letters or type put down at random would produce a grand poem. (*c*) It is always insisted on as a certain truth, even by the Agnostics in their scientific researches; for, when they find any fossil which has a regular shape or mark, they claim it as an undoubted proof of human, *i. e.*, intelligent, workmanship. Therefore order in the effect supposes intelligence in the cause.

222. *Proof* 3. **The moral argument** proves that there is a supreme Lord to whom all men are responsible for their moral conduct. It is as follows: All men when in the full possession of reason, in any part of the world, in all stages of society, among all races, even among newly discovered tribes, agree in the firm conviction, which acts as a constant check on their passions, that there exists a supreme Lord and Master to whom they are responsible for their moral conduct. Now, this firm and universal judgment cannot be erroneous; else it would show that it is natural for man to judge falsely, and the human intellect, instead of being the faculty of knowing truth, would be the source of a universal deception.

223. **Objections: I. Against the metaphysical argument.**
1. This argument is too abstruse to be reliable. *Answer.* It is, on the contrary, an obvious application of the analytical and common-sense principle of causality: everybody judges as readily that the world must have had a first cause as that a house must have had a builder.
2. Science must confine itself to the tracing of physical effects to physical causes. *Answer.* Physical science may do so, but philosophy must investigate the highest causes.
3. Evolution can account for all things physical. *Answer.* Evolution does not even touch upon the real origin of the world, but only on its development; even if the theory of evolution were true, there would still have to be a Creator of matter before that matter could begin to change its forms.
4. A self-evolving world might be a necessary being. *Answer.* Impossible. The series of evolutions must have had a beginning, a first stage; if that stage were necessary, then it could not change; besides, the world is proved in *Cosmology* (Thesis I.) not to be self-existent.
5. Although every single being in the world were contingent, the whole collection might be necessary. *Answer.* There can be nothing in the collection which is not supplied by the parts, especially when it is essentially excluded from the parts. Besides, the collection is both finite and mutable, and a necessary being is not such. (No. 103.)
6. From the existence of a contingent being we cannot conclude to that of a necessary being; for we should thus have more in the conclusion than in the premises,

viz., the necessary in the conclusion and only the contingent in the premises. *Answer.* We have the necessary being in the premises; for we have in the major that everything existing must have a sufficient reason, and in the minor that only a necessary being can truly be the ultimately sufficient reason of contingent beings.

7. There is no proportion between a contingent and a necessary being. *Answer.* There is no proportion of entity, but one of necessary dependence.

224. **Objections: II. Against the physical argument.**
1. Not every thing in this world exhibits the disposition of means to an end. *Answer.* It is enough for our argument that many things do.
2. But many things are evidently out of order; therefore it is clear that the Creator is not very wise. *Answer.* More than enough order is conspicuous in the universe to prove the Creator immensely wise, beyond all our conception. Besides, it cannot be proved that anything is out of order: a thing may not be arranged in the way that we might prefer; and yet it may, for all we know, be excellently arranged. Similarly, an ignorant man may not see the use of all the tools found in an artist's studio, but it would be foolish for him to say that they were useless.
3. But a world created by an infinitely wise and good God should be perfect. *Answer.* It should be relatively but not absolutely perfect. (No. 117.)
4. But the order of the world proceeds from the physical laws, and these result from the natures of the bodies; thus there is no need of an intelligent Ordainer. *Answer.* The natures of bodies proceed from the Maker of them: if they are well suited *to*

their ends, it is because the Creator has so suited them.

5. All the order of nature may be a mere accident. *Answer.* This would mean, in other words, that the most wonderful effect may be without a sufficient cause; for blind chance is not a sufficient cause of order.

6. The order of nature results from evolution by means of natural selection, the survival of the fittest, etc. *Answer.* If it were true that such evolution had taken place, it would only make the order displayed in the world more admirable; for he who would make a machine of such a nature that it should evolve a number of other machines in wonderful variety, and in an ever-increasing perfection of details, would thereby exhibit far more intelligence than if he were to make all these machines separately. Therefore this objection, whether true or false, is not against our thesis.

7. An adaptation of means to an end does not require intelligence; *e. g.*, the bee without intelligence builds its honey-comb most symmetrically. *Answer.* The bee and all brute animals, in following irresistibly the promptings of their instincts, display the wisdom of their Maker, just as a machine displays the skill of the inventor.

225. **Objections: III. Against the moral argument.**

1. Our judgments concerning our moral duties and responsibilities are due to education. *Answer.* They may be developed and perfected by education; but they are so essential to man that they are known even without education and amid all varieties of education.

2. This sense of responsibility comes from some passion or other, *e. g.*, from an idle fear of punishment. *Answer.*

The passions would rather prompt a man to throw off restraint, to do what he likes, while it is our moral judgment that is a constant check upon our passions. As to the fear of punishment, it is a consequence, not a cause of our sense of responsibility.

3. The sense of responsibility simply results from the intellectual apprehension of right and wrong. *Answer.* It also implies the judgment that there is a law obliging us to do the right and avoid the wrong, and that there is a Law-giver who enforces this law, for there can be no law without a law-giver.

4. There have always been atheists; therefore the judgments in question are not universal nor essential to man. *Answer.* We grant that there have been in many ages practical atheists; there have also been a comparatively small number of theoretical atheists, who maintained for a portion of their lives that there is no God. Some of these may, perhaps, have convinced themselves, or may have been convinced by others, that the existence of God was doubtful; but history does not tell of any sensible and sincere man who felt an habitual conviction through life that he was not responsible for his moral conduct to a supreme Being.

5. We find learned men who are really convinced that man is only matter, and therefore irresponsible for his acts. *Answer.* From the fact that such men as Pyrrho, Hume, Fichte, Berkeley, etc., argued against the certain existence of bodies, it does not follow that they firmly believed in their own theories; so, likewise, it does not follow from all the theorizing of materialists that they *bona fide* consider themselves as irresponsible heaps of matter, unless it be that abnormal

surroundings, or abnormal conditions of mind or heart, have extinguished in them the ordinary light of conscience. We do not know whether such a case is possible; but if it be, it is not from abnormal states that the judgments of man's common sense can be gathered.

226. Some pretend to prove the existence of God *a priori*. Now, to reason *a priori* means to reason from a cause to an effect; and as God has no cause, His existence cannot possibly be proved by such a process. But such theorists confound an *a priori argument* with an *a priori judgment;* they really mean that the judgment 'God exists' is *a priori*, or analytical. This is called the **ontological argument**, because it pretends to prove the existence from the very essence of God. This argument is specious but fallacious, and the more to be reprobated because the matter is so important. For those who see through the fallacy may be led to suspect that the existence of God is incapable of solid proof.

227. The ontological argument has been **variously proposed** by well-meaning men, such as Descartes, Leibnitz, and even by St. Anselm; it always comes to this: " God is the infinitely perfect Being; but the infinitely perfect Being exists, else He would not be infinitely perfect; therefore God exists." The middle term 'infinitely perfect Being' is ambiguous; in the major it is taken *abstractedly*—*i. e.*, it is a mere definition of the abstract term 'God'; the existence is not meant to be asserted even implicitly, but only referred to conditionally, *i. e.*, if He exists. In the minor the same middle term is used with a new meaning, *i. e.*, **concretely** and, as including existence, unconditionally. It is a trick of logic, which may escape the detection of many, but it is nevertheless a sophism.

It is true that the existence of God is immediately knowable in itself; it is even the first truth in the *ontological* order; but it is not immediately known to us, *i. e.*, in the *logical* order, but it becomes known to us by means of an obvious process of reasoning *a posteriori*—*i. e.*, from the effects to the first Cause.

CHAPTER II.

THE ESSENCE OF GOD.

228. The **essence of a thing** is that which constitutes it intrinsically, making it what it is; it is the note or notes without which a thing can neither exist nor be conceived.

We shall consider in this chapter: 1. The difference between the physical and metaphysical essence of God. 2. The infinite perfection of His physical essence. 3. The simplicity of His physical essence.

ARTICLE I. PHYSICAL AND METAPHYSICAL ESSENCE OF GOD.

229. **The physical essence** is the essence viewed exactly as it is in the being itself, not introducing into it such distinctions as do not belong to it in the objective reality. Now, there are no real distinctions in the essence of God, as we shall show further on; therefore His physical essence is simply the sum total of His perfection.

230. But **the metaphysical or notional essence** of a being is its essence as conceived by us, *i. e.*, as it is traced out by our mind, and marked out in different perfections with logical distinctions, which are not objectively real, though they have a foundation in the reality. The metaphysical essence is viewed as distinguished from the attributes, and, in a created being, as distinguished from the accidents. In God there are no accidents; for He necessarily is all that He is. Now, the essence as distinct from the attributes is conceived as, (*a*) so proper to a being as to distinguish it from every other being, and (*b*) so primary that all the attributes flow from it.

231. **The metaphysical essence of God**, therefore, must be that perfection in God which is conceived by our finite intellect as, (*a*) so peculiar to God that it distinguishes Him from all other beings, and (*b*) so primary or principal that all His other perfections flow from it. Now, this perfection seems to be *self-existence;* for (*a*) it distinguishes God from all other beings, since a self-existent being can be proved to be necessary, independent, infinite—in a word, to be God; and (*b*) it is primary in Him, since from it all His other perfections flow and can be logically proved.

232. We have said that **God's physical essence** is the sum total of His perfection; and we shall now proceed to prove two theses with regard to it: 1. That God contains all possible perfections in an infinite degree. 2. That there is no real distinction of any kind between those perfections.

233. **Thesis II.** *God is infinitely perfect.*

Explanation. We mean by a *perfection* any real entity, anything which it is better to have than not to have. A being is infinitely perfect when it has all possible entity in the highest possible degree. It is clear at once that God, being the cause of the world, must have all the perfections that are actually in the world; for there can be no perfection in the effect which is not in the cause. But besides, He must have, we maintain, all perfections that are intrinsically possible, *i.e.*, all that imply no contradiction. We must, however, distinguish between *pure* perfections—*i. e.*, such as imply no imperfection, *e. g.*, knowledge, goodness, justice, power, etc.; and *mixed* perfections—*i. e.*, such as imply some imperfection, *e. g.*, reasoning, which implies that some truth was first unknown. Now, we mean that God has all pure perfections *formally* or as such, and the mixed He possesses *eminently, i. e.,* in a better way, without any imperfections.

Proof. Whatever the necessary Being is, it is that necessarily; but God is the necessary Being; therefore, whatever He is, He is that necessarily. Therefore, if there is any limit to His perfection, that limit is necessary; *i. e.,* further perfection is excluded by the very nature of His physical essence; in other words, the entity or perfection of His being would exclude some further perfection. But no perfection excludes other perfection, or is incompatible with further perfection; there can be no contradiction between good and good, entity and entity, but only between good and not good, entity and non-entity, perfection and imperfection. Therefore no perfection can exclude any other perfection; hence no perfection is excluded either in kind or in degree; therefore God is infinitely perfect.

234. **Objections:** 1. Our finite intellect cannot know the nature of the infinite Being. *Answer.* We cannot know the nature of the infinite Being adequately, but we can know many things about it; for they are applications of first principles—*e. g.,* that there can be no effect without a cause, that no effect can be greater than the cause, that entity or good as such is not opposed to entity, but to non-entity, etc.

2. The Holy Scriptures warn man not to search into things too high for him: "He that is a searcher of majesty shall be overwhelmed by glory" (Proverbs xxv. 27). *Answer.* It is not too high, but most appropriate for man to know his Creator, that he may reverence Him as he ought: "For the invisible things of God from the creation of the world are clearly seen, being understood by the things that are made: His eternal power also and divinity; so that they

(the ungodly) are inexcusable" (Rom. i. 20). But we are warned not to criticise the ways of God when they surpass our understanding: it is unreasonable for creatures to require of the Creator that He shall render them an account of His government of the world.

3. We ought not to ascribe human perfections to God; else we make Him an anthropomorphic God. *Answer.* Since all creation is some representation of God's perfections, there must be an analogy between the perfections of creatures and the perfections of God; but there is only an analogy. Human perfections are not predicated of God univocally, but always with a difference; and thus God is not made an anthropomorphic or human God. Our view of God is true as far as it goes, but it does not do full justice to God; thus, we say that a picture is a true representation of a statue, though it is unlike the statue in certain respects.

4. It is better, with Agnostics, to call God the great Unknown than to represent Him inadequately. *Answer.* This plea is not even plausible, though it is one of the most specious pretexts of modern infidelity. Inadequate knowledge, acknowledged to be inadequate, is better than total ignorance of any great truth—it is true as far as it goes; but to call *Him* unknown of whom we know so much is a violation of truth, a negation of what we know. Besides, it is most unjust, since it deprives the Creator of the honor which is due to Him by His creatures; for who will worship the Unknown, even though it be spelled with a capital U? It is also most injurious to society; for it throws doubt upon the final accountability of men, and thus destroys the only adequate sanction of the natural law.

ARTICLE II. THE PERFECT SIMPLICITY OF GOD.

235. We have seen that all perfections belong to God; we must now prove that they are all really one, not distinct from one another except in our manner of conceiving them: this is meant by saying that God is perfectly simple. For **simplicity**, as explained in *Ontology* (N). 90), is the perfection which makes a being identical with all that is in it; while **composition**, the opposite of simplicity, implies a distinction of parts. Composition is *real* when the parts are distinct from one another in fact, in the compound object itself; it is *logical*, or mental, when the distinction is only between our concepts. Now, we do not pretend that there is no distinction between the various concepts which we form of God's perfections, that we do not trace logical distinctions in Him; in fact, we cannot help doing so, and our mental distinctions have a true foundation in the reality. For we cannot take in all the being of God at a glance; we learn His essence, as it were, piecemeal from what we observe in creatures, whose perfections must have some prototype in His own nature; therefore we affirm distinct attributes of God, and we have reasons to do so. But we are now to show that the perfections of God which correspond to our distinct concepts are not really distinct in Him; they are but the different aspects under which we view the same reality.

236. **Thesis III.** *God is absolutely simple.*

Proof. That being is absolutely simple which excludes every kind of real composition; now, such is God; therefore He is absolutely simple.

The minor may be proved: I. *In general.* Any real composition must consist of finite parts, else the parts would be equal to the whole; but no union of finite things can make up an infinite being, as God is; therefore He does not consist of parts. II. *In particular.* God excludes all composition.

1. Of *physical parts:*
   (*a*) Of *integral* parts; for integral parts make up quantity, and in the infinite being they would have to make up infinite quantity; but an infinite quantity actually existing is absurd.
   (*b*) Of *substantial* parts, such as matter and form; for each part would be finite, and no union of finite things can make the infinite.
   (*c*) Of *accidental* parts; for nothing can be accidental in the necessary being.
2. Of *metaphysical parts*, viz. :
   (*a*) Of *essence and existence ;* for existence is essential to the necessary being.
   (*b*) Of *substance and accident ;* for the accident would be something finite and the substance something finite; and these two finite things would constitute an infinite being.
   (*c*) Of *power and act ;* for the infinite Being has essentially all perfection, and therefore all action, since action is more perfect than mere power of action.
   (*d*) Of *essence and attributes ;* for all its attributes are essential, are its physical essence.
   (*e*) Of *some attributes and other attributes ;* for if these were really distinct from each other, they would be finite, and finite things would make up an infinite being.
   (*f*) Of *genus and species;* for the genus and the specific difference would be finite. Besides, God is not in any genus; nothing is univocally predicated of Him and of a creature. (No. 16.)

(*g*) Of *species and individual;* for God is essentially whatever He is, and therefore His very individuality is essential to Him.

237. Some important **corollaries** flow from this thesis: 1. That God is a substantial act, a *pure act* without potentiality or power as distinct from action or from the reception of any further perfection, one infinite act, embracing all the objects of His activity. 2. That matter, which is essentially potential, cannot be God nor part of God; and therefore that Pantheism, which makes all things God, is an absurdity. 3. That the nature of God is not divisible; and therefore that, once we learn by Revelation that there are **three really distinct Persons in God,** we know that they must have the same individual nature; nor can there be a real distinction between the nature of God and the Persons, but only between the Persons as such, so that the Father is not the Son, and yet He is the same being as the Son.

238. **Objections:** 1. Holy Writ attributes hands and feet to God, as also passions, all which supposes an organism. *Answer.* Holy Writ usually presents God to us in figurative language wisely adapted to our manner of understanding, viz., in connection with our imagination.

2. Pantheists argue that an infinite substance excludes all finite substances, and therefore whatever exists must be a part of God *Answer.* There is no contradiction between the existence of the infinite substance and that of finite substances; these are not to be conceived as bodies which naturally exclude one another from the place they occupy.

3. But if God has all entity, He contains all creatures, for these are entities. *Answer.* God contains all entity eminently, but not the formal entities that

constitute the creatures. It is proper to remark here that various modern theories are implicitly pantheistic, making the world the one necessary being. Now, **Pantheism** is not only metaphysically absurd, as proved in the first chapter of *Cosmology*, but it is also destructive of morality among men; for if we are God, or parts of God, we certainly can do no wrong, we are not responsible to a supreme Judge and Lord; each of us is fully justified in doing as he pleases. With such a doctrine there is an end to all moral obligation, and there would soon be an end to human society.

CHAPTER III.

THE QUIESCENT ATTRIBUTES OF GOD.

239. We have stated above (No. 231) that self-existence is generally held to be the **metaphysical essence** of God; by which we simply mean that when our mind, incapable of understanding the infinite being by one concept, forms partial concepts of His perfections and strives to put order in its knowledge, we designate self-existence as its essence, but only a quasi-essence—*i. e.*, as the note from which all the other perfections discerned in God flow, after the manner that attributes do from the essence of a created being. These perfections or **attributes** of God may, for convenience' sake, be classified under two heads—namely, His *quiescent* attributes, those that do not formally regard action, and His *operative* attributes, which formally regard action.

We are now to treat of the former class, and we shall consider in particular the unity, the immutability, the eternity, and the immensity of God.

240. **Thesis IV.** *There can be only one God.*

Proof 1. If there were more gods than one, they either could or could not will opposite effects; if they could not, they would not be free and independent, not infinite; if they could will such effects, they could not give efficacy to their contradictory wills, they could not be all-powerful. But a being that is not every way infinite is not God.

Proof 2. If there were more gods than one, there would be various infinite beings; but this cannot be. For, being infinite, such gods would have all perfections, and therefore everything that the one had the other would also have; they would then not differ except numerically. But they could not differ numerically; for this would suppose that their individuality would be really distinct from their essence, since the essence is really separated in the second god from the individuality of the first. But we have seen that there is no real distinction between the essence of God and His individuality. Therefore there is only one God.

241. **Objections:** 1. The arguments just laid down would prove as well that there can be but one Person in God. *Answer.* They prove only this, that everything in God is one individual Being, and such are really the three divine Persons.

2. The consent of nations was at one time in favor of polytheism. *Answer.* Most nations considered the so-called gods as subjects of one supreme Being, the one only God.

3. One infinitely perfect God will not account for the evil that is in the world. *Answer.* The creature is the cause of the moral evil; and, as to physical evil, God can cause it; for He does not owe His creatures anything, and it is not unworthy of Himself to give them a finite happiness of mixed enjoyment and suffering, especially since men can turn their sufferings into merit. As for the sufferings of the brute animal, they are far less than we often imagine. (See *Dublin Review*, Jan., 1888, "The Ethics of Animal Suffering," Vaughan.)

4. But an infinitely perfect God could not create a being capable of doing moral evil. *Answer.* This we absolutely deny: in giving us a free will God gives us a very good thing, and He does so for a very good

purpose, that we may honor Him with it and benefit ourselves; if we abuse His gift, He knows how to draw good out of evil, exercising His mercy in pardoning and His justice in punishing.

242. Among the civilized nations the unity of God is now universally recognized. In ancient times, though the worship of many gods was a wide-spread error among the masses, it found little favor with the philosophers, except in the form of **dualism**, which supposed two necessary beings, the one all good and the other all evil. In the beginning of the Christian era the Gnostics borrowed that error from the Persians, and made it popular in several parts of Europe. Afterwards the Manichæans, and later on the Albigenses, adopted the same absurd theory. It was revived in the sixteenth century by the erratic Pierre Bayle, the author of the *Historical and Critical Dictionary*, but it is now universally abandoned. The only ground for the theory was the difficulty of reconciling the existence of one infinitely good God with the presence of evil in this world. They imagined, therefore, that evil proceeded from an evil being, which they supposed could not have been produced by a good cause, and therefore they considered it as self-existent. Bayle conjectured that the good and the bad principles had made a compact to blend their works with each other. It would be difficult to imagine a more unphilosophic error. For a being all evil would have no perfection, and therefore no entity at all; and a being that would be driven to make a compact with the evil principle would be either wicked or weak, certainly not the infinitely good God. This is one of the many examples which the history of philosophy affords, showing us how self-conceited theorizers will often refuse to accept some well-established truths owing to some apparent difficulties, and, rather than modestly acknowledge

the limitation of their intellects, build up systems full of wild conjectures and flat self-contradictions.

243 **Thesis V.** *G d is absolutely immutable.*

Explanation. We maintain that there cannot be changes intrinsic to God; there may be extrinsic changes, changes in the relations between God and creatures, as when the world began to exist and thus God became its Creator, or when Lucifer fell and was thenceforth hated, while before he was loved by his Maker: in such cases all the intrinsic change is on the part of the creature.

Proof. An intrinsic change supposes the removal of a perfection or entity, or the addition of a perfection, or the exchange of one perfection for another. But nothing of the kind can occur in God; for, since all His perfections are necessary, He cannot lose them, and, having all, He can acquire no more, nor exchange one for another.

244. **Objections:** 1. God is free; therefore He can change His mind. *Answer.* He has all the perfection, but not the imperfections of free will; now, the power of changing one's mind implies an imperfection.

2. God is influenced to change His will by the prayers of His creatures. *Answer.* He knew from eternity all future prayers, and therefore He determined from eternity what He would do in consideration of those prayers. When we delay to determine a conclusion, it is either because we are without proper information, or because we do not know what is best, or because we are sluggish or timid; God has no reason to delay His choice.

3. If God cannot change, He cannot threaten and yet pardon. *Answer.* He determined from eternity to threaten conditionally, and execute His threat or pardon according to the circumstances which He foreknew.

Further difficulties on this point will be answered further on, in connection with the liberty of God (No. 256); others were considered when treating of human liberty (No. 199).

245. **Thesis VI.** *God is eternal.*

Proof. Eternity, as beautifully defined by the Christian philosopher Boëthius, is "the simultaneously full and perfect possession of a life that has neither beginning nor end"— *Interminabilis vitæ tota simul et perfecta possessio;* now, such possession belongs to God. For,

- (*a*) Since God is a self-existent, and therefore a necessary being, His life is without beginning and without end; because He is immutable, He must possess His life simultaneously in all its fulness; and because He is infinitely perfect, He must possess it perfectly.
- (*b*) Since God is absolutely simple, there is in Him no real distinction between power and act, nor between one act and another; He is, therefore, one pure and substantial act; therefore He possesses the fulness of His life, not as broken up into moments, but simultaneously; and because His existence is His very essence, His full enjoyment of life is without beginning and without end.

246. **Objections:** 1. All reality must be in God; but time is a reality; therefore it is in God. *Answer.* Every pure perfection or reality is in God formally; but time is not a pure, but a mixed reality, for time is the measure of successions in finite beings; as such it implies an imperfection or limit of existence which, of course, cannot be in God. Time is, however, eminently in God; for eternity contains all the perfection of time.

2. Eternity, as explained in the proof of this thesis, would seem to be full at each moment; but we

co-exist with some of those moments: therefore we co-exist with eternity. *Answer.* We co-exist with God, who is eternal, but not with the eternity of God. For we cannot say that eternity is full at each moment, but that it is not divisible into moments. Eternity may be said to co-exist with each moment, and yet each moment does not co-exist with all eternity.

247. **Thesis VII.** *God is omnipresent and without limit.*

Explanation. 1. The **omnipresence** or ubiquity of God means His presence in all existing things, and therefore in all real space; His **immensity** means His essential existence without limit of space, so that there is no real or possible space outside of Him. 2. Besides, the omnipresence of God, as implying a relation to creatures, cannot be predicated of Him unless creatures exist—it is a relative perfection; but His immensity is an absolute perfection of His being, and as such it had no beginning. 3. God's immensity should not be imagined as something extended; for whatever is extended has quantity and therefore cannot be infinite. But it is with the immensity of God in respect to space as it is with His eternity in respect to time: He is whole and entire wherever He is and whenever He is.

1st Part. God is omnipresent. Proof. All creatures exist for no other reason than that God gives them existence and keeps them in existence. But He cannot act where He is not present; for nothing can be a cause where it is not, since there it is nothing, and nothing cannot produce any effect. Therefore God is present in everything.

2d Part. God is unbounded. Proof 1. Else He would have limits of some kind, and therefore would not be truly infinite. *Proof* 2. He would not be all-powerful to create if He were confined to any space; but He is all-powerful, therefore He is not confined to any space. The major proposition is evident; for if He were confined to any space, He could not create beyond that space, since a being cannot act where it is not; therefore He would not be all-powerful.

248. There are **three ways in which God is in a creature**: 1. By His *essence*, *i. e.*, by existing in that creature. 2. By His *power*, *i. e.*, by working in that creature, giving it existence and everything it has. 3. By His presence, knowing the creature and in some cases making Himself known to it. It is very different with creatures; thus, a king may be said to be throughout his kingdom by his power, to be present to his troops when he reviews them, but he is essentially or substantially confined to the narrow compass of his body.

CHAPTER IV.

THE OPERATIVE ATTRIBUTES OF GOD.

249. The **operative attributes** of God are those which imply action; they are His *knowledge*, His *will*, and His *power*.

ARTICLE I. THE KNOWLEDGE OF GOD.

250. Since God is absolutely simple, His knowledge, subjectively considered, cannot be made up of different ideas, but must be identical with the one substantial act, which constitutes His essence. Objectively considered, His knowledge may be distinguished according to three classes of objects, into which all things that are knowable may be divided: 1. His knowledge of **pure intelligence** embraces His own essence, as imitable in possible creatures. 2. His knowledge of **vision** comprises His own essence in itself and all that is ever actualized in creatures, whether past, present, or future. 3. His **conditional knowledge** regards all that any creature would do under any circumstances; it is styled *scientia media*, because it holds a middle position between the knowledge of actual and that of possible beings. For instance, the assertion "If Cæsar had not been slain, he would have assumed the royal purple" is either true or false; we do not know whether it is the one or the other; but we say about all such propositions, "God alone knows." This is what we mean by His conditional knowledge.

251. **Thesis VIII.** *God knows all things possible and all*

things actual, *whether past, present, or future; and even all that any free creature would do, in any given case.*

Proof 1. *Direct.* Since God is infinitely perfect, He must know all truth; but there is truth in any judgment that may be formed on any of these matters or in the contradictory of that judgment; therefore God must know it. For instance, the assertion "If Cæsar had not been slain, he would have assumed the royal purple" is true, or its contradictory is true; now, all truth must be known by an infinitely perfect being.

Proof 2. *Indirect.* If God did not know all these things, He could not govern His creatures with infallible wisdom; He might be disappointed, taken unawares by an unexpected free act of man or angel; He would thus not be infinite in wisdom.

252. **Objections:** 1. If God knows what any person's will would choose to do in a given case, it must be because He knows the nature of that will so intimately as to see what that will must choose in a given case; therefore that will *must* make that choice, owing to its very nature; therefore it is not free. *Answer.* We grant that a will which *must* act in a certain fixed way is not really free; but that is not the way with our will, nor with God's conditional knowledge of our choice in a given case. He knows what we would choose, not because we *must* so choose, but only because we *would* so choose; for that we would, is an objective truth and a knowable truth.

2. That which has no being cannot be an object of knowledge, but conditional acts never happening have no being. *Answer.* They have no physical, but they have logical being; for judgments can be formed about them, and those judgments have truth or falsity.

3. What God knows will happen must necessarily happen, and therefore it cannot be a free act. *Answer.* The word 'necessarily' has two meanings: it will necessarily, *i. e.*, infallibly, happen, for what is future is infallibly future, just as what is past is infallibly past; but it will not happen necessarily, *i. e.*, without freedom; just as our past acts were free when we did them: knowledge does not destroy liberty.

4. The explanation given makes God's knowledge of what we would do dependent on our choice; but God cannot in any way depend on any creature. *Answer.* God's knowledge, subjectively considered, is independent of all creatures, for He does not receive His power of knowing from creatures; but, objectively considered, knowledge necessarily supposes the object known, and it argues no imperfection in God that His knowledge of our free acts supposes our free acts and is consequent on our acts.

253. The attribute of **wisdom** may, in one sense of the word, be ranked with that of Divine knowledge; for wisdom often means the knowledge of things in their highest causes. Thus considered, all the knowledge of God is properly denominated wisdom; for He knows all things as they stand related to their highest causes. In another and more usual sense, as St. Thomas fully explains (*Contra Gentes*, c. i.), wisdom comprises both knowledge and action, and means the proper direction of things to their highest ends. As such, God's wisdom is manifested by the effects of His providence, of which we shall treat in connection with His power. (No. 266.)

ARTICLE II. THE WILL OF GOD.

254. **The will of God** is not, like ours, a power passing occasionally into acts, but it is one act loving and willing

all that is necessary, viz., His own essence, and determining freely what contingent things shall be, and what others shall not be, allowing meanwhile for the free choice of His intelligent creatures.

God's love of creatures is nothing else than His will to bestow happiness. This will is often conditional, His actual conferring of benefits being made dependent on the free acceptance of intelligent creatures, whom He earnestly desires to make happy. His will viewed as antecedent to free acceptance is called His **antecedent will**; viewed as taking into account the acceptance or refusal of free creatures, it is styled His **consequent will**. The latter is always efficacious; but the antecedent will may remain inefficacious, because the creature refuses to comply with the required conditions. We shall consider the will of God under three aspects: as *free*, as *holy*, and as *good*.

255. I. **Freedom**, or **liberty**, is the power of choosing between two or more things: (*a*) The power of choosing whether a thing shall be or not be is called **liberty of contradiction**. (*b*) The power of choice between two contraries, such as good and evil, is **liberty of contrariety**; a defect is implied in the power of choosing evil, and, of course, it is not in God. (*c*) The power of choice between one thing and another not contradictory is the **liberty of specification**; we attribute to God liberty in all its perfection.

256. **Thesis IX.** *God is free in all His external acts.*

Explanation. By external acts we mean all His acts in regard to creatures; and we maintain that God from eternity, by a single act of His will, determines affirmatively or negatively all possible questions concerning all possible creatures, so, however, as not to interfere with the free acts of His free creatures. His act of determining is not free as to its entity, but as to its term; *i. e.*, He must determine every question, but He can determine it as He pleases, compatibly with His infinite perfections.

Proof 1. A well-ordered will is in conformity with a perfect intellect; now, a perfect intellect directs that what is necessary shall be willed absolutely; what is unnecessary, freely. But all created things are unnecessary, therefore God wills them freely.

Proof 2. If God were necessitated to will anything outside of Himself, this necessity would arise from Himself or from another being; but it could arise from neither. 1. Not from another; for all other beings are contingent, and therefore cannot necessitate their own existence. 2. Not from Himself; for this would suppose that there is something wanting to Him, some want to be supplied by creating, which could not be supplied by not creating; but this cannot be, else He would not be infinitely perfect, and His perfection would require a finite complement in order to become infinite.

257. **Objections**: 1. God cannot do wrong; therefore He is not free. *Answer.* The power of doing wrong implies a defect of the intellect or the will; it is not a perfection of liberty.

2. Liberty supposes potentiality, *i. e.*, something that may be or not be; but there is no potentiality in God. *Answer.* It supposes potentiality on the part of the term or object willed, on the part of the creature, not on the part of the Creator.

3. A free act is contingent, for it is not necessary; but God's acts are necessary. *Answer.* God's act is necessary; the contingency is in the object or term.

4. If God were free, He could change His decrees; but He cannot. *Answer.* God can do nothing inconsistent with any of His perfections; now, a change of

design would suppose that He has learned new motives for deciding, or that He changed His mind without reason. Besides, though the matter is far above our grasp to explain fully, there is but one act in God; hence no change is possible, and still that act is free with regard to creatures.

258. **Holiness,** or **sanctity,** means the love of what is right or morally good, and the hatred of what is wrong or morally evil; viewed as an attribute of God, it may be defined, the immutable will of God to act in conformity with His perfection, in a manner worthy of Himself. Perfect sanctity is evidently essential to the infinitely perfect Being.

259. **Thesis X.** *God is infinitely good.*

Proof. Goodness has various meanings, in each of which it is infinite in God. 1. Goodness, as a *transcendental*, is being, viewed as desirable; in this sense it is clear that God is infinitely good, inasmuch as He is infinite being, and therefore an infinite object of desire. 2. Goodness may be taken in the moral sense of conformity to the law of reason; it is then synonymous with *sanctity;* it must be perfect in the infinitely perfect Being. 3. Goodness is often taken in a relative sense, and signifies an earnest will to make others happy; it is then often called *bounty* or *beneficence*. In this sense it is infinite as an attribute of God; for it has been proved *a priori* that the self-existent Being is infinitely perfect. His bounty, however, is not infinite in its manifestations or effects, for all the works of God must be finite in finite creatures. Therefore we cannot prove *a posteriori* that God is infinitely bountiful.

260. **Objections:** 1. If God possessed infinite moral goodness, He would manifest His hatred of sin by not allowing sin to exist. *Answer.* God, indeed, detests sin infinitely and forbids it absolutely; but there are

two ways in which hatred of sin can manifest itself, viz., by preventing its existence, and, without preventing it, by repairing the evil with full compensation. God often chooses the latter way; He punishes some of the guilty with endless punishment, and He has Himself made an atonement of infinite merit for the sins of men. (Nos. 115, 118.) (See on this matter "A Sceptical Difficulty against Creation," by Rev. R. F. Clarke, S.J., *American Catholic Quarterly Review*, April, 1887.)

2. If God were infinitely bountiful, He would make all His creatures happy. *Answer.* He would seriously wish all to be happy, we grant; He would make them happy against their will, we deny. The manifestation of His goodness must have a limit, which it is for Him to determine, or to place, if he so chooses, in the determination of man's free will.

Article III. The Power of God.

261. Thesis XI. *God is omnipotent.*

Proof. Omnipotence is infinite power; now, power is a perfection, something which it is better to have than not to have, and the self-existent Being has all perfections; therefore He is omnipotent.

262. **Objections**: 1. God cannot create all possible things together, because they would constitute an infinite number; therefore He cannot do all things. *Answer.* He can do all things; but anything self-contradictory is not truly a thing. The fact that all possible things cannot be actualized together is not owing to any limit in God's power, but to a necessary limit in all finite things; for these cannot co-exist without making a number,

and an infinite number of things actually existing is absurd.

2. God cannot create a square circle, nor an infinitely perfect being. *Answer.* Both these involve contradictions; for square denies the roundness essential to a circle, and a creature, by the very fact that it is a creature, cannot be infinitely perfect.

263. **Thesis XII.** *The preservation of created beings requires at every moment the active influence of God's power and will.*

Explanation. We do not mean that God need protect every creature against other creatures or against the action of the natural laws; but that all and any created being would cease to exist, if God ceased for a moment actually to will its existence, just as the figure of a body of water would at once cease to exist if the vessel holding it were destroyed.

Proof. The present existence of a contingent being cannot, by itself, be the cause of its future existence; for the cause must contain the effect, and the present existence does not contain the future existence. Therefore another cause must exist for the permanence of that being. If this other cause be itself unnecessary or contingent, it, too, will be unable to exist and act just then, except in virtue of another cause giving it then and there existence and power of action. And thus no contingent being could continue to exist from one moment to another, except in virtue of an influence not itself contingent nor dependent, which is nothing else than the power and will of God. This may be illustrated by reflecting that the strength of a manufactured article depends on the strength, or power of permanence, of the material of which it is made. If no material were used, there could be no power of permanence, except as far as the maker continued to give it existence; now, all creation is not made out of a pre-existing material; therefore its preservation depends at any moment on the active influence of the Creator.

264. By a similar reasoning it may be proved that God not only keeps all things in existence, but that He actually **concurs with every act** of every creature. For creatures depend on God totally—that is, according to all their entity; but there is in every act an entity which is beyond the mere power of acting; therefore the act also, and not merely the power, must depend on God.

265. **God's concurrence with a free act** of a creature does not in the least interfere with its liberty; for by the very fact that He makes the being free He concurs with it in acting one way or another, as the free will chooses. The free act is man's and it is God's, but with a difference: as a boat is supported by the water, propelled and directed truly by the efforts of man, but by means of the water; so human actions proceed truly from man, but with the concurrence of God.

266. The **Providence** of God is the wisdom whereby He directs things to their proper ends.

Thesis XIII. *Every event in the world is directed by Divine Providence.*

Proof 1. This is a dictate of common sense; for all men look up to God as the supreme Controller of every one's destiny, and all nations, even while believing to some extent in fate, as some did, still prayed to God as the Dispenser of good and evil.

Proof 2. It is the part of wisdom to direct all things to their proper ends by proper means; but God is infinitely wise, since He is infinitely perfect; therefore He directs all things to proper ends by proper means. Now, He could not do so unless He directed every event in the world; therefore He directs every event in the world.

267. **Objections:** 1. All men agree that some things

happen by accident, but accident means the absence of design. *Answer.* All agree that things happen which are not the result of design on the part of men; but they do not deny that everything which happens is willed or permitted by Almighty God. If God specially and directly intends anything with regard to any creature, it is said to proceed from a special providence of God; else it is attributed to the general providence of God, who sees and wills distinctly all the consequences of the natural laws.

2. At least the events proceeding from human design are not directed by the providence of God, *e. g.*, the wicked plots of murderers. *Answer.* The physical actions of even the worst men and the effects of such actions cannot exist except with the permissive will and the actual concurrence of God; He can and does direct even these to proper ends not intended by the evil-doers, *e. g.*, that He may increase the merit of His martyrs and of the good in general. Therefore Holy Writ says: "We know that to them that love God all things work together unto good" (Rom. viii. 28).

3. It were unworthy of God to mind little things. *Answer.* No more than it is unworthy of a good painter to mind every detail of his painting. Besides, the most perfect creature is as nothing compared to God, and nothing is little when viewed as directed by Him to a high purpose.

4. If God rules all events, men need and can do nothing. *Answer.* This were true if God ruled all events without regard to the actions of men; but not if, as is the case, He allows free causes to act freely, knowing, meanwhile, how to draw ultimate good from present evil.

5. A wise Providence would punish crime and reward virtue; but this is not always done in this world. *Answer.* It only follows that it will be done in the next world, where God has an eternity to manifest His goodness and His justice.

6. If there were a Providence, there would not be so much misery and so much inequality among men. *Answer.* Much of the evils of life comes from the vices of men, which God need not hinder for the present, but which will be atoned for in due time. Often sufferings and inequalities are part of His grand design of sanctifying souls. Besides, there is no reason why God should treat all His creatures alike; on the contrary, the poet has truly said:

> "Order is heaven's first law, and, this confessed,
> One is and must be greater than the rest,
>   More rich, more wise;
>   This who denies,
> Denies all common sense."

THE END.

ALPHABETICAL INDEX.

I. refers to the Logic; II., to the Mental Philosophy; 1, 2, 3, etc., to the paragraphs.

Abstract, ideas, I. 11, 122 to 124, 148; II. 176, 182; number, 38.
Accident, one of the predicables, I. 13; opposed to substance, II. 49, 50, 58, 59.
Accidental cause, II. 77.
Act, pure, I. 237.
Action, II. 50, 55, 63 to 65, 78, 79, 85.
Actual, being, II. 6, 12; division, 91.
Adaptation of means to end, II. 150.
Aevum, II. 70.
Agnosticism, II. 103, 216, 217, 219, 234.
Ambiguous middle, I. 57.
Analogy, I. 16, 50 to 52; II. 10.
Analytic, judgments, I. 17, 63, 125 to 127; reasoning, 64 to 66.
Anatomy, II. 157.
Angels, I. 13 to 16; II. 139, 141 to 143; species fixed, II. 155.
Anselm, St., II. 118.
Answering objections, I. 55.
Apparent conflict, of reason and Revelation, I. 3; of sciences, 68.
Appetite, II. 191, 192, 195, 196.
Appreciation, power of, II. 167.
Apprehension, I. 9, 75 to 77.
Argumentation, I. 22.
Argumentum ad hominem, I. 54.
Aristotle, II. 48, 101, 127.
Atheists, II. 219, 225.

Atomic theory, II. 131, 133.
Attribute, I. 13; II. 36; of God, 239.
Authority, I. 152 to 156.

Beauty, II. 46, 47.
Begging the question, I. 58.
Being, II. 6; actual, possible, real, 7, 8, 12; logical, physical, 11; not a genus, 13; determination of, 14; possible, 17 to 27; necessary, 97.
Belief, I. 153.
Berkeley, I. 144.
Boscowich, II. 130.
Brute, animals. I. 148; for man, II. 138, 152; soul, 146 to 148.

Categorical, propositions, I. 21; syllogisms, 23.
Categories, II. 48.
Causality, limits to, II. 85; principle of, 86 to 88.
Cause, defined, II. 74; formally, materially, 76; material, formal, substantial, accidental, final, 77 to 79; efficient, 81; first, second, properly, accidentally, principal, instrumental, free, necessary, moral, physical, 83; contains effect formally, eminently, virtually, univocal, 84; has reality, 85
Certainty, I. 70, 71, 78, 112, 113;

Alphabetical Index. 181

e'ements of, 84; philosophical, 85; species of, 86, 87; existence of, 89 to 99; criterion of, 165 to 170; sources of, 100 to 164.
Change, II. 98, 99, 105.
Chemistry, II. 128, 133.
Circle, exercise of the, I. 69.
Clear ideas, Descartes', I. 168.
Cognition, II. 159; sensible, rational, 175, etc.
Cognoscive powers, sketch of, I. 100 to 111.
Common objects of sense-perception, I. 148.
Common sense, I. 156 to 164; the, 103; consent, 159.
Composition, II. 91; and division, I. 57.
Comprehension of ideas, I. 16, 20, 25.
Conception, concept, I. 9.
Conceptualists, I. 124; II. 184, 185.
Conclusion, I. 24, 25, 29.
Concrete, ideas, I. 11; number, II. 38.
Concurrence with second causes, II. 264, 265.
Condition, II. 82.
Conditional knowledge, II. 250 to 253; propositions, I. 21; syllogisms, 35.
Conjunctive, propositions, I. 21; syllogisms, 37.
Consciousness, I. 111, 114 to 118.
Consequence, consequent, I. 29, 32.
Constructing syllogisms, I. 24, 25.
Contingent being, II. 96, 97, 220.
Copula, I. 19.
Cosmology, II. 4, 100.
Creation, II. 106 to 108; purpose of, 113 to 115 : of the soul, 211.
Criterion, ultimate, of certainty, I. 165 to 170; of a true miracle, II. 124.

Criticising syllogisms, I. 31, 32.
Crystals, II. 129, 140.

Darwinian theory, II. 208; see "Evolution."
Descartes, II. 134; methodic doubt of, I. 95, 96; clear ideas of, 168.
Determinations of being, II. 14.
Dialectics, I. 6, 7.
Dialectic syllogism, I. 49.
Difference, specific, I. 13.
Dilemma, I. 41, 42.
Disjunctive, proposition, I. 21; sylgism, 36.
Distant action, II. 85.
Distinction, II. 40; of the sciences, I. 67.
Distributed ideas, I. 16.
Doubt, I. 78, 82; methodic, 95, 96.
Dreams, I. 147; II. 168, 170.
Dualism, II. 243.
Dynamic theory, II. 130, 133.

Effect, see "Cause."
Efficient cause, II. 81.
Elements, of certainty, I. 84, 88; of matter, II. 126.
Eminent cause, II. 84.
Enthymeme, I. 38.
Epicherema, I. 43.
Equivocal, cause, II. 84; terms, I. 16.
Equivocation, I. 57.
Error, I. 78 to 83.
Essence, specific, I. 13; defined, II. 28; physical, metaphysical, 30; eternal, 31; knowledge of, 32 : of God, 228.
Eternity, II. 70, 245, 246; of punishment, 118, 215.
Ethics, I. 1.
Eucharist, Holy, II. 58, 134.
Evasion, I. 54.
Evidence, mediate, immediate, I. 18;

defined, 167; the ultimate criterion of certainty, 169, 170.
Evil, II. 45, 241, 242, 267; spirits, 123 to 125; I. 147.
Evolution, II. 156 to 158, 208 to 210, 226.
Exemplars, II. 20, 21.
Exemplary cause, II. 80.
Exercise in reasoning, I. 69.
Existence, II. 33; of God, 220, etc.
Extension, of ideas, I 16; of propositions, 20; of predicate, 21; of bodies, II. 127, 132 to 134.
Extreme terms, I. 29.

Fallacies, I. 56, etc.
Falsity, I. 73; II. 42.
Fichte, II. 102; I. 144, 145.
Figment of reason, II. 7.
Figure, II. 136, 140.
Final cause, II. 77 to 79.
First, fact, principle, condition, I. 98; principles, 60, II. 35; cause, 83.
Foreknowledge, II. 199; 250 to 252.
Form, of syllogism, I. 19, 29; of living bodies, II. 144, 203 to 206; matter and, see "Matter."
Formal, cause, II. 77, 84; objects of sciences, I. 67; object of metaphysics, II. 3, 8, 133.
Free, will, the source of error, I. 81; cause, II. 83; will, in man, 194 to 199; in God, 255.

Genus, I. 13 to 15.
Geology, II. 111.
Glory, II. 115, 153.
God, defined, II. 219; exists, 220 to 227; essence of, 228; perfection of, 233, 234; simplicity of, 235 to 238; attributes of, 239; unity of, 240, 241; immortality of, 243, 244; eternity of, 245, 246; omnipresence, immensity of, 247, 248; knowledge of, 250 to 253; will of, 254 to 257; holiness of, 258; goodness of, 259, 260; omnipotence of, 261 to 263; concurrence of, 264, 265; providence of, 266, 267.
Goodness, II. 36, 43; kinds of, 44.
Growth, II. 140, 143.

Habiliment, II. 50, 73.
Harper, Rev. Thos., II. 14, 41, 133.
Highest genus, I. 14.
Holiness, II. 258.
Hume, I. 145; II. 53, 123.
Huxley, I. 10, 164; II. 123, 155, 199, 201, 209.
Hypnotism, II. 124.
Hypothesis, I. 53.
Hypothetic, proposition, 21; syllogism, 34 to 37; impossibility, II. 96.

Idea, I. 9; abstract, concrete, 11; singular, particular, universal, 12; distributed, 16; primary, 119 to 121; not innate, II. 178, 180; how acquired, 180 to 183; of being not that of God, 15, 16; of infinity, 95.
Idealism, I. 144; II. 102.
Identity, II. 39, 57.
Ignorance, I. 78, 82.
Imagination, I. 105; II. 165.
Immanent action, II. 65.
Immensity of God, II. 247.
Immutability, II. 98; of God, 243, 244.
Impenetrability, II. 135.
Indirect reasoning, I. 54.
Individuality, II. 41.
Induction, I. 44 to 48, 170.
Inertia, II. 138.
Infinite, II. 92 to 94; idea of, 95; perfection, 253.
Inhesion, II. 58.
Inner sense, I. 103 to 105, 115; reliable, 139 to 141.

Instance, I. 54.
Instinct, II. 149 to 152.
Instrumental cause, II. 83.
Intellect, I. 107, 112, 113, 148; in action, receptive, II. 177, 182.
Intellectual, memory, I. 110, 128 to 131; life, II. 139.
Intelligence not in brutes, II. 148.
Intuitions, I. 152.
Invincible error, I. 80.
Irrelevant conclusion, I. 58.

Judgment, I. 17, 18, 108; *a priori, a posteriori*, etc., 17, 18, 63; speculative, practical, 79; analytic is reliable, 125 to 127; consequent on sense-perception, 142 to 151; of common sense, 156 to 164.

Kant, II. 71, 130.
Knowledge, of possibles, II. 19, 20; of essences, 32; of God, 250 to 253; see "Cognition."

Language, II. 189, 190.
Laws of nature, II. 119 to 125.
Leibnitz, II. 45, 53, 130, 206, 212.
Liberty, II. 194 to 199; essence of, 197; kinds of, 255; of God, 256, 257.
Life, II. 139, 140.
Local motion, II. 137.
Locke, II. 34, 53, 57.
Logic, I. 2, 5; formal, material, critical, 6, 70.
Logical, order, I. 61; truth, falsity, 73 to 77; being, II. 11; distinction, 40; relation, 62; whole, 91.
Lunacy, I. 118, 145.

Major, terms, premises, I. 23 to 29; 32, etc.
Material, logic, I. 6, 70; cause, II. 77.
Materialism, II. 216.

Matter, of syllogism, I. 19, 29; not self-existent, II. 104 to 107; divisible, 126; and form, 127, etc., 144.
McCosh, II. 53.
Memory, I. 106, 110; reliable, 128 to 131; sensible, II. 166.
Mesmerism, II. 123, 124, 172 to 174.
Metaphysical, certainty, I. 86; essence, II. 30, 230, 231; truth, 72; whole, 91.
Metaphysics, I. 1; II. 2 to 4; formal object of, 8, 133.
Method, I. 59 to 67.
Methodic doubt, I. 95.
Middle term, I. 29.
Mill, J. S., II. 184.
Minor, term, premise, I. 23 to 29, 32.
Miracle, II. 121 to 125.
Modal accidents, II. 59; distinction, 40.
Monads, II. 130.
Moral, truth, I. 72; falsity, 73; certainty, 86, 87; II. 123; cause, 83; possibility, 18; good, 44, 45; evil, 115.
Mosaic account of creation, II. 111.
Motion, II. 69, 137.
Multiplicity, II. 38.
Mysticism, II. 186.

Nature, of a being, II. 34; laws of, 119 to 125.
Natural, appetite, II. 191; theology, 4, 218.
Necessary, being, II. 96, 220; cause, 83.
Negative argument, I. 54.
Nominalists, I. 124; II. 184, 185.
Notion, I. 9.
Notional, essence, II, 230, 231.

Objections, answers to, I. 55.
Objects of, sense-perception, I. 148.
Occasion, II. 82.

Omnipotence, II. 261 to 263.
Omnipresence, II. 247.
Omniscience, II. 253.
Oneness, see " Unity."
Ontological, order, I. 61; proof of God's existence, II. 226, 227.
Ontologists, II. 187, 188.
Ontology, II. 4, 5.
Operative attributes of God, II. 239.
Opinion, I. 78.
Order, I. 61; in the world, II. 122, 221, 224.
Organs of sense, I. 102; action of, II. 195.
Origin, of the world, II. 101; of ideas, 175 to 184; of language, 190; of the soul, 207 to 212.

Paleontology, II. 157.
Pantheism, II. 101, 103, 237, 238.
Particular, ideas, I. 12; propositions, 20.
Passion, I. 83; II. 50, 61, 63 to 65.
Perception, I. 145 to 148; II. 160 to 163.
Perfection, II. 43; absolute, relative, 117; of the world, 117, 118.
Person, II. 55; identity of, 57.
Phantasm, I. 10, 115.
Philosophic certainty, I. 85, 91.
Philosophy, defined, I. 1; divided, 1; important, 4.
Phrenology, II. 201.
Physical, being, II. 11; good, 44; evil, 45; beauty, 46; certainty, I. 86, 90, 91; II. 123; possibility, 18; essence, 30, 229, 232; cause, 74; whole, 91; laws, 119 to 125.
Physics, II. 1.
Physiology, II. 157.
Place, II. 50, 66.
Plants, II. 139, 141 to 143; 152 to 154.
Plato, II. 101, 127, 212.

Porphyrian tree, I. 15.
Positivists, II. 34.
Possibility, intrinsic, extrinsic, II. 17; moral, physical, 18.
Possible beings, II. 6, 7, 12, 17 to 27, 94; knowledge of, 19, 20, 94, 253; dependence of, on God, 22 to 27.
Posture, II. 50, 72.
Potentiality, II. 127, 128.
Power of God, II. 261, 263.
Predicables, heads of, I. 13.
Predicaments, II. 48.
Predicate, I. 19; extension, comprehension of, 20.
Pre-established harmony, II. 206.
Prejudices, I. 83.
Premises, I. 23, 25, 29, 60.
Preservation of created things, II. 263.
Primary ideas, I. 119 to 121.
Prime matter, II. 127.
Principal cause, II. 83.
Principiant, II. 74.
Principle, of identity, contradiction, excluded middle, II. 35; of sufficient reason and causality, 86 to 88
Probable reasoning, I. 49.
Procession, II. 74, 75.
Proper objects of sense-perception I. 148.
Property, I. 13.
Proportion, II. 47.
Propositions, I. 19; kinds of, 21, 33
Providence of God, II. 266, 267.
Psychology, II. 4, 139.
Punishment, II. 115, 118; eternal, 215.
Pure act, II. 237.
Purpose, of work, of workman, II. 112 to 115.
Pythagoras, II. 101.

Quality, II. 50, 61; of proposition, I. 20.

Quantity, II. 50, 60, 93, 94; of proposition, I. 20.

Rational, cognition, II. 175, etc.; appetite, 191, 192.

Real, being, II. 7, 8; relation, 62; distinction, 40.

Realists, I. 124; II. 185.

Reality of causes and effects, II. 85.

Reason, I. 109.

Reasoning, I. 22; rules of syllogistic, 32; demonstrative, probable, 49; indirect, 54; *a priori, a posteriori*, 62, 63; analytic, synthetic, 64 to 66; gives certainty, 132 to 134, 170.

Redemption, II. 56.

Reduplication, II. 135.

Reid, I. 160.

Relation, II. 50, 62.

Retort, I. 54.

Revelation, I. 3; II. 111, 118.

Rules of syllogism, I. 31, 32.

Sameness, II. 39.

Sceptics, I. 93, 94, 97, 99; II. 85.

Schoolmen's, the, system, of matter and form, II. 127; of origin of ideas, 182.

Science, I. 5; formal objects of a, 67.

Scotus, II. 101.

Self-contradiction, I. 54.

Self-existence, II. 104, 220, 239.

Sensation, I. 135, 136; perceives concrete objects, 137; is reliable, 142 to 147; limits of its reliability, 139 to 141; how effected, II. 161 to 163; where effected, 164.

Sense, outer, I. 101, 102, 138, 142 to 151; inner, 103, 104, 138 to 141; common, 103, 163, 164; perception, II. 160; objects of, I. 148.

Sensible, memory, I. 106, 128; II. 166; judgments, 167; appetite, 191 to 196.

Sensitive, cognition, II. 159 to 167; life, 139.

Simple apprehensions, I. 8; truth of, 75 to 77.

Simplicity, II. 90, 145; of the soul, 200; of God, 235 to 238.

Singular ideas, I. 12; propositions, 20.

Sleep, II. 168, 169, 172.

Somnambulism, II. 171.

Sophisms, I. 56.

Sorites, I. 39, 40.

Soul, the form of the body, II. 144, 204 to 206; the human, is simple, 200, 201; spiritual, 202, 203; when created, 211, 212; survives body, 213; immortal, 214.

Space, II. 67 to 69, 137.

Species, I. 13 to 15; Eucharistic, II. 134; of plants and animals are fixed, 156, 157; impressed, expressed, II. 162, 163.

Specific difference, I. 13 to 15.

Spinoza, II. 52, 101.

Spirits, II. 66, 137; I. 147.

Spiritism, II. 174.

Spontaneous, II. 193.

Subordinate, genus, species, I. 14.

Substance, II. 49, etc.

Substantial, cause, II. 77; principle, 132, 144, 145.

Suffering, II. 241, 267.

Sufficient reason, II. 86 to 88.

Supposit, II. 55.

Suspicion, I. 78, 82.

Syllogism, I. 23; construction of, 24, 25; abridged form of, 27; affirmative, negative, 28; parts of, 29; valid, 30; rules of, 31, 32; hypothetical, 34 to 37.

Synthetic, judgment, I. 17; reasoning, 64 to 66.

Term, I. 10, 16, 29, 31, 32.
Thomas, St., I. 91; II. 41, 108, 110, 118, 127.
Time, II. 50, 70, 71.
Traditionalism, II. 179.
Transcendentals, II. 9.
Transient action, II. 65.
Transubstantiation, II. 99.
Trinity, the Holy, II. 74, 237.
True, beauty, II. 47; good, 44.
Truth, I. 72 to 77; II. 36, 42.
Tyndall, II. 155.

Ultimate, criterion of certainty, I. 165 to 170; particles of matter, II. 127.
Undue assumption, I. 58.
Unity, II. 36; kinds of, 37; of God, 240, 241.
Universal, ideas, I. 12, 13, 122, 224; direct, reflex, II. 183, etc.; proposition, I. 20; major, 25; cause, II. 84.

Universe, II. 100; see "World."
Univocal terms, I. 16.

Valid, syllogism, I. 30; induction, 48.
Vegetable life, II. 139.
Virtual cause, II. 84.
Vital, principle, II. 127, 129, 139 to 148; acts, 59.
Voluntary, II. 193.

When, II. 63, 70.
Whole, II. 91.
Will, II. 181, 192; antecedent, consequent, 116; of man is free, 198, 199; of God, 254 to 258.
Wisdom of God, II. 253.
World, II. 100; origin of the, 101 to 110; age of the, 111; perfection of the, 117; purpose of the, 112 to 115.

A PRACTICAL INTRODUCTION TO
English Rhetoric:

Precepts and Exercises.

By Rev. Charles Coppens, S. J.

$1.25. *(Discount is allowed to Schools.)*

Speaking of the "Rhetoric", Very Rev. Rudolph Meyer, S.J., said: "The best thing I ever did for education was to urge Father Coppens to publish that book."

"We have taken some of the most popular and approved text-books in use in our best schools and compared them with this new Introduction to English Rhetoric. The result is in every way—and in some parts to an exceptional degree—favorable to the latter.—*American Catholic Quarterly Review.*

We are happy to add another to the list of text-books for Catholic Schools of which one can write only in terms of unqualified praise. Its author, the Rev. Charles Coppens, S.J., is already well-known through his admirable "Art of Oratorical Composition." His two books, taken together, contain the entire course of rhetoric as studied in colleges and universities. But The Practical Introduction to English Rhetoric, taken alone, must have a far wider sphere of usefulness, being perfectly adapted for the higher departments of academies for girls, and for the use of the teachers themselves in the lower departments of schools for either sex, or in schools where so extended a course of rhetoric does not enter into the plan of study.—*Pilot.*

The book is the result of thirty years of work as a professor of rhetoric in various colleges conducted by the Jesuit Fathers in this country. It is a classbook, but it would make a useful and interesting book in the library of any man who admires and loves to cultivate good English. From the examination we have given the work we feel justified in pronouncing it the best English book on rhetoric that has yet been published.—*Michigan Catholic.*

The Art of
Oratorical Composition:

Based on the Precepts and Models of the Great Masters.

By Rev. Charles Coppens, S.J.

$1.25. *(Discount is allowed to Schools.)*

"It is a clear, didactic exposition, with such illustrations from modern sources as will make it practical under our circumstances. But it is also a text-book, which is saying something apart from its general merits, as teachers will understand. . . . . Least of all has Father Coppens reason to guard himself against distrust, for he simply proves his strength by the grasp he has of the masters in his profession. . . . . For seminaries, we find here the entire course from preparatory school to the class of sacred eloquence in theology."—*American Catholic Quarterly Review.*

Father Coppens has been, over twenty-five years, a Professor of Oratory in the United States, so that he brings to this book not only the full equipment of a master of the art, but all the invaluable skill in imparting his knowledge to be acquired only, and after long trial, in the rostrum of the teacher. Father Coppens' is perhaps the most practical class book on the speaker's art yet offered to American schools. . . . Father Coppens, wherever it is practicable, lets the acknowledged masters of oratorical composition speak for themselves, so that his pupil is made familiar, and in their own words, with the leading precepts of the great writers on oratory among both the ancients and moderns.—*Catholic World.*

www.ingramcontent.com/pod-product-compliance
Lightning Source LLC
Chambersburg PA
CBHW032102220426
43664CB00008B/1101